NEW PLAYS USA 2

New Plays USA

James Leverett, *Editor*

New Plays USA 1

Lee Breuer, *A Prelude to Death in Venice*
Tom Cole, *Dead Souls*
David Henry Hwang, FOB
Emily Mann, *Still Life*
OyamO, *The Resurrection of Lady Lester*
Adele Edling Shank, *Winterplay*

NEW PLAYS USA 2

Edited by
M. ELIZABETH OSBORN
and GILLIAN RICHARDS

Introduction by
RICHARD GILMAN

THE PLAYS

Secret Honor
Donald Freed and Arnold M. Stone

Food from Trash
Gary Leon Hill

Mensch Meier
Franz Xaver Kroetz
translated by *Roger Downey*

Buck
Ronald Ribman

Mercenaries
James Yoshimura

Theatre Communications Group   New York   1984

New Plays USA is published biennially by Theatre Communications Group, 355 Lexington Ave., New York, NY 10017.

Designed by Soho Studio.

Manufactured in the United States of America.

ISBN 0-930452-35-6 (cloth)
ISBN 0-930452-36-4 (paper)
Library of Congress catalog card number: 83-645685

First Edition.

Contents

Selection Committee for
New Plays USA 2

New Plays USA 2 was supported in part by a generous grant from Home Box Office, Inc.

The playwrights whose plays appear in this volume are recipients of Playwrights USA Awards, also funded by Home Box Office, Inc.

NEW PLAYS USA 2

Preface

It was the Greek philosopher Heraclitus who first set down the maxim that you can't step into the same river twice. I doubt if he was obliquely referring to some now lost collection of pre-Aeschylean drama which he was editing at the time, but the wisdom of that old sage of flux has resonance for me as I contemplate the process that has produced the second volume of *New Plays USA*. You really can't step into the same theatre twice either, by virtue (the main virtue, I think) of the ephemeral nature of the art itself: the one-time meeting of performers and audience on their respective ways through life and history. And how much more disconcertingly fluid it all becomes when the theatre into which you are trying to step is in fact the sum of hundreds of theatres doing thousands of productions for millions of people in every part of a vast country. This is an accurate if dizzying description of the American National Theatre as it has come into being over the past generation, regardless of those who still try to confine it to a couple of densely populated dots on a map. The book before you, by virtue (again, the main virtue) of how it came to be, is a representation of that theatre. And of that nation.

In his introduction to *New Plays USA 1*, Michael Feingold found in that first volume of the series a "manifesto" of American playwriting in all of its colorful variety. Indeed, although no one had planned it that way, when the complex and comprehensive selection process (which I shall describe later) was complete, we had in book form an extraordinary cross section of a heterogeneous culture: *A Prelude to Death in Venice*, a highly experimental performance poem by Lee Breuer; *Dead Souls*, a translation-adaptation of a Russian classic by Tom

Cole; *FOB*, a provocative meeting of Orient and Occident by David Henry Hwang; *Still Life*, a documentary drama of the Viet Nam experience by Emily Mann; *The Resurrection of Lady Lester*, a mood song evoking the great black saxophonist Lester Young by OyamO; *Winterplay*, a hyperreal comedy of West Coast life by Adele Edling Shank.

If with that collection we step out far into the Heraclitean stream, with *New Plays USA 2* we step in deep. As Richard Gilman points out in his introductory essay, the plays are unified in a common "mood or morale" of serious political concern. This is not at all to say that the contents of the first anthology lack political dimension—the political in both cases taken in its broadest sense of the human soul finding itself in the larger contexts of society. But the collections differ utterly in focus and tone, which brings me back to the Heraclitean theme: The world has changed in the two years separating the two books and so necessarily has that most social of art forms, the theatre.

Does the *New Plays USA* series show more than other anthologies about the direction in which our theatre is moving? Perhaps not; or perhaps any collection, no matter how casual, would reveal something if one is looking for revelation. However, to use the pollster's parlance, here is no random sample. It is a controlled selection made by the most elaborate, comprehensive system I know anything about. Thanks to Gilman's introduction, you can get a good sense of the spirit in which the choices are made. The following describes a bit of the history and the nuts and bolts of the choosing.

We must start with a theatre that has been radically transforming itself over the past 20 years. What was a world almost totally dominated by the commercial marketplace called Broadway has now diversified and decentralized into hundreds of permanent theatres spread through almost every state in the nation, which like symphonies or museums depend on government, foundation and corporate support for much of their sustenance. These are the nonprofit professional institutions often identified as regional, repertory or resident theatres, although none of those terms adequately describes them in all their variety of artistic aim, organization and locale. Now most plays that find their way eventually to Broadway and other commercial venues—aside from giant musicals, imports and a dwindling number of boulevard comedies—have their origin in one of these far-flung theatres. And many more have a full life without ever entering the commercial arena.

Yet as a result of both decentralization and tremendous growth in the production of new work, the lines of communication which transmitted who was doing what where were strained to breaking. This situation was not helped as script publication, that traditional means of dissemination, shrank to a trickle of mainly Broadway hits, British imports and a few classic chestnuts. How could a production in Seattle instigate another in Atlanta and a third in Milwaukee? How could teachers and students become familiar with not only the drama of the ages, but also that of last year? And how could people both here and abroad find out about the array of American dramatic writing being created beyond the tight spotlight of Broadway and its immediate environs?

An idea evolved to use the facilities of Theatre Communications Group, the national organization of nonprofit theatre, to mobilize the resources of its over 200 member theatres, the very ones most responsible for the great surge of new play production. These theatres would submit new scripts from their seasonal repertoires to a selection process on a national level. The plays chosen in this process would be circulated in manuscript form to what would eventually become an international subscribership interested in reading, studying and producing contemporary American work.

The Ford and Rockefeller Foundations, the National Endowment for the Arts and, later, the New York State Council on the Arts provided the funds for this huge, unprecedented undertaking and *Plays in Process* was born. Since its start in 1979, *PIP* has circulated 53 new scripts in addition to information about hundreds more. Playwrights credit this system with over 60 productions, as well as many other benefits, such as grants, commissions and residencies, which added visibility brings.

The other, equally important aspect of the project came to fruition with the publication of *New Plays USA 1* in 1982. Whereas *Plays in Process* is primarily a service for theatre professionals and students, distributing scripts that have not necessarily reached their final form but still need the polishing that further production can bring, the *New Plays USA* series has quite different aims. The contents of these anthologies are selected from two seasons of *PIP* scripts and published as part of an ongoing record of the state of the art of American playwriting. These books are meant to demonstrate that plays have a double life, on the page as well as on the stage. No less literary endeavors than novels, poetry or essays, plays should be accorded the same attention and respect. Over the long haul of history, the life of a play, and of more importance, the life, growth and health of a body of dramatic literature, depends at least as much on publication as performance.

The five plays in *New Plays USA 2* were selected from 26 chosen for *Plays in Process* during the 1981–82 and 1982–83 seasons. These were selected from hundreds of scripts which TCG theatres nominated after having given them full productions, which were in turn picked from the thousands routinely submitted to those theatres every year. The anthology plays are wonderfully rich and varied, but behind them is the not so apparent diversity both artistic and geographic of the theatres that produced them: *Secret Honor* originated at the Los Angeles Actors' Theatre; *Food from Trash* won the Actors Theatre of Louisville's Great American Play Contest; *Mensch Meier* was given its American premiere by The Empty Space in Seattle; *Buck* was coproduced by New York City's American Place Theatre and Playwrights Horizons; *Mercenaries* came from the Interart Theatre, also in New York.

The writers in *New Plays USA 2* are also the first to receive Playwrights

USA Awards. Home Box Office, Inc. put a capstone on the whole *Plays in Process* project when it established these substantial grants as a means of insuring the existence of a continuing pool of dramatic writers from which all performance media can draw. Such funding buys writers time to write and gives careers a boost toward security.

Like the first one in the series, this anthology contains a translation— Roger Downey's translation of *Mensch Meier* by the Bavarian playwright Franz Xaver Kroetz. The presence of this work, which seems as at home here as the strictly native pieces, upholds a fundamental tenet of the project: Dramatic translation and adaptation require skills as rare and demanding as playwriting itself and should be judged on the same level. This philosophy, coupled with the profound new influences now abroad in our culture generally, has led to a project growing out of *Plays in Process/New Plays USA* to discover, translate and publish works from the vast repertoire of Hispanic drama.

Behind any book is always an army of people who deserve thanks and acknowledgment. In the case of this one, the group is particularly large, including all of the artistic directors, dramaturgs and literary managers from TCG theatres who nominated works for the project—plays on which they had lavished their personal expertise and loving care, as well as the resources of their theatres—and, of course, the playwrights, translators and adapters without whom neither the theatre nor the project could exist. Special thanks must go to Bridget Potter, Home Box Office's vice president for original programming. Without her commitment to new American dramatic writing, the Playwrights USA Award would never have happened. And finally, my deepest gratitude to that extraordinarily dedicated and multitalented group, my fellow members of the *Plays in Process* and *New Plays USA* selection committees: Elinor Fuchs, theatre critic and author of the prizewinning play *Year One of the Empire*; Richard Gilman, teacher, theatre critic and author of, among other works, *The Making of Modern Drama*; Emily Mann, director and playwright whose Obie award-winning *Still Life* appears in *New Plays USA 1* and has received numerous productions here and abroad; Robert Moss, artistic director of the Hangar Theatre in Ithaca, New York and founder and former producing director of Playwrights Horizons in New York City; Julius Novick, drama critic for *The Village Voice*, professor of literature at the State University of New York, Purchase, and author of *Beyond Broadway: The Quest for Permanent Theatres*; and Howard Stein, chairman of the Hammerstein Center for Theatre Studies at Columbia University.

JAMES LEVERETT
December 1983

Introduction

Richard Gilman

If I'm right in taking one of my implicit assignments in this introduction to be that of writing about the current state of our drama, it would be helpful if I had a governing notion or perception, a rubric under which things might be arranged, linked, seen to express some prevailing method or concern. At least this makes for a more seductive commentary than one that sees only the wayward and untidy, if not quite the chaotic. Well, to the possible disappointment of journalists on the one hand and academics on the other I've no trend to report, at least in stylistic matters. There's been no surge of technical innovation in the two years since the first *New Plays USA* appeared; if anything this second volume is a bit more conservative in strict aesthetic terms, but that doesn't constitute a trend either.

Time operates peculiarly on culture; imaginative works keep on being produced out of different epochs of the mind, which isn't at all the same as different epochs of the calendar. Tradition runs alongside experiment, the "old" novel is concurrent with the new and, in regard to my subject here, narrative or linearly structured plays, dramas of "character," go right on being written along with performance pieces, plays of circular instead of progressive action and those that rest on images more than "stories."

The plays in this book are traditional, then, insofar as they have plots (more or less), recognizable characters, a movement in time to a denouement (more or less). The avant-garde is still out there, of course, but because of its predominantly non-literary nature, few of its products came into our purview, and none found its way into this book. After all, like the military unit from which it takes its name, the avant-garde in any art sometimes grows repetitive in its reconnoiterings, may sit down to rest or even fall asleep for a while. I don't know if that's what's happened to our theatrical avant-garde, but it seems to me rather in retreat right now.

In any case the plays printed here ought to be satisfying to all but the most fanatic adherent of the new. And in fact they *are* new in a certain way, something I'll come back to. I ought to say that the members of *PIP*'s selection committee, of which I was one, didn't concern themselves with finding a common stylistic bent or theme that would make for a "coherent" anthology. The coherence is there but it doesn't lie in anything that would interest a trendmonger.

We went on the principle that we'd choose only those plays, out of the hundred or more we read (and in some cases saw), to which we could give strong, if not necessarily unqualified, assent as discrete, independent works of dramatic imagination, no matter in what mode they were constructed or what they were "about." And when we voted it was with a remarkable unanimity, considering the multiplicity of points of view, credos and experiences we brought as a group to the matter.

I think that the five plays at hand are representative of the best that are being made in America at pretty nearly this moment. Well, if there isn't a common style to them, or even a predominant one, is there something we can call a common theme or preoccupation? I remember that when I ran the playwriting program at Yale there were thematic cycles in the plays submitted by writers applying for admission. In the late sixties and early seventies there were many plays about Viet Nam, in particular about the troubled lives of American draft-evaders in Sweden or Canada, and a spate of dramas based on the Manson killings (including a couple of full-scale musicals!). And then there were clusters of Ionesco-like or Pinter-like dramas about the absurdity or the non-communicativeness of it all, and dramas about Watergate, and our nostalgia for the thirties or fifties, and ecology.

Now to write a topical play, especially a political one, has always seemed to me a great danger artistically. The language (the jargon often) of the moment, the sense of crisis, the lofty principle, the itch to prod, cajole, *change things*—and then the wind shifts and you're left with something thin and rapidly becoming archaic. Beyond that, what's at present of high interest and importance may turn sour as a subject, as material for the imagination; the importance may remain but the issue's been squeezed dry, exhausted as a lode for the mind to work—slogans crowd out insights, ready-made emotions substitute for those that have to be wrought.

The noteworthy thing about the five plays in this book is that while they share no common subject or what we usually call "theme" they're all in one way or another propelled by what I would describe as a common state of mind or morale. More than that they're all "topical" or political, but in a sense that gets them past the dangers I just spoke of. The best plays we read were those in which the psychic and the social fuse, the private and the public merge; in them the political takes on its widest, most useful implications for dramatic vision, as the organization of life, the communal arena of values, and so goes beyond program or indictment. Yeats wrote that we make "poetry" out of the quarrel with ourselves but "rhetoric" out of that with others.

The division isn't so sharp in these plays but it's there. The self is engaged while the external reality—society, political realms, the facts of power—is probed, laid bare, mourned over. The state of mind or morale I spoke of before is indeed a sorrowing, a lament, overt or more hidden. From the most obviously "political" of the plays—Donald Freed's and Arnold Stone's *Secret Honor* and James Yoshimura's *Mercenaries*—to the least—Franz Xaver Kroetz's *Mensch Meier*—these dramas speak of what we are all suffering.

And so in their different ways they testify to our moral, social and, without making anything clinical of it, psychic condition, as, to be sure, plays do at any time. But we are more self-conscious of what we're like and of the means we use to tell ourselves what we're like than most other ages have been, and so plays like these are peculiarly immediate witnesses to our lives as well as artifacts fashioned from them. Since this is a dark period (darker than others? for the sentient mind such comparisons have no meaning) the plays reflect it and are therefore suffused with pain, anger, threat and absence: of sustaining structures, trust, a sense of honor, a sense, finally, of assured humanity.

But they're eloquent in varying degrees, and eloquence is one kind of triumph over despair. They're surprising too. I look at the Richard Nixon play and think: Who could have imagined another play about *him* or that anything at all new could be said? Yet this strange play, so unlikely in its starting-point, so seemingly vulnerable to all sorts of objections, *works*, by which I mean exists powerfully as dramatic vision while the ideological and political demurrers to the very subject lose their force. The proof of its risky victory seems to me to lie in the startled, half-grudging remark of one reviewer that it "humanizes" its protagonist. Yes, of course: It returns him from an abstraction, a malefic emblem, to disheveled, ambiguous, painful presence, someone not all that far from the rest of us.

James Yoshimura's *Mercenaries* can be seen as a scathing attack on American policies in the Third World, especially its clandestine and unofficial ones, and Gary Leon Hill's *Food from Trash* as an equally scathing indictment of ecological waste and pollution. The plays indeed have motivations of anger and outrage, they deplore all right, but that isn't what gives them status as dramas. In the case of *Food from Trash* an ideological or sermonizing impulse breaks through near the end, giving off an echo of both the thirties and the sixties.

But this lapse doesn't come close to being a fatality. For almost all its way *Food from Trash* offers an extraordinary tale of life on the margins, of that nearly hidden dehumanization of our society that goes on beneath or at the back of the flagrant ravages that power works. It is more or other than an outcry against institutionalized greed and rapacity; more profoundly it's a piteous vision of deracination and the destruction of dignity.

In the same way *Mercenaries*, while on the surface a political drama, moves past its obvious targets to compose a portrait, both ferocious and grimly funny, of trapped souls, in this instance those of some American hired guns lost in the bewildering world of what we euphemistically call "international relations." Plebeian, shaped by Viet Nam, poor slobs all, dumb and crude and venal, they're as much victims of the cold, terrifyingly impersonal operation of power as they are its small cogs, and that Yoshimura has made us care for them is his play's victory.

Ronald Ribman's *Buck*, dramaturgically perhaps the most complex of these plays, appears to have no political dimension, yet it's there, if we go back to the notion of the political I sketched earlier. The climate in which Buck Halloran, the TV director, works is depraved, corrupted beyond thought of remedy. He tells his co-worker in regard to the series of reenactments of sensational killings they're filming, "I want the truth up there, Charlie, the truth!" But the shadowy, infinitely vulgar magnate who "owns" it all says, "Talking [or truth] is a crock of shit." Apparently a familiar tale of idealism brought down by the rapacity of commerce, *Buck* is more deeply a fable of innocence and suffering and a vision of truth under desperate siege: Society has been *organized* this way.

The remaining play, Franz Xaver Kroetz's *Mensch Meier*, requires a word of explanation about its inclusion in this volume. What's a play by a German writer doing in a book called *New Plays USA*? Well, look at that title again: It's not "New American Plays" or "New Plays by American Writers." As I said earlier the book is composed of plays recently "made" in America, and I chose that word deliberately. *Mensch Meier* has been brilliantly translated by Roger Downey and that is the technical basis of its eligibility. More than that it has been and is being produced here, given a new incarnation by our theatre. I think its presence in this volume testifies to a breaking down of walls and is a blow at aesthetic jingoism.

Whatever brings it to this book, *Mensch Meier* is a wonderful play, immensely affecting and almost wholly deceptive in its appearance. At first glance it seems a familiar enough naturalistic study of lower or working-class life, filled with evidence of a beleaguered existence. But Kroetz is no conventional naturalist. What he exposes isn't so much the material or even emotional suffering of his characters as their loss of parts of the self, their having been *diminished*. The worst pain of all is that they have no capacity to "see through their situation," as Kroetz has said of his plays' characters in general, and this is because they've been rendered "inarticulate" by the society at large. They suffer dumbly, and if this isn't ultimately political, this totally unheroic tragedy of human waste and loss which society keeps on staging, then I don't know what is.

As I read over these pages I see a vocabulary of oppression and melancholy. Yet I don't think these plays will leave the reader with a feeling of despair. In this regard I'd like to recount something that took place at a Thanksgiving dinner I shared in recently. A tradition in this family is that everyone, from the youngest child capable of it, has to read something before the feast is served, a poem, a little story, whatever. My hostess, the novelist Ann Roiphe, read a poem by her 20-year-old daughter and prefaced it by saying that while the poem was sorrowful and even despairing the *fact* of it having been written was the heartening thing. Art, she said, is one of the few ways we have to oppose darkness, affirm the spirit, and this is beyond the question of its being "hopeful" or the reverse in its statements. This book of plays offers several more examples of that.

Richard Gilman is the immediate past president of the American Center of PEN, the international association of writers. Currently a professor of drama at Yale University and drama critic for *The Nation*, Gilman has won the George Jean Nathan Award for drama criticism and the Morton Dauwen Zable Award for criticism from the American Academy and Institute of Arts and Letters. He is the author of numerous books on theatre, including *The Making of Modern Drama* and *Decadence*.

Secret Honor

The Last Testament
of Richard M. Nixon:
A Political Myth

Donald Freed
and
Arnold M. Stone

About Donald Freed and Arnold M. Stone

Donald Freed's prizewinning play *Inquest*, about the Rosenberg-Sobell case, played on Broadway in 1970. He has received a grant from the Office for Advanced Drama Research, the John Larkin Award, and a prize as one of the International Gandhi Centennial Finalists. *The Glasshouse Tapes*, which he edited, received a California Gold Medal journalism award. Freed is the author of the "novel of fact" *Executive Action* (adapted for film with Dalton Trumbo), and of *Agony in New Haven*, which deals with the Black Liberation movement.

Currently lecturing in the philosophy of literature at Mount Saint Mary's College in Los Angeles, Freed has taught linguistics, world literature, anthropology and philosophy at UCLA, UCI and USC; and in a special project at Yale University he brought together Erik H. Erikson and Huey P. Newton for an historic dialogue and book, *In Search of Common Ground*. *The Spymaster* was a Book-of-the-Month Club selection in 1981 and is now being adapted for film, as is *Death in Washington: The Murder of Orlando Letelier*. Plays awaiting production in 1984 are: *Solidarity!, Circe & Bravo, The White Crow (Eichmann in Jerusalem)* and, in collaboration with Harold Lieberman, *The Gandhi Problem* and *Hogs Run Wild!*

Arnold M. Stone's distinguished legal career includes both private and government service. For three years he was an intelligence analyst with the National Security Agency, and later spent four years as a Department of Justice attorney, supervising federal investigations into organized crime and racketeering. Stone now practices in Los Angeles in the firm of Stone & Rohatiner. He is also a partner in a literary publishing house, The New South Company. He has long been a student of U.S. history and foreign policy.

Production History

Secret Honor was nominated for TCG's *Plays in Process* script circulation series by Bill Bushnell, producing/artistic director of Los Angeles Actors' Theatre. It was presented there under the title *Last Tape (and Testament) of Richard M. Nixon* as part of LAAT's fifth annual Festival of Premieres from June 7 through September 3, 1983, and won the top Louis B. Mayer Playwrights' Award as best new play of the festival.

Robert Harders directed. Set and lighting were designed by Russell Pyle, sound by Jon Gottlieb and costume by Michele Jo Blanche. Diane White and Adam Leipzig coproduced the festival. The cast was as follows:

Richard M. Nixon . . . . .Philip Baker Hall

Producer Robert Altman brought the LAAT production of *Secret Honor* to New York City, where it opened at the Provincetown Playhouse on November 8, 1983.

Playwright's Note

This is a play of "Fact" and of "Cruelty." The biographical and political material is well known to historians; the legal case is abstracted from documents prepared for the House Judiciary Committee as it confronted the impeachment process in 1973 and '74. The rest is our burden—authors and audience: We made the man and we broke him. He is of us, simply, and we must come to terms with him, at last.

Characters

RICHARD M. NIXON

Time

The 1980s.

Place

The study of Richard M. Nixon.

The Play

Secret Honor

The Last Testament
of Richard M. Nixon: A Political Myth

The study is official, expensive, formal. Everywhere are signs and symbols of the Imperial Presidency. Oversized photographs of Eisenhower, Kissinger and Woodrow Wilson look down from the walls. Stage Right is a fireplace, near it a comfortable chair. Upstage Center is an alcove with shelves for books and liquor. Stage Left is a piano. A large desk dominates the study. On the desk are an expensive tape recorder, a microphone, a telephone and the inevitable legal pads.

RICHARD M. NIXON is discovered seated Stage Right, lit only by firelight, staring into the flames. HE is dressed expensively but soberly. HE finishes his drink, then crosses the dark room to a closet Upstage Left and exchanges his suit coat for a red smoking jacket. HE uses a panel of dimmer switches near the door Upstage Right to light the room to his satisfaction. HE listens at the door, peers out suspiciously, then locks the door. HE goes to his desk, unlocks a drawer and lifts out a large box. HE opens the box and checks the gun inside. Finally HE begins the painful process of activating the tape recorder.

Testing: one, two, three, four.

HE *rewinds, plays. Silence.* HE *looks closely at the machine then sits back, removes a tape cassette from his pocket and inserts it into the machine.*

Testing: one, two, three, four.

HE *rewinds, plays. Harpsichord music comes from the machine.* HE *clicks it off.*

Shit.

HE rewinds and records.

Testing: one, two, three, four. . . . Roberto, I told you that this thing doesn't . . . it doesn't . . . it's got a bad, uh, you know.

HE rewinds, plays. The same music comes from the machine. HE clicks it off.

Cocksucker.

HE removes an instruction manual from a desk drawer. Consulting the manual, HE prepares the machine for recording. HE rewinds, records.

Testing: one, two, three, four. . . . Roberto, this is for "Eyes Only," for, uh, our eyes, uh . . .

HE rewinds, plays. This time we hear his voice. HE approves and replaces the manual in the desk drawer. But when his recorded message ends, music continues from the machine. HE sits back and listens to it for a moment. Then, ready to begin, HE clicks off the machine. HE rewinds, records.

Uh, Roberto. Send that, uh, call Mr. Stein at my publisher's to pick up that package I gave you. And tell Mrs. Nixon that I, uh. . . . Never mind. . . . I hear that the gardener's, uh, Fernando's, wife is in the hospital. Send her a new portable radio. A good one. But, uh, don't use my, uh . . . make it anonymous, okay? No, say that it's from, uh, "Friends of a Free Cuba," uh, Cuba Libre.

HE stares at the turning tape for a moment.

Okay. Side One. Day and date, et cetera. Then, uh, then I'll write the prayer or the plea or the, uh, the, uh, uh, the prologue . . . you know. . . .

HE stops recording and rises to pour a drink, then resumes taping. HE speaks rapidly most of the time. Even his stumbles and stammers make up a part of the staccato scansion of his compulsive chatter. But when HE assumes the role of the lawyer we can see and hear the formidable figure who rose to the acme of power.

Your Honor, may we take the matter of the pardon first. It solved nothing. A complete fake, because, you know, if there had been a trial and, uh, the rest of it . . . if I had gone to prison, well, then, you know, I'd be a free man today. A free man. . . . Because a pardon has two definitions. Now, first is the legal aspect which excuses a convicted man from punishment. Then there's the general meaning of a pardon which is to forgive. . . .

HE *stops and sips drink.* HE *stares into space and chuckles mirthlessly, then resumes in the third person with power and gravity.*

Your Honor, my client has been driven almost mad. He can never be made whole. Because he faced, as you shall see, the country he loved more than life itself faced with . . . yes, civil war and tyranny. You will hear how he has had to carry the most terrible secrets of all locked up inside his breaking heart and, uh, beating mind. Now, you have read the reasons for the Watergate affair in the press, but today my client is going to reveal to you the *reasons behind the reasons!* And you, ladies and gentlemen of the American jury, you alone shall look at the face that is under the mask, that is . . . under the mask. You alone shall judge his life. . . . Your Honor, my client has never been convicted of anything. Therefore he was not qualified, technically, for a pardon. Nevertheless, he has suffered, uh, banishment and extremes of libel and slander for which there is no remedy. Now, as to the general definition of a pardon . . . *there has been no forgiveness here!* So it's all been a sham. . . . No trial, no conviction, no legal punishment. Instead, Your Honor, my client must suffer lifelong personal punishment, torment, for what has been called the, uh, "good of the nation," and so forth. But if the nation knew the real truth then I would be in the position of de Gaulle, for instance. Because I had to withdraw because of . . .

HE *pauses, then clicks off the recorder.* HE *rises and tries to telephone. No answer.*

. . . de Gaulle. Or Mao . . .

Realizing the machine is not recording, HE *clicks it back on.*

Mao! You know, he was a kind of lone wolf, too. He said to me once, "I am alone with the people, waiting." I'll never forget that moment, the gooseflesh came out. And if the American people knew what happened—not the break-ins and all that crap!—knew what really happened, then we'd have a situation like . . . . But the true story could never be told during my lifetime, Your Honor, because the nation could not have stood it. Take the, uh, killing of President Kennedy and the Warren Report, and so forth. The country could not have stood the whole story. So, it was a blessing when, uh, what's-his-name, uh, Ruby shot Oswald. Now, I'm not saying that two rights make a wrong, but it was a godsend when that patriotic, uh, nightclub owner shot, uh, uh. . . . And this would have been the same thing. The American citizen is like the child in the family that you can't, uh, you can't, uh, *you can't!*

HE *laughs. His mood shifts sharply.*

You see, I always understood the Kennedy brothers. The four boys. My brother Harold—we were four brothers, too—he had the same charisma. A big, brash redhead, and the girls all, you know. . . . T.B. G'damn T.B. up and down both sides of the family. It got my little brother Arthur in 1925 and Harold in 1933. In those days you went to . . . well, my mother, she took Harold to Arizona for the dry air, and I went along in the summer to work as a barker at the carnival, at the, uh, Slippery Gulch Rodeo . . . that son-of-a-bitch wrote that I was a shill for a crooked card game. Well. . . . But Harold chased around and drank and had a good time for awhile, at least, I guess. . . . Sure, while I was shovelling manure in the G'damn rodeo stables and my mother was scrubbing their stinking floors to get money for that, uh, my old man called it "a fat-cat lunger clinic." Yeah, my old man, he was, uh, he was. . . . But Arthur was the worst.

> As HE discusses the death of his younger brother it is as if HE were talking to an angel in heaven.

Only seven years old and the favorite in the family. Meningitis fever up to 105 degrees.

> HE punches off the machine, mutters to himself as HE refills his glass. Then HE goes to a cluster of old photos on a shelf and stares at one.

Awful pain. His eyes were black and beautiful, sparkling with hidden fire. His eyes . . . beckoning us to come on some hidden journey beyond riches. A mass of brown curls, a little sailor suit. How he suffered. Oh, God, and Mother, too. It should have been me! It should have been me, kiddo. But it won't be long now. G'damn T.B.

> HE returns to the machine and presses the record button.

G'damn T.B. That's why we came to California in the first place, for the G'damn climate . . . and then they all die anyway. And I'd lay there at night figuring how I could . . . the sound of the Santa Fe railroad was the sweetest sound I ever heard. . . .

> HE lurches quickly to a shelf, takes down a book and looks up his 1968 acceptance speech before the G.O.P. Convention. HE stands and declaims it once again with full power.

"Tonight I see the face of a child. He is black, he is white. He is Mexican, Italian, Polish. None of this matters. What does matter is that he is an American child. . . . He is American. . . . He sleeps the sleep of childhood and dreams its dreams. . . . Yet, when he awakens, he awakens to a living nightmare of poverty, neglect, and despair."

> HE looks up from the book, out into the great amphitheatre of memory.

"I see the face of another child. He hears the train go by at night and dreams of faraway places he would like to go. It seems like an impossible dream. But he is helped on his journey through life: a father. A gentle Quaker mother. A great football coach. A courageous wife and loyal children. Tonight he stands before you . . . nominated for President of the United States. You can see why I believe deeply in the American Dream. For most of us the American Revolution has been won, the American Dream has come true. I ask you to help me make that dream come true for millions to whom it is an impossible dream today."

HE *bows and basks in absent applause, past music. Then, returning to the present,* HE *crosses to the machine.*

Roberto, would you please erase everything back to "I see the face of a," uh, "a child." Thank you. And would you send a. . . . The Kennedys stole the 1960 election in Chicago and they all told me to blow it wide open but, again, there are some things that you can't, the public, uh, they can't. . . . Oh, shit!

HE *returns the book to its place on the shelf.*

Roberto, send Fernando's wife a basket of fruit, too. A big one. . . . Poor woman, she. . . . Okay. Now, you see, Your Honor, the so-called Watergate is just, uh, copping a plea, a misdemeanor, a third-rate burglary. Watergate was nothing more than a convenient hook upon which to hang my client's political body because before anyone in the world ever heard the word Watergate, the Nixon Presidency was over. Your Honor, my client had, as you know, stood the acid test of six major crises, but this was something of an entirely different magnitude. This wasn't like '52 when I could go to the public with my side of the story.

HE *recalls the painful past and recreates the famous 1952 Checkers speech to the TV cameras.*

The whole country was waiting. Ike had already dropped me like a. . . . When the cameras came on I was going to quit the race. . . . I promised Pat, uh, my wife, that. . . . Well, she *believed* in me then and I couldn't, uh, when someone believes in you, you can't, uh. . . . Well, after I lost in California in '62, I really was going to get out of it for good. In fact, I wrote it down and carried it around in my . . . in my . . . wallet. . . .

HE *takes out his wallet, removes the promise written on the back of an old photo of Pat and stares at it.*

And I would have. But I couldn't. . . . But in '52, she did still believe in me. But I couldn't. Down in South America, they spit on her. My God, I am so sorry for that. But I couldn't . . . I couldn't just quit with my tail between my, you know, legs like that.

Leaping up, HE *is back at the moment of destiny.*

". . . And my wife doesn't wear a mink coat, you know, she wears a good Republican cloth coat . . . and my little dog Checkers. . . ." And I cried and the public cried with me and Ike, the old man, he couldn't get rid of me. . . . Yes! I could always cry in public. Dr. Birdsell, my dramatic coach in school, always said that I was the most melancholy Dane he had ever directed. . . .

HE *rises with a curious power and speaks the familiar lines with a simple potency.*

"To be, or not to be, that is the question,
Whether 'tis nobler in the mind to suffer
The slings and arrows of outrageous fortune,
Or to take arms against a sea of troubles,
And by opposing, end them. To die, to sleep . . ."

HÈ *crosses to pick up the fireplace poker.*

". . . and by a sleep to say we end
The heartache and the . . . the, uh, the, uh . . ."

HE *is suddenly enraged.*

Villain, villain, smiling, damned villain!

HE *whirls to face the portrait of President Eisenhower.*

Remorseless, treacherous, lecherous, kiiiindless villain. . . . O, vengeance!

HE *lunges toward the portrait, poker upraised to plunge, then freezes.*

I'm not your stinking caddy now, you old . . .

HE *returns the poker to the fireplace.*

They used to say that Adlai Stevenson was Hamlet, but it was me who was really Hamlet. And Ike was the King. I never even got to see all the rooms in the White House until Johnson became President. Ike. One time he introduced me to a crowd as Nick Dixon. Ike! He'd drag his coattails and then jerk them away and leave me high and dry so that I was running. Always running. Trying so hard to make the team that I was always offsides. Just like my old man. He sold the lemon grove, *then* they discovered oil on it. Well, not me. Not to the manner born. I had to pretend not to see all the snubs and sniggers. Had to keep up a front. "Welcome to Denmark."

HE *brightens.*

God, how I used to love to act. That was the real fun. The Whittier *News* said that I was very good, and that "for no extra charge you can watch Dick Nixon try to manipulate his fencing foil." Ha!

HE *lunges with an imaginary foil.*

"Get thee to a nunnery. I say we shall have no more marriages. Those that are married already shall live . . . *all but one!* To a nunnery, go."

HE *laughs and descends deeper into memory.*

When I was thirteen, my first debate: "Resolved: Girls are no good." And I won! Then, next was, "Resolved: Cows are better than horses." I always hated girls but I couldn't keep away from them. Well, in high school you can't. . . . So, what I did, I founded the Orthogonian Society . . . all boys—square shooters—uh, no girls. And our motto was the four B's: "Beans, Brains, Brawn, and Bowels!" And we had a . . . we used to . . . uh . . .

HE *recalls his theme and sings with a youthful exuberance.*

"ALL HAIL THE MIGHTY BOAR
OUR PATRON BEAST IS HE
ECRASONS L'INFAME
OUR BATTLE CRY WILL BE:
BROTHERS TOGETHER WE'LL TRAVEL ON AND ON
WORTHY THE NAME OF ORTHOGONIAN."

HE *strikes a high-school debater's pose.*

Resolved. . . . Resolved to win! Period. Because that's the system. You take either side, it doesn't matter which, and go on the attack. It's like football. No, no. It's like poker: the winners make jokes and the loser says "Deal! Deal! Deal!"

HE *takes a drink and calms down.*

Roberto, erase all that crap . . . back to, uh, the lesser of two evils, back about before the break-in. Thank you.

HE *grabs a legal tablet and begins to talk with great force, in and out of character.*

Your Honor, there were three Charges of Impeachment brought against me and none of them could be proved. They all knew that. Kennedy's hit man, John Doar—and he had a hundred bloodhounds working for him—and they told him—and we have ways of knowing this, Your Honor—they told him: "There is no case against the President. Period." Your Honor, the impeachment process itself was simply the grandest cover-up of all. There can only be—and you know this, Your Honor—one impeachment charge and that is "Treason, Bribery, or other High Crimes and Misdemeanors." Well, so they brought a load of . . . well, we gave 'em a load of chicken-shit charges against me. And none of them stuck. And none of their theories, either. And I know what was going on inside the Judiciary Committee: the "Tip of the Iceberg" theory or the "Narrow Escape" theory or the, uh, "Robber Baron" baloney and all that crap. Oh, then there was the "Higher Standard of Conduct" theory.

HE *roars with laughter.*

That's rich! The Founding Fathers caused the White House to be built in a swamp in the first place, for Christ's sake, and Congress up on a G'damn hill. The Founding Fathers were nothing more than a bunch of snotty English shits who never trusted any elected President to begin with. So, why, then, Your Honor, did my client resign, *voluntarily?* Why did he give them a sword? When the fact is that Richard Nixon not only need not have quit but, in fact, could have stayed on beyond. . . . Your Honor, something happened to my client. The year is 1945. . . . Okay, Roberto, that's the end of the, uh, prologue. The next part is 1945 through 1952. So, uh, make a separate, uh, watchmacallit, for each, uh, uh, you know. . . . Okay. Now in 1939 I went to Cuba after I almost got disbarred for signing some client's name to a, uh. . . . Roberto, would you erase all that, please? They wanted me to stay in Cuba but I was so damned wet behind the ears and then the Navy came along. . . . Your Honor, I'm trying to tell you about 1945: I was just getting out of the Navy and an ad appeared in the Whittier *Daily News* . . . I will never forget it. It said, "WANTED: YOUNG MAN INTERESTED IN RUNNING FOR CONGRESS. VETERAN PREFERRED." And it listed the name of some committee to contact. So I took some of my poker winnings and flew out there in my uniform.

HE *rises to speak as the young naval officer.*

"If the choice of this committee comes to me, I promise to wage an aggressive and vigorous campaign based on a platform of practical liberalism. . . ." Well, it was those men. I answered the ad and I met those men. The Committee of 100 they were called. Well, the names changed over the years: Committee for a Free Iran, a Free Guatemala, Free Congo, Free Taiwan . . . always Taiwan. And the men, they were a certain kind of . . . well, the men came and went with the years. But I always knew them as the Committee of 100. Well, they selected me, Your Honor, and they took my client up to Bohemian Grove and that's where the China Plan was. . . . That's where I got the message. Up there in Bohemian Grove, deep in the California redwoods, with the guards and the dogs and the prostitutes from Guerneyville. At the Caveman Camp. And this young man, Richard Nixon, this boy from a poor family who'd never had a break, never had a chance was overwhelmed by these big men on the Committee of 100. Because these men showed him a vision of the riches and the power of this world. And he drank—drank in their words and visions—and he had a little sip of their liquor, too . . . this poor boy who couldn't drink, didn't know how from his strict Quaker background. And he may have said and done some things up there that came back to haunt him twenty-five years later in 1972 when the real China Card was played. . . .

HE *leans back, remembering.*

But that first night up there, I couldn't sleep. All night long I could hear the guard dogs howling, the big German shepherds, but way off in the distance. And then the men, they were singing and dancing. . . . Oh, yes, football songs. All night long. They were singing football songs . . . far off . . . waaay off . . . in the . . . distance. . . .

HE *sits at the piano and softly plays the "Notre Dame Fight Song." HE hits a sour note. HE turns to the microphone.*

It's a little out of . . .

HE *turns back to the piano.*

But you were my mother's piano and that fucking museum is not going to get you.

HE *resumes playing and finishes the song.*

And the whores . . . oh, yes, these were men. These were not homos from Westchester County or Cambridge. Not, uh, old money or the better sort. These were Armenians, Italians, Irish and, uh, assorted "white trash" . . . men! And what they wanted was a political laboratory and that is what they made California into; as a kind of proving ground for later on when they, uh, uh. . . . But the men! These were real men, big men with hair on their chests. Rough and tough and they had the contacts. And here was me, a complete loser. The punching bag on the football team, Coach called me. Just like my old man, you know. He could never make a go out of any G'damn thing, either. He insulted every boss or customer he ever had. But they lied about my old man. He may have been a strike-breaker, yes, but he was never a barn-burner. Never! So . . . so. . . . But you see why these football songs were music to my ears!

HE *plays a rousing reprise of the "Notre Dame Fight Song."*

But it was the words. That was the real music to my ears. Look, I'd been a loser all my G'damn life. At last I'm gonna be a winner. Me, old number twenty-three. You know what Coach always said? He said, if I could run the ball the way I ran my mouth winning debate prizes, well, then, ha, ha. . . .

HE *moves away from the piano.*

But these guys dancing with the hookers, they were real winners. I couldn't dance worth a G'damn. As a matter of fact, my old man *wouldn't* dance because he said that it gave him a, uh, it "aroused" him. Uh, me too. Oh, you can imagine I took a hell of a kidding on that. So you know what I did? When I ran for high-school student president, I promised a liberal dress *and* dance code . . . and I won!

HE *picks up a family picture of his father from the desk.*

The old man. . . . God, he hated politicians. So there's me saying, "Yes, Father, I'm going to be an old-fashioned lawyer, I won't take any bribes." Crap! If he'd gone beyond the sixth grade, poor bastard, he'd've known that we're all crooks. It's not his fault, though. He had a worse childhood than I did. Wandering, a rolling stone, poor old bastard. Handy with the G'damn strap, too . . . but that was all to the good, Your Honor, because. . . . Did I used to hate it when they called me "Nicky," "Nicky,"—oh, boy—but I had the last laugh when I won that scholarship to Duke. But, you see, I still wasn't a winner, yet. I mean, a winner doesn't have to break into the Dean's office like I did to find out what his grades are. Sure, I graduated third in my class but when we went to New York to interview for some big-time law firms, it was a different story. I was out of my league, and I knew it. But I also knew this: that New York was the big time, the big, big money. New York with the clubs and the fast track. In New York money talks! Yes, sir! Yes, sir! Talks! Talks! Talks! Yeah! Yeah! Yeah! Anyway . . . I wanted to join the Dulles brothers' law firm . . . Sullivan and Cromwell. Thick, plush carpets. Fine, oak panelling. Quiet . . . fine. . . . East-Coast shits, that's what they were. Well, my two friends, they did get taken on by one of the big firms. Uh, I did not. So, then I tried to join the F.B.I. and, uh, well, I got turned down again. Hoover, I worshipped Hoover. Then years later, that son-of-a-bitch tried to stab me in the back, too. But the point of this, Your Honor, is that here is a young man—basically a loser . . . a hard-luck kid—exposed to these big men. He just flunked out on the F.B.I. test, then he came to California where his first case almost ruined the little law firm of Wingert and Bewley, who had only taken him on out of respect for the defendant's grandfather, Franklin Milhous. So, after that I had to get out of town. So, I went to Cuba and, uh, then the Navy came along and I got stuck on that G'damn island playing poker. . . . But the point of all this, Your Honor, is that the Committee of 100 had a plan. And that was it in '46, and '48, and '50, right on through. I was very young and . . . they gave me the blueprint. Do you understand that? Crooks and Communists were to be the target; you know, go after the Reds. That's when Murray Chotiner came into the picture because, Murray, he was the link to Lansky and Ratner and, uh, the Mob and, uh, all the rest. . . .

HE *grabs a yellow legal pad and begins to scrawl madly. The pencil breaks but* HE *shouts on.*

What Hiss and the Kennedys—all those East-Coast pricks—never understood was, is that I would be a winner because I was a loser! That's right. I dream of failure every night of my life. And that's my secret. To make it in this rat-race you have to dream of failing every night. That's *reality!* Jews, Niggers, Reds, Kikes . . . new Nixons, old Nixons. . . . *Because I am an American!* A real American. The forgotten American, that's me. I'm not some rich Ivy League prince that thinks he's a winner. We shoot that type down in the street like dogs. We send those people to prison. See, what the big shots thought is that I was a dog-catcher. Yes! *I was!* And I am. And a used-car salesman. *Sure! Fine!* And a siding and shingle man. Because I knew that, today, the dogcatcher is king! And all those crooks and shysters, the mobsters and lobsters, I mean, lobbyists, and every well-fed, I mean, welfare bum and tramp in the country . . . *that is your Palace Guard!*

HE *pushes away from the desk and, laughing, rides the swivel chair across the room.* HE *stops and stares back into the past, 1960.* HE *is sad, wistful.*

I could have won in 1960. I could have beat Kennedy. But the C.I.A. told him about the "Track II" operation against Castro. They told Kennedy and then he out–Red-baited me by attacking Castro and that made *me* look soft. And they promised me that the invasion, the, uh, "Executive Action" against Castro would take place before the election. God, how they screwed me! I could have won! I could have beat Kennedy.

HE *foams with grief and rage.*

And I was the one with the "5412 Special Group" who had planned the whole thing in the first place. And I'd have bombed 'em, oh, how I'd have bombed them! But Castro was smart . . . oh, boy. . . . When Eisenhower wouldn't meet with Castro when he came to this country before the election . . . and then the son-of-a-bitch went up there and had lunch with the colored waiters at the G'damn Theresa Hotel in Harlem. And I would have got him. We already had the poison, for Christ's sake. We tested it on some monkeys.

HE *gestures warmly to the heavens as* HE *recalls Kennedy.*

Ah, but, Jack, Jack, Jack. . . . He was a big, good-looking Irishman with that shock of hair. Like my brother, Harold. He had the same charismatic. . . . And the women, they all jumped up and down whenever he. . . . And his wife. She was a G'damn clotheshorse. My wife was forty-eight G'damn years old, for Christ's sake. And what was she? Thirty? I went to their wedding. And Jack liked me. Yes, he did, he did. He even congratulated me when I beat Helen Gahagan Douglas. His old man contributed money to my campaign. Of course, it's true that we were black Irish and they were. . . . But, we both had our tragedies, though. The four brothers, uh, the boys. . . . And the Catholic thing. I never, uh, I never used it. I didn't. . . . Then the debates came along. Everybody said I was like Cicero. They said, "How well he speaks." But when Demosthenes spoke they all said, "Let's march! Let's march!" G'damn Jack. He was something else.

HE *turns bitter and drinks.*

And I got rattled when the press got hold of the Howard Hughes loan to my brother for that wacko scheme of his to sell "Nixonburgers." Then Haldeman calls Martin Luther King a "nigger" on the telephone. But the worst was three days before the election when I slipped and called for "Peace *and* Surrender." That was the dumbest thing I ever did.

HE *stops, stares at photographs.*

My poor G'damn dumb brothers. I had to put 'em all under surveillance because of Vesco.

HE *laughs hysterically.*

Then my brother Don's kid, he runs off and joins some dirty hippy commune and they had to get some private investigator to wade through all that crap and drag him back by the ears and put him to work for Vesco. Oh, Jesus Christ, my G'damn family alone could have ruined me!

HE *gets himself another drink.*

I still couldn't sleep at night right up to the election. And I could have neutralized the Hughes thing because the Committee of 100, they were tapping her, tapping Marilyn Monroe. Well, the Kennedy boys, they were all big studs like their old man. Like my brother Harold. And I'll tell you something else, too . . . that's what killed them! That's right. There were no women allowed up at Bohemian Grove . . . not *real* women. We were a different type from that Kennedy crowd. I was a different type. I never . . . I didn't . . . I never.

HE *launches back into his confession.*

But I didn't quit. Not even in '74 when I could've . . . I really should've . . . I could have burned the tapes and stonewalled it and let the big boys shoot it out up at Bohemian Grove. And let the country go Fascist by 1980. We're talking shooting it out in the streets, I mean civil war in this country by 1977. . . . So, you see why I had to withdraw, to lay my life on the line to stop them. Stop Fascism. *And* Communism. And the G'damn Yankees—Ford—they get the Presidency, anyway, and that fucking Bush and the cowboys they get the C.I.A. And what the hell do I get for following orders for thirty G'damn years . . . a fucking pardon and disgrace?! I tried to give 'em their dirty little war in Chile . . . but that Allende, he was a worse whoremonger than you know who. . . . But they didn't have to kill him . . . like that. Not . . . like that.

HE *returns to the tape.*

But I could have hung tough and called out my political base. I could have called out Main Street against Wall Street. But I didn't. I said, *I'll* go. And I did it for them. For the little people. For Maggie and Jiggs. For my people. For all the forgotten ranchers and farmers, people just like my old man: the cabdrivers, the grocery-store clerks, the cockroach capitalists, the travelling salesmen. The forgotten Americans, the Silent Majority. In their name I said screw all the wise men, all the tough guys who've sold us out and stabbed us in the back. Look, I was not elected President on some other planet! *I am America!* I am a winner who lost every battle up to and including the war. I am not the American nightmare . . . I am the American dream! Period. And that is why the system works. Because I am the system. Period!

HE *drops the microphone onto the desk and angrily paces the room, remembering and recalculating old strategies.*

So I talked and I stalled and then finally I unleashed Haig and that provoked the "Saturday Night Massacre." Oh, yes! This was before I went crazy and they had to bring in the Army to shoot me down on the floor of the Oval Office.

HE *whispers into the microphone.*

Oh, yes, they would have done it, all right. There was a "Sinister Force" loose in the White House, but it sure as hell wasn't me. In the end, I was just an "unindicted co-conspirator" like everybody else in the United States of America.

HE *crosses Upstage for another drink.*

You were right, Mother. There never was a "new" Nixon. I'm a square. Always have been . . . but . . . I believed in the system. And that's what I did. I got out to protect the system. To protect the Presidency.

HE *recalls the good old days.*

God, how I loved being President . . . I cannot tell you. The walks on the South Lawn with the dogs and the girls. And the White House. I used to love the. . . . And the Lincoln Study. I used to love to sit in the Lincoln Study with the fireplace burning and the air conditioning on, thinking about Lincoln and Washington . . . what a liar he was, huh? And the putting green. I used to love the . . . I couldn't even hold the. . . .

Chuckling, HE *mimes swinging a golf club.*

But the Rose Garden . . . it was so beautiful. . . . And the yacht. Oh, yes, the Sequoia . . . how I used to love to sit topside on the fantail of the Sequoia . . . down the Potomac . . . back to the Navy Yard. Sipping drinks with a friend and talking "geopolitics". . . . Ahhh, God, God, God. . . . Oh, and the jiga . . . the jiga . . . the, uh, *colored* waiters bringing up steaks from the galley. And the breeeeeze! Gee, we had fun. Oh, Kissinger and that crowd, they used to like to read the pornographic novels and swing. But I was a Navy man. I was at home on the Sequoia. I was at peace . . . I was. Oh, I really used to enjoy calling in plays to the Redskin coaching staff on the white phone, and going over the bombing targets in Cambodia with Henry on the red phone . . . at the same time! That's fun!

For a moment, HE *is lost in the ecstasy of a favorite memory. But then his mood shifts.*

Yeah, we were having such a . . . we were just going along and. . . . But then, the press, and the liberals . . . they got in there and . . .!

HE *turns abruptly to the door, listening.* HE *quietly crosses to the desk, picks up the gun, and tiptoes back to the door. With the gun at the ready,* HE *unlocks the door and puts a hand on the doorknob.*

I don't know who you are out there. But if you want me, you come in here and get me. 'Cause I don't give a shit!

Ready to attack, HE *flings the door open. There is no one there.* HE *looks down the hallway and turns back, aware of his overreaction.* HE *shuts the door and returns to the tape, tight and secret.*

Roberto, when CBS calls don't, uh. . . . Just remember what I told you. The press and the liberals . . . they're yellow. Sure, they hated me . . . 'cause they were scared, too . . . shitless. Because I was their messboy, and you're mine. And your turn is coming, Señor. And when you new guys, you Cubans and, uh, all you immigrants start taking over for us . . . watch out for the liberals! The colored found that out—when it was too late—that it was the North not the South that. . . . And they will—oh, yes—the liberals will come after you just the way they came after me. And that's what made me . . . their fear! And remember this, Roberto, I knew who I was . . . *nobody*. All they knew was that they did not want to be me! So they don't exist. So don't you be afraid of 'em. Ever. *Never*. And remember this: it was not the press and the liberals that got Joe McCarthy . . . it was the Army. So you use 'em. Let 'em use you. Get in bed with 'em. Fuck 'em. *Cuba Libre!*

HE *leans back in his chair and rubs his forehead.*

And I still can't sleep. I still have the nightmare. But it is the American nightmare. . . . Uncle Sam, he's the American nightmare. He's become a pitiful giant, an old man, being eaten alive by an army of Ellsbergers and Ralph Naders and Jane Fondas. All led by Hiss. *Alger Hisssssssssss!* And the Red rats of the Roosevelt, I mean the Rosenberg Spy Ring and all the campus bums. . . . All Jews, you know. Every G'damn one of 'em. Lansky and Ratner . . . all big "anti-Communists." And even Chotiner, Murray, he's a G'damn, uh, Jew. The Committee of 100 wouldn't touch any of 'em with a ten-foot pole but when it came time to hide the bodies in the closet, then they'd pick up the phone and call Chotiner and he'd contract Miami and the Jews. Well, I beat 'em, the Jews . . . almost. It was the Committee of 100 that I couldn't handle and the China-Plan people. So that, Your Honor, is why we had to invent "Deep Throat" and use Watergate . . . to get out with a pardon. Oh, God. . . .

HE *sighs deeply and drinks.* HE *tries the telephone number again. No one answers.* HE *hangs up.* HE *then looks about the room for something. Unable to find it,* HE *throws things and curses.*

Where the hell did I put that . . .? God damn it! Dirty fucking Cubans, they're all. . . . Where the hell did they put that . . .? Nuts! *Where is my mother's album?* Oh, yeah. It's behind the Kissinger crap.

HE *pulls a book from a shelf and reads the title.*

American Foreign Policy . . . Henry "Asshole" Kissinger!

HE *throws the book over his shoulder and grabs another book from the same area on the shelf.* HE *discards it in a similar manner and repeats with another book, and another.*

Kissinger! Kissinger! Kissinger! I don't owe a single one of 'em a G'damn cent, much less an apology.

From the now-cleared shelf area, HE *removes an old, black family album which* HE *hugs to his chest.*

Only you, Mother; you, I owe.

He flips through the album, mumbling and smiling. HE *comes across a piece of his mother's lace on a page and presses it to his lips.* HE *then finds an old letter.*

Oh, no. . . .

HE *reads.*

"Dear Master: The two boys that you left with me are very bad to me. Their dog Jim is very old and he will never talk or play with me. One Saturday the boys went hunting . . . while going through the woods one of the boys tripped and fell on me. I lost my temper and bit him. He kicked me in the side . . . I started to run. . . . When I got home I was very sore. I wish you would come home right now. Your good dog, Richard."

HE *sets the album on the desk and kneels in his chair.*

"Now I lay me down to sleep. . . ." Arthur used to say that little prayer for Mother. "If I could die before I wake. . . ."

His eye is caught by the portrait of Kissinger directly opposite on the wall.

What the hell are you staring at? Kissinger, that asshole! He wrote that I was praying for guidance after the Watergate, on the rug that the Shah gave me. Judas son-of-a-bitch!

HE *is livid, choked.*

Wait till "Deep Throat" tells the American people the truth about Dr. Shit-Ass.

HE *crosses to the microphone, making sure that this part gets on tape.*

How Dr. Shit-Ass took a fortune from the Shah and how he and that other guy fixed the Shah up in New York with a bunch of nice young boys. "Deep Throat" is going to strike again! I made you and I can break you. You slimy, two-faced, brown-nose, ass-licking, kraut, son-of-a-bitch!

HE *crosses to the portrait and offers Kissinger a Bronx cheer.* HE *laughs so hard that* HE *falls onto all fours. Then his own laughter turns on him and* HE *clutches himself in pain.*

Mother, have mercy on . . . your good dog.

HE *tries to shake himself out of it.*

Stop this crap! Think of something good. Like what? Oh, yes. Playing King of the Pool with Bebe down at Key Biscayne at two A.M. in the morning . . . that was fun . . . splashing around in the. . . . Come on what else . . .? Dinner in Pompano Beach at the Cork 'n Screw! Hobo steaks and ice creams and, uh . . . pistachio was my . . .

HE *turns and glares at the portrait of Kissinger.*

That turd, Kissinger! They gave him the Nobel Peace Prize and me they called the Mad Bomber. I had to do it, I promised to get us out with *honor.* I couldn't go *soft.* I was in Russia during the heaviest part of the bombing in Cambodia and the Russians, they suffered, too, you know, in the war. They lost twenty-five million. And I knelt at the monuments in Moscow. I read the diaries of the children. The dead children.

HE *covers his face, shaking.*

And they gave that whoremaster the Nobel Prize and me they called monster, freak, Juke, Callicak, the Mad Bomber. They said I stole the silverware from the White House. The fucking "Madman Theory" was Henry's idea in the first place to scare the North Vietnamese. And that fat fuck is telling everyone that I'm nuts and all the time he thinks he's Napoleon or, uh, Metternich. . . . And then those kids, tearing up Washington after Cambodia. Fuck 'em. Those kids will not judge me. I couldn't sleep. I went down to the Lincoln Monument to talk to them. And all I could think of to talk about was football. God, I was so ashamed. God damn it! Those kids will not evaluate my life. Because I am a Quaker, for Christ's sake. My mother used to say that . . . "There is no path to peace . . . peace is the path. . . ." That's what my mother said.

HE *sits back at the desk and picks up the microphone.*

Roberto, would you erase everything back to, uh, the Committee of 100? Thank you. . . . Your Honor, the Committee of 100 were winners. Real winners. Not me. Not yet. I wasn't a winner yet but I wasn't a quitter. *Never!* The Hiss case was the key. Because the Hiss case proved to the Committee of 100 that I could manage a crisis. That I could save the Committee if they . . . that I could save the country. All right. Let's take the Hiss case. . . .

HE *rises, galvanized, reliving the crisis. The microphone is in his hand as* HE *dictates.*

If Alger Hiss could look down his Ivy League snoot at the House Un-American Activities Committee and get away with it then HUAC was through, I was through, the Committee of 100 was through. Now what do I do? I've got ten days to prove that Alger Hiss is a high Communist agent in our State Department or else, they'll say, we've been made a laughing stock by a clever psychopath named Whittaker Chambers who's set the Committee up to fail once and for all.

HE *stops, remembering.*

Psychopath? Whittaker was . . . brilliant. . . . He was the only one I could. . . . We . . . we used to sit, just the two of us, uh . . . underneath the, uh . . . rocking, just rocking. . . .

From the depth of his memory HE *begins to talk into the microphone as if it were a telephone.*

. . . Yes, Whittaker, I understand. You have been a disciple of the devil and now you are . . . on God's side? No, no, I know that you're serious because I told you about my mother and the Quakers, and everything. I'm coming over to see you tomorrow. Well, because misery loves company, that's why. Look, Whittaker, we all get low sometimes and then we need cheering up. We need someone to talk to man to, uh, you know, straight from the, uh, the, uh . . . yeah. . . . I feel that way about you, too. You go to sleep, Whittaker. We are going to use your plan . . . because . . . there is no way we can prove that you and Hiss were in the Party at the same time . . . but we can prove that you and Hiss knew each other . . . very well . . . that you were very close. That you were both "creatures of the Party. . . ." And you're what, now? Both "creatures of the government . . .?" I see. Well, there you go. Whittaker, you go to sleep now and . . . Whittaker, listen, listen. . . . "Now I lay me down to sleep. . . ." Uh-huh, uh-huh, uh-huh, uh-huh. Yes. Pleasant dreams.

The "conversation" over, HE *discovers the telephone/microphone in his hands.* HE *struggles for control of himself and returns to his desk and the formality of his dictation.*

But the Hiss case brought my client national fame. However, in politics, victory is never total. As an aftermath to the Hiss case, for years afterwards, my client was subjected to an utterly unprincipled and vicious smear campaign. But the Committee of 100 saw that I had saved the day. Alger Hiss was in jail for perjury. Whittaker Chambers was . . . dead. And I was on top . . . I was . . . I was on top. But . . . well . . . the stress, you know. So I had to, uh, get away. And I went down to Bebe's boat, in Biscayne, and we talked about it afterwards, Bebe and I, and that's where we decided that I should go after Helen Gahagan

Douglas in the 1950 Senate campaign in California. Now, Helen Douglas, uh, she was a strong woman, uh . . . uh, noble-looking, uh, uh, she, uh . . . beautiful is what she was. In fact, she was the kind of woman that I, uh, well, she had a, uh . . . I've always been, uh . . . that kind of woman always, uh. . . . I liked her. . . . Shit. I could have beat Helen Gahagan Douglas without all the dirty tricks. But Chotiner and the Committee already had the money coming in from Florida and everywhere. And those jackasses from USC—the USC Ratfuckers they called themselves—they paid those students to throw eggs at her and plant the rumors that she was a Red and that she wore pink underwear and that her husband's real name was Hesselstein or Brown or some G'damn thing. . . . All that hurt *me* in the end. Look, I was thirty-seven years old, for Christ's sake. . . . I had nothing against Helen Gahagan Douglas. As a matter of fact, I, uh, I felt that she . . . she . . . I felt she was . . . she was the kind of woman that I, uh, uh. . . . *But she was the leader in the drive to take away the offshore oil rights from the companies. Period. Chotiner and the Committee wanted her dead and I was to be the hatchet man. Period.*

HE *turns his back to the microphone, hiding for a moment.*

So, my idea, then, was to run as above party. You know, as a kind of "Republicrat." Oh, yes! A "Republicrat" and . . .

HE *crosses to the piano and plays the melody of "Happy Days Are Here Again."*
HE *sings.*

"THE REDS, THE REDS, THE REDS, THE REDS,
ATHEISTIC, GODLESS, SPYING REDS;
HIDING UNDER DEMOCRATIC BEDS;
OH, THE REDS, THE REDS, THE REDS. . . ."

HE *turns to the microphone, enjoying himself again.*

That's what the country believed then and I believed it, too. In fact, my platform was: "I believe in America, and I believe in real estate." *And* "the Reds, the Reds, the Reds, the Reds."

HE *does an energetic dance across the room, then stops and begins pacing, talking fast and low.*

That's when the first "Dump Nixon" campaign began. See, I got soft and I let Alger Hiss's wife get away from me because she was a Quaker. But I learned my lesson. Oh, yeah . . . you gotta be hard on . . . these women, they're the worst kind of. . . . "Dump Nixon?" Never . . .! That's when the G'damn L.A. *Times* started calling me "Tricky Dick" and the cartoons with the jowls and the stubble. Look, I had feelings too, you know. My family had to stomach all that crap. Making me look like a G'damn tramp. All right. Sure. I am. I am a tramp. There I am down in the sewer waiting for my turn. A slimy slug crawling towards the White House down there in the swamp where the Founding Fathers put the G'damn White House in the first fucking place. The *Post* and the *Times*. We'll get those bastards because they deserve it. Lording it over the whole country like that! We'll make *them* bums. Because I was not dumped . . . I walked away. But I didn't quit. Because I have got the patience . . . that's right. They did not call me "iron butt" in law school for nothing. Go ahead, laugh, laugh, laugh. Sure, I drove Pat to her dates with other men before we were married. And what of it? Nobody dumps Nixon. And the *Times* and the *Post* and the rest of the G'damn country tried to shaft Nixon and all the other forgotten Americans. And Ike. Even Ike. Ike tried to get rid of me in 1956 and I said to him, I said, "Shit or get off the. . . ." Because—listen to this—Nixon, only Nixon, could dump Nixon . . . yeah!

HE *crosses back to the desk and gestures to the tape recorder.*

Tapes. G'damn tapes. They were an invasion of the public's privacy not mine. And everybody knows anyway that where there are tapes, there are tapes of tapes, for Christ's sake. "Expletive deleted." Shit. The whole public mind is one great big, fat expletive deleted as far as the Eastern Establishment is concerned. And that's why they hated me . . . because they hate the ordinary American who lives down there in the armpit of this country between New York and L.A. And the tapes are just one more G'damn set of lies.

HE *stares at Eisenhower's portrait.*

Me, a liar? That's rich. The one thing my Quaker mother really cared about was telling the truth. Not being President . . . telling the truth. After she died in 1967, that's when I wrote the words I spoke at Miami at the convention when I was nominated: "We must commit ourselves to the truth . . . to see it like it is . . . to tell it like it is . . . to see the truth, to find the truth, and to live the. . . ." To live the truth. Christ, if only they'd let you. The Committee of 100 big boys wanted plenty of things—you can believe that—but the truth was not one of them. Look, if the American people want truth and moral leadership, we'll give 'em truth and moral leadership. But that's not what they want. They just want you to be tough, that's all. Lie, cheat, steal, kill . . . but win, for them, win, win, *win*! Fuck the people. Shit. All the people want is a white man, or, uh, a white house, a white horse, or, uh, a white horse on a white house! Look, if you *lose*, then they use the word "morality." We were losing in Vietnam, then the Kennedy crowd starts talking "morality." Those clowns get caught in the Watergate . . . if you get caught then we talk morality . . . because that's the system. My mother is a saint and I'm a liar—what?—because I'm her son.

HE *addresses the Eisenhower portrait.*

You could afford to take the high road. I couldn't. You delegated, I had to do all the dirty work . . . right from the beginning! You sat up there and you said, "Can't somebody do something about that Castro fellow?" I heard you say that. Then *I* had to go out and pull the G'damn trigger. Hypocrite!

Enraged, HE *turns away from the portrait and then back to it and straightens the frame against the wall.*

My mother was a saint and I'm a liar because I'm a man who . . . who. . . . I just wanted to get some power, that's all. I mean, without power, you can't even . . . . Shit. And then I answered that G'damn ad in that G'damn paper for a Congressman and then I just, I, uh. . . .

HE *stops, slumps and turns down the lights in the room.* HE *stares into the fireplace and records in a low, secretive voice.*

Well, Your Honor, they call the tune. The Committee of, uh. . . . They took me back up there, you know, to the Grove. No drinking this time, also no, uh . . . strictly business. "The American future lies to the East. The great free markets of the Pacific Rim are the American Destiny. Dick, you are going to be President of the United States . . . it is only a matter of time. President of the Pacific Rim and Taiwan will be yours." I will never forget Arnholt Smith's voice. "Taiwan will be your trigger finger. Your trigger finger!" Then somebody—Chotiner, I think—said something in Yiddish and all those jerks from Miami laughed. And then, Haldeman's father, the old man, he whispered in my ear, "Taiwan is the China Plan. The shaft, the arrow that would plunge into the body of the East." I was drawing a long bow that night. Well, I found that out later. But that night, I just walked in that redwood forest all by myself.

HE *roams the darkened study.*

They told me that the China Plan would be my Excalibur. A plan for good, for peace, they said. For greatness! My Camelot. I could hear those men laughing and singing . . . but out there in the night, among those giant trees . . . I just embraced one of those giants and accepted my fate. I wanted to give not to receive. Yes, of course I knew they were using me, but I thought if I can use them to get some power. . . . I could still hear them out there . . . laughing and singing in the distance . . . but I didn't care. . . . Because the stars were so bright, and the moon bathed me in light, and I could hear the Russian River calling my name in the blackness of that darkness. And I was a part of the night, a child of those mammoth trees. And I loved my country, and I loved my God—I did— and I loved those giant trees. . . . Well, I should have run away through the night—escaped—and let those trees protect me from those men who were waiting for me back there at the Caveman Camp. Do you understand? My life ended that night. God forgive me. . . . So many dirty things. I had no one to talk to. I was getting pressure from above. Pressure from below. Where is that Deep Throat when I need him. I need to leak . . . how they made me do it. The bareknuckle boys, the cowboys from Vegas and Phoenix and Houston and Los Angeles. And if I tried to get away, there were the faggots from Boston and Georgetown and New York coming after me. . . . They were still out there, laughing, singing, pissing on the redwoods. Do you think they were laughing at me? I'm not a complete fool, you know. I knew that this was the crossroads. I knew I either had to go all the way with the China-Plan people or suffer the consequences. That's right. I knew . . . out there in that wilderness . . . that I was signing a pact with the Devil. And I thought of my mother and I prayed for guidance. Just the way I'm praying now . . . at this, another crossroads . . . the deepest crisis of my life.

HE *looks to heaven.*

Oh, God, help me again to do the hard thing. . . . I can feel Mother's eyes right now beaming down on me, searchlights of truth burning into each crisis in my miserable life. . . . Mother, do you remember when Harold lay dying in Arizona and we fought together, you and I . . . you by his bedside and I was out barking—arf, arf, arf—trying to bring in a little money to help out? Mother, do you remember. . .? "Step right in, step right in. Win your fortune on the inside. Step right in. Step right in. Meet real men from the California goldfields and from Old Mexico . . . on the inside. . . ." And then I would come home, and you would tell me what a good boy I was. And I would tell you how I was going to grow up to be Abraham Lincoln. "Step right in. Step right in. Riches and heart's desire . . . on the inside!" Mother? Do you remember? "Riches and heart's desire. . .?"

HE *falls to his knees, sobbing, near the breaking point.*

Mother, have mercy on your little dog. Mother, do you remember your little dog? Arf . . . arf . . . arf. . . .

HE *rises, staring at the portraits in the room, the real objects around him, to regain his equilibrium. Slowly, HE makes his way back to the desk and the microphone.*

Your Honor. . . . This is it!

HE *goes for the whiskey and brings the bottle back to the desk with him.*

I did not have a choice. I had to get out, resign right after the election, get the pardon *or* follow the Committee of 100's orders to prepare for a public mandate—that's right—a constitutional amendment . . . *a third term* for my client, Your Honor. A third term. And whatever happened to me after that, that was my problem. . . . Look, it would have all come out in the end, anyway, because the Patman Committee—Congressman Wright Patman—was following the *money*. . . . The American people must understand why I could not level with my lawyers and burn the tapes . . . they were stabbing me in the back, anyway . . . fuck 'em. Anyway, the Patman Committee was following the money that was coming into the Committee to Re-Elect the President. Now, *CREEP* had money in Taiwan, of course, Hong Kong, Singapore, Rangoon. . . . Millions and millions of dollars . . . all put there and handled by my old China-Lobby gang, the Committee of 100, and CREEP, and "Democrats for Nixon" and all the dummies and fronts that have been riding on my back all my G'damn life. But, Patman, he was a Texas radical, you know, and bright, and he was onto something . . . and he knew it. I mean, this money was flowing into the Committee to Re-Elect the President . . . *after* the President had already been reelected in 1972. After the biggest landslide in American history. And Patman, he was watching this cash and he's asking why is all this money still coming into the Committee and especially he wants to know why is all that money coming in from Asia . . . . Well, Your Honor, that money was to be used to re-elect Nixon in 1976 . . . you know, "Stick with Dick in '76," and all that shit. And all this money is being kicked back from Saigon. While old Henry's out there talking about "Peace Is at Hand," or some shit, the Saigon government is sending back millions in U.S. aid. Now understand this . . . this is money that we had originally sent to them . . . they're sending it back to me. . . . All through a network of fronts that we had set up all throughout the Pacific Rim. . . . Now, the Committee of 100 told me that they didn't give a shit if I went to China and got in bed with Chairman Mao. I mean, they didn't give a shit about Communism. What they told me was, is that they had to have me in the White House for eight more years because it involved—what else?—money . . . and *power!* Millions for the Bohemian Grove guys and billions for the Mob because of the, uh, the . . . heroin . . . thing. . . . The Committee of 100 and their buddies, the cowboys from Vegas and Phoenix and Houston. . . . Look, I was not the only one! They can't buy everybody. They found that out in 1960. But you can't cross 'em. These people are not the Rockefellers. No, they can't buy everything . . . but they sure as hell can shoot you down in the G'damn streets. Period. They can do that. . . . And they would've done it, too.

HE *rises before the microphone, struggling to keep control.*

All right. . . . Ladies and gentlemen of the American jury, your hour has come. Consider the crisis: it is the morning after the smashing victory mandate of November 8, 1972. My client, Richard Nixon, has just received the word from the Committee of 100. And that word was: "Here is the plan." Point one, of that plan, ladies and gentlemen: continue the war in Vietnam until 1976 . . . whatever the cost. Point two: accept a draft for a third term in '76 or *take it*. And point three: seal the deal with China against the Soviets and then carve up the markets of the so-called Third World. . . . That's it. Period. That's the word that my client received from his masters. And you know who they are. Oh, yes! You know who they are and you know exactly what you would have done. My client, Richard Nixon, the leader of the Free World, on November 9, 1972. . . . Look, I had to make a terrible decision. Slip away . . . like a G'damn *clown* . . . just disappear from the pools of light . . . *or*, burn the tapes . . . but then that meant going public. And if I did that, they would have put me in a G'damn lunatic asylum because . . . they got a million guys down there . . . they would've found some new boy, taken him up to the Grove and prepared him for '76 or '80. So, what then, Your Honor, did my client do? He took the hardest possible way: he chose to orchestrate the tapes like a great drama! He chose Secret Honor. Yeah. Secret Honor . . . and public disgrace. But in your heart, you know that he was right. . . . I did want to be Abe Lincoln. But I found out that the world is nothing more than a bunch of second-generation mobsters . . . and their lawyers . . . and the P.R. guys . . . and the new-money people who made theirs in the war . . . and the old-money crooks who made theirs selling slaves and phony merchandise to both sides in the Civil War. I didn't look for this . . . I didn't want it, but I sure as hell found it! And I'll tell you something else: that's what public life is all about . . . and if you can't stand the burnt then you, uh, you, uh, get, uh . . . ah, you know what the hell I'm talking about.

HE *sits at the desk.*

So, I had to find some way to leak the tapes. I needed to have a deep background source, a "Deep Throat." I had to find a way to destroy that huge '72 popular-vote mandate. I would've been unbeatable in '76 and . . . I just couldn't run, anymore. . . . So, uh, Dean, uh, Al Haig carried the ball on the tapes. He cut Henry off at the pass in Paris . . . and then the Judas son-of-a-bitch turned out to be a Rockefeller traitor all the G'damn time. . . . See, they knew I had to go because . . . they wanted their man—Ford—in there for six more years. And they would have got him, too . . . except he had to pardon me and thereby destroy his chances for re-election in '76, poor bastard!

HE *laughs maniacally, enjoying, even in his own despair, the bad luck of someone else.*

Well . . . John Dean, John Dean, John Dean! John Dean did me a favor. I would have had to *invent* John Dean. What the hell. He was young . . . he had to watch his ass. I have nothing against John Dean. In fact, I *like* John Dean. I have nothing against any of 'em. We are all nothings, small fry compared to the big guys. They buy us and sell us every four years. I sold my soul at Bohemian Grove for shit. I kissed Rockefeller's ass and he shit all over me. And they do, you know, that's what they do! They fly from New York to L.A. shitting every step of the way on all of us. And they've got a million guys down there. They can send down to Central Casting and get some dummy that looks good on the tube like, uh . . . some Arrow-collar killer type who'll. . . . All right. . . . Wall Street is asking for Agnew. So you know what I did? I gave 'em Agnew. That fucking Agnew . . . he was taking bribes with both hands, for Christ's sake. You know what Agnew did one time? He took a turkey and two hundred dollars, right in the office! Fucking asshole. But they wanted more . . . they wanted everything. Because I was their hole card . . . I was their China Card. You know what I thought they were trying to do with me? I thought they were trying to make me into *King Richard the Turd!*

HE *is beside himself with laughter but now stalks back to the microphone.*

You understand what I'm saying here? The Rockefeller gang was shafting me from the rear and the China-Committee big boys had me by the nuts up front. And the only card that I had to play against the Committee was the Hughes thing, and, uh, of course, I had the, uh, uh . . . heroin . . . connection. And then I had the Kennedy, uh, uh . . . but, I had to be very cautious because Lunt and Hiddy, Krough and Caulfield—the Watergate guys—they were all ex-C.I.A., and ex-this and ex-that . . . and those bastards knew where the bodies were buried. So, I couldn't just go rushing in there and. . . . Meantime, this money is still flooding into the Committee to Re-Elect the President. And Patman, he's watching this . . . I mean, this money is coming in from *Asia* . . . from Flying Tiger, from Air America—dropping millions of dollars—from the Bank of Seoul, the Bank of Rangoon, and the Bank of Taiwan—especially the Bank of Taiwan—and Patman, he's watching all this money . . . and Patman—he's funny—he said . . . he said . . . "Where the fuck is all this money coming from. . .?"

Overwhelmed by the absurdity of it all, HE *falls to his knees behind the desk, laughing, but then sobers at the situation's implications for himself.*

. . . They almost had me. . . . I fed 'em Agnew, I opened the door a little bit for Rockefeller . . . but that wasn't enough. . . . I was trapped, I had nothing left, I was going on nerves because, you see, if they . . . catch me . . . it means . . . the . . . firing . . . squad. . . .

His aria chokes him. HE *stumbles over to the wastebasket and vomits. His face is ravaged and torn, his breathing hoarse.* HE *fights for a shred of dignity.* HE *takes off his tie and smoking jacket.* HE *mops his face.*

Your Honor . . . make no mistake about it. If they catch me . . . it does mean the firing squad. There would be no pardon for prolonging the war in Southeast Asia in exchange for vast sums of money . . . American tax money. A fortune in blood to be used to finance a third term for my client. Your Honor, the country would have boiled over . . . because this blood bribery would have meant the death of thousands of American boys. . . . I didn't want that. . . . I didn't. . . . Who the hell wants to go down in history as a traitor who took bribes to keep a fucking war going. . .?! So, that's why I led the press and the Congress to the tip of the wrong iceberg. That's why I gave them a trail of "Crimes and Misdemeanors" to follow . . . so that they wouldn't find out about the "Treason and Bribery" and put me in a cage like a common traitor!

HE *makes a final, heroic effort.*

Ladies and gentlemen of the jury, the prisoner in the dock is guilty of one crime only . . . and that crime is being Richard Milhous Nixon!

HE *drops, deflated, back into his chair.*

I just wanted . . . some power . . . that's all. . . . I thought if I had some power I could . . . without power you can't even.. . . .

HE *speaks to the portrait of Woodrow Wilson.*

I know you understand this. You had power in World War I. When you've got it, it's nothing. Nothing! They broke your heart, too, didn't they, with the League of Nations?

HE *crosses to the portrait, whispering.*

You know what they wrote about me? They said, at the end, that I was running around the White House, crazy drunk, talking to the pictures on the walls. . . . I was lonely, for Christ's sake. I needed someone to talk to besides . . . a machine. . . .

HE *addresses the heavens.*

I just wanted to be a man, that's all . . . not a dog, not a nothing. . . . A real man. . . . Mother? Do you understand this? A long time ago, they took me up there to the . . . and all I was trying to do was . . . and because of the . . . they had me in a, uh. . . . Mother? Mother? *Mother. . .?! I know what I did.* . . . Mother, tell me who I am. . . . Please . . . tell me . . . who I am. . . .

HE *crosses to the desk.* HE *pulls the revolver to him and stares into the barrel.* HE *confronts his fate.*

What . . . Mother . . . I did not elect myself. They elected me. Not once. Not twice. But all my G'damn life. And they would do it again . . . if they had the chance. They said they didn't trust me. They said let Dick Nixon do it . . . and I did it!

HE *rises.*

They said they wouldn't buy a used car from me . . . but they gave me the biggest G'damn vote in American history. And then they flushed me down the toilet . . . and they wanted me to stay down. They wanted me to kill myself.

HE *grabs the microphone.*

But I won't do it. If they want me dead, they'll have to do it.

HE *stares front, indomitable.*

Fuck 'em!

Blackout.

END OF PLAY

Food From Trash
Gary Leon Hill

About Gary Leon Hill

Born in Nebraska, Gary Leon Hill is a writer, photographer and filmmaker. His films *Horizontal Violence* and *A Day Late and a Dollar Short* were funded in part through grants from the National Endowment for the Arts and the Nebraska Arts Council. He made *Energy and How to Get It* with Robert Frank and Rudy Wurlitzer on a grant from the Corporation for Public Broadcasting. Among his other films are *Stonebust, Crime* and *Cure*. Hill is currently working on a full-length play *Soundbite* and on a one-act play commissioned by Actors Theatre of Louisville.

Production History

Food from Trash was nominated for TCG's *Plays in Process* script circulation series by Julie Beckett Crutcher, literary manager of Actors Theatre of Louisville. Co-winner of the 1982 Great American Play Contest, *Food from Trash* was presented by ATL as part of its seventh annual Humana Festival of New American Plays, from February 23 through April 3, 1983.

Jon Jory directed. The set and lighting were designed by Paul Owen, costumes by Karen Gerson and sound by Richard Sirois and Larry Hickman. The cast was as follows:

Sudden Pisanger	Bill Smitrovich
Leatha	Nora Chester
Lomar	Amy Appleby
Butch Cobb	Robert Schenkkan
Bob	John Pielmeier
Alma	Helen-Jean Arthur
Phil Cobb	Andy Backer
Sarge	Ray Fry
CB	Helen-Jean Arthur
Running Joke	Kent Broadhurst
Son	Will Oldham
Freddy the Cop	Gary Leon Hill

Playwright's Note

The vision and spirit of Jon Jory and Actors Theatre of Louisville in their premiere production of this play spawned an operatic event with five sets, three cars, one full-scale operational garbage truck built from scratch, smoke, fog, explosions, wraparound sound and graphic contamination. Theirs was a full-blown commitment that stunned the senses. It was spectacle.

But *Food from Trash* can be staged with less extravagance. The theme is waste, which is both poison and a potential source of energy and power. The essential action is hauling and sorting this waste. The central image is the back end of a garbage truck: a black hole of appropriate dimensions which both eats and shits garbage. Bags full of garbage are hauled by Sarge and Pisanger, swallowed and disgorged by the truck, sorted through by Running Joke. Pisanger's red toolbox is emblematic of his potential transformation and should be on-stage at all times. The computer read-out he finds is conspicuously with him, stuffed in a back pocket.

The following description of stage areas, which ATL fleshed out to the last detail, can be treated as a model from which to draw sketches. I leave it to the producer/director/designer to decide the amount of detail necessary to render this landscape, but insist that the play is "about" a toxic environment only insofar as that environment is seen and understood to exist on every level including the cellular level of the inhabitants of the landfill. *Food from Trash* is "about" the relationships of people who are poisoned.

GARBAGE TRUCK: The rear end of a Leach Packmaster truck with hydraulic shafts, chains, operational hopper which lifts out of the way, and a dumping blade to disgorge garbage. Front blade moves up into the truck to pack garbage.

TRAILERHOUSE: Suggestion of a kitchen counter, refrigerator, couch, low table, telephone, CB radio, bed, garbage can. Predominant lighting: sodium-vapor yellow from above, purple gloom of video from one side.

ALMA'S BAR & GRILL: Lightweight chairs and a Wurlitzer jukebox.

INDUSTRIAL REFUGE, INC.: Phil Cobb's office, lit hard from above by a bank of fluorescent lights.

THE TANKS: A circular storage tank with a narrow climb of steps snaking down its outside surface. Garbage bags, auto parts, assorted salvage. One 30-gallon barrel sits upended in a 55-gallon barrel. A 12-inch sewer pipe drips thick yellow drainage. A five-inch pipe sticks up out of the ground about three feet.

Characters

SUDDEN PISANGER, muscled, older than his 36 years; garbageman, husband, father and natural-born mechanic.

LEATHA, 35, Sudden's wife.

LOMAR, teenage foster daughter of Leatha and Sudden.

SON, nine-year-old son of Leatha and Sudden.

BOB, 30, garbageman, drinker, husband, father.

CB, voice of Bob's wife Francine.

PHIL COBB, 55, the boss, owner-operator of Industrial Refuge, Inc.; bald, horn-rims, jumpsuit.

BUTCH COBB, 35, Phil's son, in line to take over the business.

SARGE, 60, alcoholic, garbageman, lift on one shoe.

RUNNING JOKE, 30s, ex-garbageman.

FREDDY THE COP, 30s, County-brown uniform, .38 Smith & Wesson.

ALMA, 50s, owner-operator of Alma's Bar & Grill.

Time

Now.

Place

Landfill dump.

The Play

Food From Trash

To Jo

For Frank

ACT ONE

The action of the play moves between the following locations: Centerstage is the LANDFILL DUMP with the GARBAGE TRUCK immediately Upstage of it; PISANGER's TRAILERHOUSE is Stage Right; the Stage Left area is shared by ALMA's BAR & GRILL and the offices of INDUSTRIAL REFUGE, INC. Upstage Right is THE TANKS.

Scene 1

TRAILERHOUSE *bedroom. Pre-dawn, purple gloom of video.* LEATHA, *sitting upright in a nightgown, pounds slow motion on* PISANGER's *naked chest. His ribcage moans a slow percussion.* HE *is rigid, numb, beyond emotion, doesn't resist or fight back as* LEATHA *pounds on him like a drum.*

Trailerhouse living room. LOMAR *rises from the couch, sheet draped from arms, and stretches in dim video spill. Dropping the sheet,* SHE *crosses into the kitchen and opens the refrigerator door. The inside light illuminates her bare legs in an oversized T-shirt as* SHE *gazes half asleep at 28 tall bottles of Coca-Cola.* SHE *pulls out four bottles and kicks the door shut.*

PHIL COBB's *car pulls Onstage,* BUTCH *driving,* BOB *in the passenger seat.*

BOB: You come down Mohawk?

BUTCH: That's right.

BOB: How's it look?

BUTCH: Dark.

BOB: Is it running heavy?

BUTCH: Bob, how long you worked for us?

BOB: Three years.

BUTCH: How's Monday run?

BOB: How heavy, though? Three loads?

BUTCH: Four.

BOB: Shit.

BUTCH: Whatsa matter, Bob? Don't you like hauling garbage?

BOB: Oh I love it, it just don't lead to nothing. There's no future in it.

BUTCH: Don't tell Dad that. He started out at sixteen with a wheelbarrow and a
pair of gloves. Now look at us—fifteen men, ten trucks, a four-hundred-
and-eighty-three–acre sanitary landfill and a 1983 Lincoln Continental.

BOB: You can train a damn monkey to walk down the street and pick up garbage cans.

BUTCH: That's what he did.

In TRAILERHOUSE *living room, tight spotlight hits* PISANGER *in the face coming
out of the bedroom, bag-eyed, underpants, carrying his clothes. Sitting in armchair,* LOMAR *aims flashlight at* PISANGER *who squints, covers his face, cusses her,
laughing.* LOMAR *shifts beam to his crotch.* HE *gives her his back and pulls up his
pants.* SHE *turns off the flashlight, crosses to the window, lights three or four cigarettes.* PISANGER *at sink.*

LOMAR: God it's back.

PISANGER: What is?

LOMAR: The stench. Couldn't sleep for the trucks driving in and out of the
dump all night and now this.

PISANGER: What trucks?

LOMAR: Those gas trucks, those ones with the real long tanks on 'em.

PISANGER: Dump don't open till seven.

LOMAR: Those tanker trucks are up and down this goddam road all night, all
summer long.

PISANGER: You're dreaming, Lomar.

LOMAR: This stink?

PISANGER: The smell of money.

LOMAR (*Turns on portable radio*): Not yours. Not mine.

PISANGER: What are you listening to?

LOMAR *extends radio at arm's length.* PISANGER *leans in.* LOMAR *draws him to
her by bringing the radio to her ear.*

LOMAR *and* PISANGER (*Singing along with radio*):
   . . . TRAIN OF LOVE'S A COMIN',
   BIG BLACK WHEELS A HUMMIN'.

Honk. Headlights sweep trailerhouse as PHIL COBB'S *car pulls up.* PISANGER *pulls away from* LOMAR; *three Cokes between fingers, passed from* LOMAR, HE *exits trailerhouse as* BOB *and* BUTCH *get out of car.*

BUTCH: Morning, Pisanger.
BOB: 'Lo, Sudden.

PISANGER *eyeballs car and sucks on a Coke.*

BOB (*Continued*): How's Leatha?

PISANGER *ignores* BOB.

BOB (*Continued*): How's your kids? How's your Chevy?
BUTCH (*Leering*): How's Lomar?
PISANGER: Where's my boat trailer, Butch? I paid you for it. You told me you'd bring it over.
BUTCH: What's your hurry? You don't have a boat so you can't use it. Your Chevy don't run so you can't pull it anywhere.
PISANGER: I'll get the Chevy running. All I need is some parts.
BUTCH: You'll need a sled by then and a pickaxe to chop through the ice with.
BOB: At least he'll catch something.
BUTCH: He'll catch a cold first and catch hell when he gets home. Ain't that right, Pisanger?
PISANGER (*Crossing to* ALMA'S BAR & GRILL): I don't know. I'd have to ask Freddy.
BUTCH: Ask Freddy about what?
PISANGER: About all those holes in the bottom of your boat.
BUTCH (*Laughing hysterically*): Axe fishing!
BOB: Don't tell that story again.
BUTCH: Hell, Freddy was down on all fours in the bottom of my new boat catching carp with his hands.
BOB: You can't catch carp with your hands.
BUTCH: You can't. He could. Freddy did. He was. I took him out there to show him my new graphite rod, my ugly stick—to *show* it to him. I never said he could use it. And he got pissed off and dropped down on his hands and knees and started scooping carp out of the lake with his goddam bare hands. (*Suddenly thoughtful*) Made me mad as hell for some reason. Didn't make no sense.

PISANGER, BOB *and* BUTCH *enter* ALMA'S BAR & GRILL. ALMA *is at the counter.*

PISANGER: Makes more sense than fishing with an axe.

BUTCH: You shoulda seen him. Freddy's fanning the air with a big old carp waggin' off his hand and I'm busting up the water with my goddam axe!

PISANGER: Catch anything?

BUTCH: Bluegill, carp, channel cat—hell yes I hit 'em. And they come up bitesize, too. (*Laughing*)

PISANGER: How many holes in the bottom of your boat?

BUTCH: I clobbered so goddam many fish you couldn't count the pieces! I stood up in the boat and yelled at Freddy, Martial Law—

BOB (*Heard it all before*): Martial Law.

BUTCH: —that's illegal to fish with your hands is against the fucking law you're paid to enforce and besides that you're so goddam drunk you're getting good at it. This is *my* boat! I drove us out here! If you don't goddam stop it I'm gonna quit being careful with this axe!

ALMA: Morning, Butch.

BUTCH: Morning, Alma.

PISANGER: How long'd it take that boat to sink?

BUTCH: About as long as it took me to talk you into buying my boat trailer. (*Laughs*) For twice what I paid for it. I come outta that one pretty good, wouldn't you say, Pisanger? Huh?

PISANGER: Yeh.

BUTCH: Huh?

PISANGER: Yeh.

BUTCH: Wouldn't you say I came outta that one all right?

BOB (*Slapping* PISANGER's *arm, patting his back, buddy-buddy*): Let his turds roll, Sudden. He ain't like us. He don't work for a living. He don't know friendship.

BUTCH: Hell, if you get your Chevy running soon enough, I might sell you the boat! (*Laughs*)

PISANGER: What do you want, Bob?

BOB: Will you take my place when I finish up today? I gotta get someplace.

PISANGER: She'll wait.

BOB: That ain't it. I don't see her anymore.

PISANGER: Since when?

BOB: Since that night you seen us out to the garage? Two days after that I went back to Francine.

PISANGER: Yeh?

BOB: Yeh. Francine used the kid on me. Had Aaron tell me he didn't want to see me drunk or throw up in his sandbox. Kids. They pull at the heartstrings. Hell, you know that.

PISANGER: If it's Francine, I know she can wait to see you.

BOB: There's a 'lectronics class starts at three-thirty over at Tech. I need to get home, clean up, get there.

PISANGER: Electronics?

BOB: Yeh.

PISANGER: I thought you were gonna get a truck and steal a garbage route.

BOB: Shhhh.

PISANGER: Run Cobbs outta business.

BOB: I said if they ever made me mad enough I would.

PISANGER: Ain't Butch running the route today?

BOB: That's what I mean. He'll be driving us around in circles. I'll never get off.

PISANGER: That oughta make you mad enough.

ALMA (*Serving* BOB *a plate of food*): Everything eats and everything is eaten. What's eating you boys this morning?

BOB (*Reading his plate*): Three eggs, toast, hashbrowns and coffee. Thanks, Alma.

ALMA: You never change, Bob. How 'bout you, Sudden?

PISANGER: I'll drink my Coke.

ALMA: And rot your insides.

PISANGER: It starts my heart, Alma.

ALMA *shakes head.*

BOB (*Eating*): Sudden, it ain't me. Look, I've had worse jobs.

PISANGER: What's worse than hauling garbage?

BOB: Ripping cheeks offa pigs at the slaughterhouse. No, it's Francine, see. She don't wanna be married to a garbageman.

PISANGER: She got you the job.

BOB: Hell she did.

PISANGER (*Tossing* BOB *a matchbook*): Giver these.

BOB (*Reading matchbook cover*): No-Fault Divorce.

Enter PHIL COBB, *laughing.*

ALMA: 'Lo, Phil.

PHIL: Good morning, beautiful.

BUTCH: Hey Dad.

PHIL: Son.

ALMA: What are you so happy about, Phil?

BOB (*Handing matchbook back to* PISANGER): I give you my rod and reel.

ALMA: You got a bottle in the car or what?

PHIL: Alma, you know I can't drink.

BOB: And my copper wire.

ALMA: You smoking something funny, Phil?

PHIL: I haven't even lit it yet.

PISANGER (*Tossing matches to* PHIL): Here, Phil.

PHIL: Thanks, Sudden.

BOB: I'll throw in all my aluminum.

PISANGER: I can't today, Bob, or I would.

ALMA: Did you get that government contract?

PISANGER: Leatha's got Weightwatchers.

ALMA: You're going to haul the schools.

PHIL: Schools, hell!

BOB: Shit.

BUTCH: Did Woolco finally pay up, Dad?

PHIL: No. I'm sending you out there this morning to shut that compacter off.

BUTCH: That'll put the screws to them. Wait'll their store fills up with garbage.

PHIL: Decided that last night, me and your mother, counting our money! (HE *pulls out a bristling chunk of money and laughs like a kid*)

BUTCH: Holy shit, Dad!

PHIL: Intuition in the fifth!

BOB (*Ears prick*): That's *my* horse! Phil! You bet him?

PHIL: Intuition? Damn right I did!

BUTCH (*Excited*): What he pay, Dad?!

PHIL (*Second thought. Signals* BUTCH *to shut up, folds money back into pocket*): Overhead.

BOB: Where's my share?

PHIL: You get a new barrel.

BOB: I give you the tip!

PHIL: And I put a new carrying barrel on the truck for you.

BOB: Phil, I give you the goddam tip!

PHIL: Don't drag this one down the driveway. Put it on your shoulder. It's the last one you get.

SARGE *enters.* HE *is 60, silver hair slicked back, dressed secondhand with style—blue suit, shoulder pads, vest, shirt, tie, a lift on one shoe, both shoes shined.*

ALMA: Sarge!

PHIL: Goddam!

PISANGER: Hey!

BUTCH: Holy cow! Back from the dead!

PHIL: Sarge, where in hell you been?

SARGE: I been in the slammer, Phil.

PHIL: You want to work?

SARGE: I got two dimes in my pocket. I gotta work.

PHIL: Sit down.

SARGE: 'Lo, Sudden, Bob.

PISANGER: You rested up?

SARGE: Oh yeh. Dried out and everything else. I guess. (*Clears throat*)

BOB (*To* PISANGER): I asked Phil for two bucks to bet that horse and Phil wouldn't do it. Then *he* bets the sonofabitch.

PISANGER *shrugs.*

PHIL: I don't suppose you got too good a breakfast in jail.

SARGE: No, they kick you out before breakfast. Save that money.

PISANGER: Yeh!

PHIL: Well, I'll buy you breakfast.

BOB: Thanks a lot, Phil.

PHIL: Son, let Sarge sit down. (*Pulling* BUTCH *out of his seat*) Alma, give Sarge something to eat.

ALMA: Ham and eggs, Sarge?

PHIL (*Sitting* SARGE *down*): There you go, Sarge.

ALMA: Short stack, coffee, toast?

SARGE: That'll fit, Alma.

PHIL: Butch, where's Running Joke?

BUTCH: Oh ain't you heard, Dad? Running Joke's gone back up to the reservation. Yeh. He's up there hanging from his tits over a pile of shit. (*Laughs real hard*)

PHIL: I told you to go get him, Butch.

BUTCH: That's the famous Indian Shit Ritual.

PHIL: Go down to the Terminal Hotel. If he's there, you tell him we need him.

BUTCH: We don't. We never did need him. And sure not now Sarge is squeezed dry. Right, Sarge?

PHIL: Sarge lost his driver's license.

BUTCH: Well, you're not going to let Running Joke drive, are you?

PHIL: Go find him, son.

BUTCH: Number twelve's not out of the shop yet and you're gonna put that dog-eater behind the wheel again?

PHIL (*Quiet authority*): Butch.

BUTCH (*Resigns*): Jesus.

PHIL: Pisanger. Stop scratching.

PISANGER (*Raking his arm with his nails*): It's getting worse, Phil.

PHIL: It'd go away if you stopped drinking all that Coke.

PISANGER: Doc Stewart says it comes from working the route.

BUTCH: Hoo hah. Now I heard everything.

PISANGER: He says it's got to be an infection of some kind I'm getting from the garbage.

BUTCH: If you could get diseased off a garbage route, don't you think I'd died of it a long time ago?

BOB: Maybe you can't get it just sitting in the truck.

PHIL: Butch.

Exit BUTCH.

PHIL (*Continued; peeling off bills*): Here, Sarge. Get some cigarettes.

SARGE: Thanks, Phil.

PHIL: I don't suppose you have any gloves.

SARGE: No.

PHIL: Alma, give Sarge some gloves. And here. (HE *peels off more dollars, gives them to* SARGE)

SARGE: I appreciate this, Phil.

PHIL: Just don't say nothing to my wife or the others.

SARGE: How do you want me to pay you back?

PHIL: When you get it.

SARGE: I will as soon as I can.

PHIL: There's no hurry about it. I'll get it out of you. (*Turns to go*) Gentlemen. Three hundred garbage cans stand out there waiting on your gentle expertise.

SARGE: Thanks, Phil.

PHIL: Bye, Alma. Bye, boys.

ALMA: Bye, Phil.

Exit PHIL.

BOB: Seven hundred cans! Sixteen thousand pounds! Eight tons of somebody else's shit! I haul two thousand houses, I haul fifty downtown stops eight times a month for that sonofabitch. He takes in ten grand a month. He gives me one hundred dollars a week.

PISANGER: He gives you *ninety-six* dollars a week and takes half that back playing blackjack in the office. But what are you going to do about it, Bob?

BOB: I'm gonna—

PISANGER and BOB (*In unison*): —complain about it—

PISANGER: —real loud. What else?

BOB: Look, Sudden, I ain't dumb and I ain't dead and I ain't given up like you have.

PISANGER: I ain't given up.

BOB: Phil's got ten years of your life—so far—and what have you got? One sad-ass trailer down by the dump. That ain't no place to raise kids, have a family, support a wife. You ain't a man.

PISANGER: What am I?

BOB: You're a dumb-ass half-dead belly-up and you're gonna *die* in the goddam dump.

PISANGER: And you're not.

BOB: Hell no.

PISANGER: 'Cause this ain't your real job.

BOB: Damn right it ain't my real job.

PISANGER: This job is only temporary for you.

BOB: Right.

PISANGER: Like life.

BOB (*Pounds table once*): AHHH!

ALMA (*Serving* SARGE *breakfast*): Bob—

SARGE: Thanks, Alma.

PISANGER: Bob, you're me five years younger and if you don't know that you're stupider than I was when I was your age.

BOB: I ain't nothing like you!

ALMA: Bob—

BOB *stands scratching his arm in a gesture identical to* PISANGER'*s.*

PISANGER: Oh no? See you out there, Sarge.

SARGE: Where at?

PISANGER: I'll pick up King Dollar. You meet me at the bottom of B.

SARGE: Okay.

Exit PISANGER.

ALMA: Bob—

BOB (*On his way out*): What?

ALMA: Three eggs, toast, hashbrowns, coffee.

BOB: Phil paid.

ALMA: For Sarge. Not every stoat in the hall.

BOB: That was *my horse*, Alma!

ALMA: Next time you give *me* the tip.

BOB (*Stomping*): I give Phil three years of my life and he ain't *never* bought me breakfast.

ALMA: You boys put together a union, you could be buying *Phil* breakfast. No union, no protection, no benefits, no bargaining, you won't stick together—what do you expect? Two thirty-seven with tax.

BOB *pays, exits.* ALMA *turns to* SARGE.

Upstage, at THE TANKS, FREDDY THE COP *appears, loading a .38 Smith &*
Wesson.

ALMA (*Continued; to* SARGE): It's good to see you again, Dugan.

SARGE: Still alive, Alma. Thought a lot about you. Peter did, too.

ALMA *sits on* SARGE'*s lap, straddles him, facing him.*

Up at THE TANKS, FREDDY THE COP *aims at a distant target.*

SARGE (*Continued; to* ALMA): Remember Branched Oak Lake?

FREDDY THE COP (*To himself*): Time's up. Last chance. Gettin' late.

ALMA (*To* SARGE): After the wreck or before?

FREDDY THE COP *fires.*

ALMA *and* SARGE *crack up laughing.*

FREDDY THE COP (*Taking aim*): Relax, Freddy. Gettin' close. Comin' in, comin' in, comin' in.

SARGE (*To* ALMA): How'd that happen again?

FREDDY THE COP *fires.*

ALMA *rotates her ass in* SARGE's *lap.* THEY *laugh.*

FREDDY THE COP: Relax. Relax. Relax.

ALMA (*To* SARGE): I'll see you later.

FREDDY THE COP *fires.*

FREDDY THE COP (*Pleased*): Ahhh. Freddy, you are one scary motherfucker. (*Laughs*)

SARGE: See you later, Alma. (HE *exits*)

Scene 2

GARBAGE TRUCK. *Out on the route. Bottom of B.* PISANGER *hooks the truck's chains to a container and hits the switch. The blade pulls back, the container lifts and garbage slides out into the hopper.* PISANGER *reverses the switch, the blade comes forward, the container drops.* HE *unchains it, rolls it out of the way as the blade shoves garbage high into the truck. The power take-off shuts off, truck idles. Mourning dove purrs.* PISANGER *shivers, wheels around.* HE's *heard something, felt something move in a blindspot.*

SARGE *drags his barrel round the back of the truck, pulls on new gloves.*

SARGE: Jimmy Plattsmouth says hello.
PISANGER: That goofy bastard back in jail?
SARGE: He bounced another check.

PISANGER *and* SARGE *start emptying garbage cans into their barrels at opposite ends of the stage, talking loud, across lawns.*

PISANGER: Insufficient brains. I heard he called the cops up and told them he was gonna drive a hundred miles an hour through downtown and they couldn't catch him.
SARGE: He was doing ninety when he went off that little bridge. Yeh. He's still there. He don't want out. Funny how many people locked up in jail don't want out.
PISANGER: It's getting worse out here.

SARGE: Looks good to me. Smells good. Feels good.

PISANGER: I'm not talking about Alma.

SARGE *laughs.*

SARGE: How you doin', though, Sudden? Really.

PISANGER: Fine.

SARGE: How fine?

PISANGER: All right.

SARGE: You get your Chevy running?

PISANGER: Not yet.

SARGE: You and Leatha? Working things out?

PISANGER (*Shrugs*): Not really.

SARGE: You ever figure out what killed your trees?

PISANGER (*Shakes head no*): Whatever it was killed the bushes, too.

SARGE: I saw Lomar's father in prison. He's one mean stupid sonofabitch. Musta been murder living with him.

PISANGER: What's he in for?

SARGE: Incest, ain't it? Delinquency of a minor.

PISANGER *bites into an apple—crack.*

SARGE (*Continued*): You still eating outta the hopper?

PISANGER: I got this offa tree.

SARGE: You don't change.

PISANGER: Come on, Sarge. I got this off that tree.

SARGE: Still eating garbage and still won't admit it.

PISANGER: Bullshit.

SARGE: Remember eating chicken out backa the Drumstick? Filling our bellies and greasing our hair at the same time. (*Runs fingers through his hair*)

PISANGER: I remember the summer you quit hauling that woman's cat shit.

SARGE: Well, Jesus, I told her to bag it. She wouldn't bag it. Just poured it down in the bottom of the can and put her other stuff on top. I took her other stuff.

PISANGER (*Laughing*): Yeh, and kept pulling the can around into the sun so it'd bake up real good.

SARGE: It kept getting fuller and I kept not taking it. Finally built up to where even she couldn't stand it. One morning she came out with another box of cat shit, lifted the lid and fell over.

THEY *empty their barrels into the truck hopper.*

PISANGER: Look at this. (HE *leans into his empty carrying barrel, pulls out a snapshot which* HE *wipes off on his pant leg*)

SARGE: Cat shit turns to industrial ammonia. It'll kill you.

PISANGER *hands snapshot to* SARGE. SARGE *raises an eyebrow.*

SARGE (*Continued*): Now if you only knew where she lived, huh?

PISANGER: She moved in over there, that yellow house. (HE *sees something else in his barrel*)

SARGE: With this fellow?

PISANGER (*Leans into barrel, pulls out a sheaf of papers—a computer read-out*): No.

SARGE (*Studying snapshot*): Got a little one, don't he? Tell you what, Sudden. You pull the truck up and I'll work her side of the street.

SARGE *laughs, exits.* PISANGER *stands, oblivious to* SARGE, *puzzling over the computer read-out* HE's *found, lips moving as* HE *reads.*

Scene 3

TRAILERHOUSE *living room. Early morning.*

CB (*Voice of* BOB's *wife Francine*): Breaker one nine, we looking for that one Queen Bee—you got your ears on, girl? Over.

LEATHA, *in chenille bathrobe, crosses to the CB radio.* LOMAR *sleeps rolled up in a sheet like an enchilada on the couch against the far wall. Coffee water simmers.*

CB (*Continued*): Breaker one nine for the Queen Bee, you copy?

LEATHA: Ten four, Cotton Candy. You're hitting me with ten pounds over here and thanks for the pills.

CB: That's all I could get is two bottles. Go 'head.

LEATHA (*Holds one bottle*): Two bottles?

CB: Just two. I'm sorry. I know how it is. I porked out after Aaron was born. Uh, Leatha. That slipped, I'm sorry. Go 'head.

Dialogue in TRAILERHOUSE *continues as* FREDDY THE COP *enters* PHIL COBB's *office at* INDUSTRIAL REFUGE, INC. HE *makes small talk with* PHIL, *who counts out money and is about to slip bills into an envelope.* FREDDY THE COP *takes bills, counts them, takes envelope and is moving out door when* PHIL *hands him a cigar. Payoff made,* FREDDY THE COP *exits and* PHIL's *attention returns to his portable video game.*

LEATHA (*To* CB): I'm fat, Francine. I know it. You know it. Sudden knows it. These'll help.

CB: You get dizzy, you stretch out.

LEATHA: You have any fun last night?

CB: I was having fun when he passed out, put it that way.

LEATHA: You gotta wean that man.

CB: Bob was born spitting up.

LEATHA: I did my time. I won't live with a drunk. Over.

CB: Tell you what, though, Leatha. Next time don't send Lomar over. Go 'head.

LEATHA: Why not?

CB: She sleep good?

LEATHA: Yeh. Still is.

CB: She ought to. She drank enough barley pop over here to flush a toilet.

LEATHA: You wanna ten-nine that?

CB: Leatha, you want more of those pills, you send the boy or come over yourself. Your little Miss Highheels I've had about enough of. She wouldn't go home. Just sat on the couch and watched and watched—

LEATHA: You got her hooked on your color set.

CB: Negatory. She was eyeballing my Bob.

LOMAR *sits up.*

LOMAR: That dumb cow.

CB: You wanna ten-nine that?

Water kettle whistles on stove.

LEATHA: Lomar! The coffee. Get the coffee!

LOMAR *doesn't budge, insolently layers her face with makeup, ignores* LEATHA.

LEATHA (Continued): Get off your butt and get the coffee!

LOMAR *ignores* LEATHA. LEATHA *crosses to the stove and pulls the kettle off the heat.*

CB: Queen Bee, you out there? Queen Bee, you copy?

LEATHA *crosses back to CB radio.*

LEATHA: I gotta back out, Francine. I'll catch you on the flip flop.

CB: Threes to you and a buncha eighty-eights. We gone.

LEATHA *cradles the CB mike and crosses to the couch, takes one corner of the sheet* LOMAR *is wrapped in and whips her off onto the floor.*

LEATHA: Get up. Get dressed. And get out of my sight.

LEATHA *exits.* LOMAR *sullenly crosses to the refrigerator, pulls out a 16-ounce Coke, uncaps it.* SHE *pops a handful of pills into her mouth and draws slow on her Coke.*

Scene 4

GARBAGE TRUCK *at* LANDFILL DUMP. *Early afternoon.* SARGE *at rear of truck.* BOB *rounds truck with a six-pack of beer.*

BOB: Here, Sarge. Welcome back.
SARGE: You shouldn't of.
BOB: It was sitting on top of that can over there.
SARGE: Somebody lost their mind.
BOB: Here's to you, Sarge. Here's to life outside the slammer.

BOB *drinks.* SARGE *doesn't.*

SARGE: I had a nice family one time I lost onna counta this shit. Kept getting drunk, getting mean with her. She finally wouldn't put up with it.
BOB: Francine drank more'n I did. Hell, she was always getting *me* drunk.
SARGE: Not anymore?
BOB: Not since the kids. Now I gotta stop? 'Cause I got kids? 'Cause she stopped?
SARGE: Lotta people wonder why a guy drinks, why he grows old. There's a lotta things people don't know.
BOB: I know I ain't quittin'.
SARGE: I'm like you. I'm stubborn. In 1967 Phil Cobb got me outta jail twenty-seven times for public intoxication. He finally said you know, I think you're so hooked on that booze you can't quit. It made me angry. I didn't take a drink for eighteen months! Phil Cobb told me I couldn't quit. I bust my ass to show him I did. (HE *pops open his beer can and draws hard*)
BOB: So now you got a busted ass and a lift on one shoe. And what's Phil got?
SARGE: The leg was my fault. I come down wrong off the back of that truck.
BOB: Phil's truck. You were working.
SARGE: My own fault.
BOB: Hell it was. Running Joke was driving.
SARGE: He made a mistake.
BOB: Sonofabitch better hope I don't see him.

Greasy forearms, face spliced with crud, PISANGER *slides out from under the truck and moves Downstage to his red toolbox.*

BOB (*Continued*): How much longer's this gonna take?
PISANGER: Getting mad, Bob?
BOB: I been mad enough to quit since I started.
PISANGER: You oughta look into the field of electronics.
BOB: Blew that. It's past noon. We still got half the route left.
PISANGER: What took you guys so long?

BOB: Butch took us out to Woolco so we could watch him disconnect that compacter. Then we spent the rest of the morning driving around in circles, Butch stroking his shotgun, looking for Running Joke.

PISANGER: You find him?

BOB: He don't want to be found. Why's Phil so stuck on him?

PISANGER: I don't know but he tried to give him a route.

BOB: What!

PISANGER: First week he worked, Running Joke started in on Phil about how he could change the route around and save gas, cut costs, be more efficient.

BOB: Ass-kisser.

PISANGER: Then right after the accident, Phil told him he could have the Air Base—he'd give him a truck and he could run the route himself.

BOB: *After* the accident?

PISANGER: Yeh.

BOB: I work three years, I get nothing. Running Joke works one week, wrecks a truck, puts Sarge in the hospital and gets—

PISANGER: What about me, Bob? Ten years on the force—

BOB: Phil blames you for not fixing the brakes.

PISANGER: Phil knows that wasn't my fault. I told Butch that morning not to drive that truck or put anybody in it. I hadn't finished with the brakes. Butch knew that when he give it to Running Joke.

BOB: Running Joke. I told Butch we could find the bastard better with a geiger counter whatever it was, you remember that time Butch had it out there looking for coins? Every time he'd point it in Running Joke's direction damn thing'd go off tick tick tick tick tick tick tick—

SARGE (*To himself*): If it hadn't been for that little lady I was staying with at the time, I'd been awful cold and awful hungry.

PISANGER (*Troubled by* SARGE, *changes subject*): How do you rip off a pig's cheek, Bob?

BOB: That fucker Running Joke is radio-reactive.

PISANGER: I'm serious, Bob. How do you rip off a pig's cheek?

BOB: I did it with a screwdriver. They had me at a table with a hundred heads in a pile like this—eyeballs looking off in all directions. Only thing still twitching is the cheeks. You stick this thing in behind the cheek and jerk it back and forth real hard till the muscles tear loose.

PISANGER: Where at?

BOB: That's Canadian bacon.

PISANGER: Farmland?

BOB: Outside Crete, yeh.

PISANGER: Did you know Janet there?

BOB (*Crooking his thumb*): With the hook?

PISANGER (*Laughing*): Yeh.

BOB: Yeh, she was crazy.

PISANGER: Job makes you crazy.

SARGE (*Drifting*): Between her and her sister they kept me pretty well satisfied both physically and sexually and everything else, so—

BOB: That sad fart.

PISANGER (*About the truck*): Try it now, Sarge. (*Approaching him*) Sarge—

SARGE pushes PISANGER away, throws beer can, stalks off around the truck.

PISANGER (*Continued; to BOB*): You dumb fuck.

Truck starter grinds. Engine turns over. The power take-off kicks in. The blade clears the hopper. PISANGER and BOB loosen the turnbuckles in back. The hopper lifts on chrome hydraulics. The front wall shoves back, forcing out a truckload of garbage in a jerking peristalsis. The hopper comes down. PISANGER and BOB tighten the buckles and exit round the front of the truck.

From deep within the mountain of garbage emerges RUNNING JOKE, in boots, maroon sweat pants, a black shirt hanging in wide ribbons, a yellow shirt hanging in wide ribbons over that, a shredding denim jacket with large pockets outside and many more inside. Standing, HE is vertical litter. HE deftly picks himself clean one piece at a time and separates the litter into piles in front of him. Something HE pockets. Another piece disappears into another pocket. Something else unseen HE rolls in the palm of his hand, then pops into his mouth.

Picked clean, RUNNING JOKE sits down in the pile of garbage and junk and rips open a bag. Birds twirp. HE laughs, deep, through time. Flash, explosion, puff of steam. Blackout.

Scene 5

TRAILERHOUSE bedroom. SON explodes up out of bed screaming, clawing nonexistent webs from face, spitting hair.

SON: MOM! MOM! (*Gasping*) It's too late.

LEATHA rushes in.

SON (*Continued*): It's already too late.

LEATHA (*Embracing SON*): Shhh, you're dreaming.

SON: I'm out in that same field running and the dirt's blowing up underneath my feet.

LEATHA: Shhhhh.

SON: Every time I close my eyes, Mom, every place I put my foot explodes orange rocks.

LEATHA: Shhh, I'm here. It's all right.

SON: Smoke's pouring in. Smoke's pouring in.

LEATHA: You're dreaming.
SON: I'm spitting fur.
LEATHA: Shhh.
SON: The earth doesn't want us.
LEATHA: Baby.
SON: Mom, am I gonna die?
LEATHA (*Hugging him close to her*): No. No.
SON: What did I do wrong?

Scene 6

LANDFILL DUMP. *Early afternoon.* LOMAR *sits in the pile of garbage where* RUN-NING JOKE *was last seen.* SHE *sorts trash.* SHE *sings to herself. Finding a 12-inch rubber dildo,* SHE *uses it as a microphone.*

LOMAR (*Singing*):
SHE DON'T LOVE YOU
LIKE I LOVE YOU
IF SHE DID SHE WOULDN'T
BREAK MY HEART—
BREAK YOUR HEART—

RUNNING JOKE *enters.*

RUNNING JOKE: Morning, Lomar.
LOMAR: Ooooh—you give me chills coming up on me like that. (*Stashes dildo in shoulder bag*)
RUNNING JOKE: You bring the kid?
LOMAR: I get tired him tagging after me everywhere I go. I got no private life. Anyway, Leatha don't want him spending time with you.
RUNNING JOKE: She doesn't know me.
LOMAR: That don't stop her.
RUNNING JOKE: She doesn't trust me.
LOMAR: She's got opinions about a whole lotta stuff she don't know nothing about.
RUNNING JOKE: Like your private life?
LOMAR: Oh she knows. Least she thinks she knows. You think I'm pretty?
RUNNING JOKE: You remind me of my sister.
LOMAR: She look this good?
RUNNING JOKE: She's beautiful.
LOMAR: You love her?
RUNNING JOKE: Love her?
LOMAR: Not today I don't mean, not with my eyes burnt holes in a blanket and a chest fulla crud.

RUNNING JOKE: Maybe too much makeup.

LOMAR: That's covering up these splotches. I'm breaking out. Something's got me good. I think it's all this repressed sex I'm not getting. (SHE *laughs too loud*) She was nice, though, huh? Your sister?

RUNNING JOKE: She was sad like you. She missed Father.

LOMAR *and* RUNNING JOKE *rip open garbage bags and sort.*

LOMAR: You ever drink blood?

RUNNING JOKE: No, but I did pills, Lomar.

LOMAR: I heard of a person once that usta work out to Farmland? He'd bring cow blood home in a mason jar and drink it.

RUNNING JOKE: Pour it in a glass of wine.

LOMAR: You know him?

RUNNING JOKE (*Reads a page he's pulled from an inside pocket*): Listen. "The quality of your being attracts your life."

LOMAR: What's that mean?

RUNNING JOKE (*Hands her the page*): I'm not sure.

LOMAR: I belong here at the dump. I feel like a pile of shit.

RUNNING JOKE (*Pointing*): *That* is a pile of shit.

LOMAR: I could tell that.

RUNNING JOKE: Some animal couldn't use that part of what it ate and got rid of it.

LOMAR: That's me.

RUNNING JOKE: You treat it right, that pile of shit will heat your home, drive a car, lift a Lear jet right off the ground and fly you—where do you want to go?

LOMAR: Kansas. I told you. You gonna take me? You told me you would.

RUNNING JOKE: You hear what you want to hear.

LOMAR: I gotta get out.

BUTCH (*Offstage*): Running Joke!

LOMAR: You gotta help me.

LOMAR *scampers Off.* BUTCH *enters with a shotgun.*

BUTCH: Running Joke. You're on our land.

RUNNING JOKE: Dad's land.

BUTCH: Mine too.

RUNNING JOKE: Mother earth.

BUTCH (*Throwing traps at* RUNNING JOKE's *feet*): Checking your traps?

The earth rumbles.

RUNNING JOKE: Just listening to your ground fart.

BUTCH: That was a truck backfire.

RUNNING JOKE: Last week it backfired, took out that stinkweed tree.

BUTCH: What stinkweed tree?

RUNNING JOKE: I watched your tractor plow it under.

BUTCH: We got nothing to hide.

RUNNING JOKE: You got a lot you're ignoring.

BUTCH: Like what?

RUNNING JOKE: Like the fact that garbage packed this tight this long makes methane gas.

BUTCH: Like the fact this land is posted "No Trespassing" every fifteen feet. I could part your hair for good right now and no white man'd ever miss you.

RUNNING JOKE (*Indicating shotgun*): With your fishing pole?

BUTCH (*Leveling shotgun at* RUNNING JOKE*'s chest*): Including Phil. He don't want you. We don't need you. You'll never haul garbage for us again.

PHIL (*Offstage*): Butch!

RUNNING JOKE: Why not?

PHIL (*Entering*): Butch! I told you to *find* Running Joke.

BUTCH: I found him. Right here. Stealing God knows what off our land. Trespassing. He's got traps set clear around the pond down there, making money off us, waltzing in and out of here at his leisure.

PHIL: I told you to find him and tell him we need him. Did you tell him that?

RUNNING JOKE: Not exactly.

BUTCH: Who is he? Do we know? Who the hell is he? Can we afford having him poke around out here?

PHIL: I gave you a direct order, son.

BUTCH: We oughta get rid of him.

RUNNING JOKE: Fucked up last time you tried it. Crippled Sarge, lost a truck.

PHIL (*To* RUNNING JOKE): That truck is taken care of and Butch is paying through the nose. Unfortunate accident. (*To* BUTCH) It won't happen again, right? That's all, Butch. I'll meet you back at the garage.

BUTCH: Dad.

PHIL: Butch.

BUTCH: Dad, we can't trust him. We don't need him. We're doing fine.

RUNNING JOKE: Just fine.

BUTCH: It's perfect!

RUNNING JOKE: What do you know about perfect?

BUTCH: Ten trucks, fifteen men and a sanitary landfill that's the first one in America with a plastic liner.

RUNNING JOKE: That *is* sanitary.

BUTCH: That's the state of the art. *Solid Waste Management* calls this one gem of a dump. Best-run dump, greatest nation of the world.

RUNNING JOKE: Greatest nation of the world.

BUTCH: We had a centerfold in *Waste Age*.

RUNNING JOKE: *Waste Age!*

BUTCH: The amount of waste produced equals the greatness of the nation. Don't it, Dad?

RUNNING JOKE: Waste makes you great?

BUTCH: It makes us boss.

RUNNING JOKE: Boss of what?

BUTCH: Of shit like you. Hell you know that. We wasted your people, we smashed your culture, we stole your land, we murdered your parents—

RUNNING JOKE: You did all that?

LOMAR enters, hovers Upstage.

BUTCH: Damn right.

RUNNING JOKE: My parents?

BUTCH: Yer an Indian, ain't you?

RUNNING JOKE: Who told you that, Butch?

BUTCH: *You* did!

RUNNING JOKE: I told you I was an alien, Butch. To the way you think. Alien.

LOMAR, from behind, shoves 12-inch dildo between BUTCH's legs and wags it. BUTCH grabs it, lets go, yells out.

BUTCH: Put that down. You don't know where it's been!

LOMAR: I got a pretty good idea.

BUTCH: Give it here.

LOMAR: Get your own!

BUTCH: Dammit Lomar! Give me the goddam—

BUTCH lunges at LOMAR. SHE sidesteps him and breaks Offstage. BUTCH runs after her. RUNNING JOKE rips open another bag of garbage.

PHIL: Looking for something?

RUNNING JOKE: All my life, Phil.

PHIL: How'd you get past the guard?

RUNNING JOKE: I came in with the garbage.

PHIL: My garbage.

RUNNING JOKE: You got a lot of it.

PHIL: What are you looking for?

RUNNING JOKE: Gold, diamonds, bags fulla money.

PHIL: You're wasting your time.

RUNNING JOKE: I found a toaster, a pair of pliers.

PHIL: Anything worth money the men already took off.

The earth rumbles.

RUNNING JOKE: They didn't take that.

PHIL: What's that?

RUNNING JOKE: That's methane, Phil.

PHIL: That was a truck backfiring.

RUNNING JOKE: That's shit turning to gas.

PHIL: There's no methane gases here. We have no trouble here with that.

RUNNING JOKE: I'm not making trouble, Phil. I'm telling you there's power underground here. We're sitting on a goldmine source of power. That should be good news.

PHIL: To who?

RUNNING JOKE: To the man who owns it, I'd say! Man like you with a fleet of trucks and a big fat car, brand-new one.

PHIL (*Proudly*): It's a Continental.

RUNNING JOKE: I know. I saw it this morning—gleaming in the sun.

PHIL: You could be driving one like it.

PHIL *and* RUNNING JOKE *exchange looks.*

PHIL (*Continued*): If you'd take up my offer.

RUNNING JOKE (*Shakes head, sorts garbage*): Lot of chrome on that car, Phil.

PHIL: First year I was in this business I found a big family album full of snapshots with little captions written up underneath each picture. The book was sixty or seventy years of a family's life. Total strangers. I could see them being born and growing up and going to school and getting jobs and having kids and funerals and birthday parties and car wrecks. Vi and me would sit down and look through that and try to imagine our own life stretched out. I used to wonder about Phil Junior.

RUNNING JOKE: Butch?

PHIL: How he'd grow up. What kind of man he'd become.

RUNNING JOKE: I'm sorry, Phil.

PHIL: Then one time I found a baby, two to three weeks old, rolled up in the want ads, bottom of a can. After that. . . (*Shakes head no*) I used to pay attention to what I was hauling. Now it's just so much a ton. Maybe that's wrong—

BUTCH *chases* LOMAR *back Onstage.* SHE's *got the dildo.* HE's *got the shotgun.*

PHIL (*Continued*): Butch! What are you doing!

BUTCH *throws a look at* LOMAR *and points the shotgun at the ground.*

BUTCH (*Squeezing trigger in denial*): Nothing.

BOOM! *The shotgun fires.* RUNNING JOKE *and* LOMAR *combust in spontaneous laughter.* BUTCH, *dumbfounded, takes in their reaction to him but not his splattered foot. Finally, in seconds, hit by pain,* BUTCH *bellows.* PHIL *hurries to him.*

BUTCH (*Continued*): Jesus Christ, my foot!

Blackout.

Scene 7

ALMA'S BAR & GRILL. ALMA *drops two oversized boxes of Kotex into a grocery bag on the counter.* SON *sits monkeying with a toy gun. From his belt, like a holster, hangs a rubber swim-flipper.*

SON: It's missing fifteen functions. It's supposed to light up and buzz and I think this here is supposed to go around and around. The death ray don't work. The spontaneous combuster I don't think ever *did* work.
ALMA: You got your batteries in upside down?
SON: No.
ALMA: They leaking?
SON: No.
ALMA: Where'd you get it? Out to the dump?
SON: No! I saved up for it. I paid eighteen dollars for it.

Stage Right, LEATHA *has come into* TRAILERHOUSE *kitchen with two armfuls of groceries. As* SHE *starts putting them away,* LOMAR *enters, laughing, wagging the 12-inch dildo.*

LEATHA (*To* LOMAR): Where you been?
ALMA (*To* SON): Eighteen dollars!
LOMAR (*To* LEATHA): Up on Venus where the men suck their penis.
LEATHA (*Snatching dildo from* LOMAR): You want to go back to County?
LOMAR: Is it worse than this? I forget.
LEATHA (*Crossing to bedroom wastebasket, throwing dildo into it*): There's no married men to seduce.
LOMAR: Hell there ain't.
ALMA (*To* SON, *about gun*): This isn't supposed to work. This was designed *not* to work, to break and not get fixed.
LEATHA (*To* LOMAR): Why don't you go find a boy your own age?
SON (*To* ALMA, *about gun*): Frankie's got one.
LOMAR (*To* LEATHA): There are no boys my age.
SON (*To* ALMA): He's got a cosmic dissembler on his and everything.
LOMAR (*To* LEATHA): There are only men my age.

LEATHA: Think of Sudden.

LOMAR (*Caught?*): I didn't mean him.

LEATHA: He's gotta work with Butch.

LOMAR: Who's stopping him?

LEATHA: You don't make it easier, hitting on his boss.

LOMAR: I ain't hitting on Butch. Jesus, whatta expression! 'Sides, Butch ain't Sudden's boss anyway. Phil is.

LEATHA: Butch'll take it over when Phil retires.

LOMAR: Butch will? God, I thought Sudden would.

LEATHA: Butch will.

LOMAR: That's not what Bob says. Bob says Butch is lucky to have a pair of gloves, screwing up the way he does.

LEATHA: You don't know that family.

LOMAR: Well, not like you do, no.

LEATHA: Lomar—

LOMAR: He is kinda cute, though.

LEATHA: For a married man.

LOMAR: You jealous?

LEATHA: Of you?

LOMAR: It could happen.

In ALMA'S BAR & GRILL, ALMA *fiddles with* SON'S *gun, using a screwdriver.* SON *moves about the bar, stung, disappointed, feeling stupid.*

LEATHA (*To* LOMAR): Finish up with this. I gotta go.

LOMAR (*Peeling off her shirt*): Butch is a teddy bear. Sudden is a goat.

LEATHA (*On way out*): Well the goat's asleep, so keep the TV down. And put your shirt back on!

LOMAR: I don't have to.

LEATHA: In *my* house.

LOMAR: Whose house?

LEATHA: The hell you don't!

LOMAR (*Kicking off her shoes*): You're not the boss of me!

LEATHA: The hell I'm not!

LOMAR: Sudden!

LEATHA: Hush up.

LOMAR: You get two hundred dollars a month to put up with your foster child. Why should I make it easy?

LEATHA: If I wasn't late for Weightwatchers, we'd settle this right now. (SHE *goes out trailerhouse door*)

LOMAR (*Following* LEATHA): Weightwatchers meets at the mall. Not at the Terminal Hotel . . . Mom!

In ALMA'S BAR & GRILL, SON *reaches high to a shelf where a glass box contains a white bone flute.*

ALMA (*To* SON, *about gun*): Well this is a piece of junk, sweetheart.

SON (*About flute*): What's this, Alma?

LOMAR (*At* LEATHA, *from trailerhouse door*): You're lucky to have a job this day 'n' age!

ALMA (*To* SON): That . . .

LOMAR (*At* LEATHA): Thank me for that!

ALMA (*To* SON): . . . is something special.

> LEATHA *exits.* LOMAR *moves into* TRAILERHOUSE *bedroom where* PISANGER *is laid out on the bed, snoring.* LOMAR *sits down across from him, sucking on a Coke, tickling his feet.*

SON (*To* ALMA, *about flute*): It's old.

ALMA: Long before you landed.

SON: I couldn't reach it before.

ALMA: You're getting big.

> SON *holds flute up to his eye and scans the room, using it as a telescope. Finally,* HE *focuses on* ALMA.

ALMA (*Continued; fanning her fingers in mime of playing a flute*): What do you hear?

> SON *lowers flute to his mouth, blows a few notes.* ALMA *grins, congratulatory, and drops broken gun into grocery bag.* SON *hands flute back to* ALMA *and moves toward door.*

ALMA (*Continued; holding grocery bag*): Don't forget to give this to your mom. And uh . . .

> ALMA *slips bone flute into* SON's *swim-flipper holster.* SON *grins and* THEY *hug.*

> *In* TRAILERHOUSE *bedroom,* PISANGER *is jarred awake by* LOMAR.

PISANGER: Ow! Goddammit, Lomar!

> SON *leaves* ALMA's BAR & GRILL, *waves.*

SON: Bye, Alma!

LOMAR (*To* PISANGER): You don't take me I'm going anyway. I'll get Running Joke to do it.

PISANGER (*Half asleep*): Do what?

LOMAR: Take me 'cross into Kansas.

PISANGER: He'll take you up to Pine Ridge and trade you for a horse.

LOMAR: You think!

PISANGER: He's an Indian, ain't he?

LOMAR: I hate Leatha.

PISANGER: She thinks a lot of you.

LOMAR: Shit she does. Looks of me makes her blow up. What would she do she knew about us?

PISANGER: Uh.

LOMAR: She'd go crazy, call the cops *and* the County, wouldn't she? Then we'd have to go.

PISANGER: We'll go.

LOMAR: I won't hitchhike. I won't take no goddam bus.

PISANGER: You'd go bareback with Running Joke.

LOMAR: Hell I did. Did you say did or would? I'm going in a car.

PISANGER: He don't have a car.

LOMAR: He can get one.

PISANGER: How? Steal it?

LOMAR: If he had to.

PISANGER: Who's going to make him? He can't even keep a job.

LOMAR: Maybe he don't want to work for Phil. Maybe he's smarter than a man should be to haul garbage.

PISANGER: He's a freak.

LOMAR: He don't need that job.

PISANGER: Who needs it? I need it? I could quit tomorrow.

LOMAR: And jump a goddam train.

PISANGER: We'll drive.

LOMAR: When?

PISANGER: Soon as I don't know when.

LOMAR: Or how.

PISANGER: When I get the Chevy running, that's how. When I get the money for the parts for the Chevy. It won't take half a day to fix that thing.

LOMAR: Trick'll be yanking it out of that tar pool it's sunk in. It's up over the wheels now.

PISANGER: I know.

LOMAR: Gets hot like this that whole back yard heaves up and down like a hairy waterbed.

PISANGER: Something will happen.

LOMAR: You wish.

Phone rings in living room. LOMAR *jumps up to answer it.* PISANGER *rolls over, covers head.*

LOMAR (*Continued; into phone*): Hello. Hi Phil. Yeh he's here. No, he's asleep. He told me not to. Yes I will. Bye Phil. (SHE *hangs up, moves back into bedroom*) That was Phil. He says if you don't go back out to the garage and grease the trucks, you're fired.

PISANGER: Well, you just call back and tell him then I'm fired 'cause I'm not going back out there.

LOMAR (*Delighted, racing back to phone*): Really?! You're going to stay here with me?

PISANGER: Oh God.

LOMAR (*Into phone*): Hello, Phil? Phooey. (*To* PISANGER) Phil's not there! (*Into phone*) Well, Butch, Phil said Sudden's fired if he don't go back out there and grease the trucks and Sudden says he ain't going back out there, so— Phil never fired Sudden? Well, by God he did over the phone. (*To* PISANGER) Butch don't know if you're fired or not!

As LOMAR *talks,* PISANGER *rolls out of bed, pulls on his pants, shirt, shoes and breaks for the trailerhouse door.*

LOMAR (*Continued; into phone*): Butch. Uh huh. Yeh I will only no he won't. He says he's staying here with me. Not coming in. Okay. Bye.

LOMAR *hangs up, moves back into bedroom.* PISANGER's *gone.*

Scene 8

INDUSTRIAL REFUGE, INC. PHIL COBB's *office.* PHIL, BUTCH *and* BOB *play cards.* BOB *is drunk and drinking,* PHIL *and* BUTCH *aren't.*

BOB: Not a damn thing!

PHIL: Quitcher bitchin', Bob.

BOB: It ain't fair, Phil.

PHIL: Who said it would be?

BOB: You treat us all different.

PHIL: I respect your differences.

BUTCH: Hell, you count on them.

BOB: All I want is a fair shake.

PHIL: That's a low goal, Bob. I'll take a hit.

BOB: I'll take a hit.

BUTCH: You'll shit and fall back in it.

Phone rings.

BOB: What I'm talking about Phil is I don't care if I never make another nickel more in wages—

Phone rings.

BUTCH (*To* PHIL): You're gone now, aren't you?

PHIL: Yeh yeh I'm gone.

BOB: —what I want is benefits.

BUTCH (*Answering phone*): Industrial Refuge. May I say who's calling? (*Hand over phone*) Uric Salts from the Woolworth Company in Minneapolis.

Laughter, shouts from BUTCH *and* PHIL.

PHIL: We want the money. We want the money, Butch!

BUTCH (*Can't believe it*): Minneapolis!

PHIL: You take it, son.

BUTCH: Me!

PHIL (*Putting money down for a bet*): He'll talk you out of it.

BUTCH (*Matching* PHIL's *bet*): He won't talk *me* out of it! (HE *swings out from under the table, his right foot encased in a huge white plaster cast, an oversized bowling ball.* HE *drops his voice*) Hello.

BOB (*To* PHIL): Like if I get sick on the job this winter or somebody else gets sick on the job so that he has to go to the hospital for ammonia, heart attack or anything else—

BUTCH (*Into phone*): Uh huh. Well I just took it out of service temporarily until I receive some money on it.

BOB: I just want him to be able to support his family.

BUTCH: If he does that there'll be no problem. I'll turn the compacter right back on.

BOB: I want to be able to be a human being like everybody else.

BUTCH: The store *was* notified.

BOB: To hell with the wages, forget it.

PHIL: Three or four times we told them!

BOB: What I want is the benefits. It's no more'n fair.

BUTCH: The store was notified about three or four times.

BOB: I mean, if we go out there—

PHIL: Bob—

BOB: —in the middle of winter—

PHIL: Bob.

BOB: —thirty degrees below zero—

PHIL: Sit down.

BUTCH (*To* PHIL): A personal check?

PHIL: No! Cash or a certified check.

BUTCH (*Into phone*): It'll have to be cash or a certified check.

BOB: —and if we go out there middle of summer, a hundred and thirty degrees *above* zero—

PHIL: Goddammit!

BUTCH: Yeh.

BOB: If we're not appreciated that much then we're not appreciated at all.

BUTCH: The only way I could take anything other than that would be to have a board meeting and some of the board members aren't here right now and I'm sure I can't get hold of them.

PHIL *cracks up laughing.* BUTCH *beams.*

BOB: Then somebody else better start taking over and hauling the garbage altogether.

BUTCH: I'm just taking orders.

BOB: All of it!

BUTCH: I—and you remember the kind of problem we got into there because we had nothing in writing and it was verbal.

BOB: All of it!

BUTCH: And I'm sure you can understand my point.

PHIL (*Grabs phone from* BUTCH, *yells into it*): NOT UNTIL WE GET THE MONEY! (*Hands phone back to* BUTCH)

BUTCH (*Into phone*): Not until we get the money. (*To* PHIL) He hung up. (HE *hangs up*)

PHIL (*Collecting the bet*): What he say?

BUTCH: He's gonna meet me at seven-fifteen with a certified check for nine thousand dollars! (*Takes bet money back from* PHIL)

BOB: Phil—

PHIL (*Punches* BUTCH): Wheee! I told you we'd get it!

BOB: Phil—

BUTCH (*Punches* PHIL *twice as hard*): I told you I could do it!

BOB (*Holding a card*): Phil, you're over. You were sitting on a queen.

PHIL: Ahhh! I didn't know I had a queen!

BUTCH: Don't you look at your cards?

BOB (*Raking in the money*): You were thinking about all that money.

Office door swings open. SARGE *limps in.*

PHIL: Wouldn't you worry about nine thousand dollars?

BOB: Phil, I worry about nine dollars.

BUTCH (*Showing* BOB *his cards*): Bob?

BOB (*Beaten*): Ah shit!

SARGE: Well, see you tomorrow, Phil.

BUTCH (Raking in money from winning hand): You still in the game, Bob?

PHIL: How'd you get along out there, Sarge?

SARGE: Fine.

PHIL: Easy as fallin' offa log, ain't it?

SARGE: Yeh.

PHIL: Bullshit. I know better than that. It's hard work. (*Gets up, throws an arm around* SARGE) You know what, you old bastard?

SARGE: What?

PHIL: I want you to stay with me till you die.

SARGE: Great. I got a job till I die.

PHIL: If you want it.

SARGE: Well if I'm gonna stay with you till I die, you're working me to death.

PHIL: Ahhhh!

PHIL *and* SARGE *laugh,* PHIL *louder than* SARGE.

PHIL (*Continued*): Sarge, you guys are all my family. If it wasn't for you guys, I wouldn't have nothing.

SARGE: Thanks, Phil. I'll get that money back to you.

PHIL: Don't worry about it, Sarge. I'll get it out of you.

PHIL *shoves a cigar into* SARGE's *mouth.* SARGE *leaves.* PHIL *returns to game. Phone rings.*

BUTCH (*Into phone*): Industrial Refuge. May I say who's calling? (*Covers phone with hand*) Gene Risks from the Environmental Protection Agency.

PHIL: I'm not here.

BUTCH: I'm sorry, Mr. Risks, Mr. Cobb is predisposed. (HE *hangs up*)

PHIL (*Shuffling cards*): Got any money left, Bob?

BOB, *drunk, slides off chair, hits floor.*
        Outside office, PISANGER *enters, wiping grease from his hands into a rag.* HE *eyes* PHIL COBB's *car, parked out front.*
        Inside office, PHIL *and* BUTCH *turn lights off and leave.*
        PISANGER *paces, spits, nervous as if being watched. Approaching the car from the driver's side,* HE *walks past it, back, looks in, stops, turns again and crosses back to his red toolbox Stage Left.* HE *tosses the rag.*
        RUNNING JOKE *stands behind* PISANGER.

PISANGER (*Taken aback*): Where'd you come from?

RUNNING JOKE: Long story. Starry galaxy.

PISANGER: I didn't see you come in.

RUNNING JOKE: I scare you?

PISANGER: You don't scare me.

RUNNING JOKE (*Crossing to red toolbox*): Good. I came to borrow some tools from Daddy Phil.

PISANGER: They aren't Phil's. They're mine.

RUNNING JOKE: All of them?

PISANGER: Damn near. The ones that aren't broke are.

RUNNING JOKE (*Opening toolbox*): You have everything you need.

PISANGER (*Closing toolbox*): People forget that around here. They take 'em out, they don't put 'em back.

RUNNING JOKE: You could open your own garage—

PISANGER: I'm keeping my tools at home now.

RUNNING JOKE: —if you wanted to.

PISANGER: I still can't find my five-eighth socket.

RUNNING JOKE (*Pulls socket wrench out of his back pocket*): This yours?

PISANGER: Where'd you get it?

RUNNING JOKE: Lomar gave it to me.

PISANGER (*Takes wrench back*): It ain't hers to give it.

RUNNING JOKE: What about your box-end combination there, your quarter-inch? You be needing that?

PISANGER: What are you doing up at the tanks?

RUNNING JOKE: Come up and see.

PISANGER: I don't want Lomar up there anymore. If anything happened to her—

RUNNING JOKE: I won't hurt Lomar.

PISANGER: She don't need help getting into trouble.

RUNNING JOKE: I know. She needs a father.

PISANGER: You're not her father.

RUNNING JOKE: I'm not trying to be. Are you?

PISANGER: No. Yeh. I'm her foster father.

RUNNING JOKE: That's a big responsibility. Are you able to respond? As a father?

PISANGER: Look asshole you keep your mouth off my life—

RUNNING JOKE (*Pulls a gear out of his pocket*): Do you know what this thing is?

PISANGER: Yeh. It's a crankshaft gear. Did you hear me!

RUNNING JOKE (*Another gear*): What's this?

PISANGER: Offa camshaft.

RUNNING JOKE: Do they fit into each other?

PISANGER: Hey!

RUNNING JOKE: The teeth?

PISANGER (*Shakes head*): They're independent. Crankshaft's down here, pushes the pistons up and down. Camshaft's in the manifold, opening closing the valves. You know that.

RUNNING JOKE: No, I didn't.

PISANGER: Letting in the mixture.

RUNNING JOKE: So they do work together.

PISANGER: Well, they're connected, yeh. They're on a chain. And they gotta be timed just right.

RUNNING JOKE: To work together.

PISANGER: Not these two.

RUNNING JOKE: Why not?

PISANGER (*Takes gear*): That's a Ford. This is General Motors.

RUNNING JOKE: General Motors.

PISANGER: Three-twenty-seven, three-fifty horsepower.

RUNNING JOKE (*Takes gear, moves toward red toolbox*): Thanks. I'll get this box-end back to you.

PISANGER (*Cutting* RUNNING JOKE *off at toolbox*): You can't have it. I'm going to need it. (HE *grabs toolbox, moves out around front of* PHIL COBB's *car*) I'm gonna need all of them. Real soon.

RUNNING JOKE *nods, exits.* PISANGER *spits, slowly turns 360 degrees.* HE *is alone.* HE *crosses to* PHIL COBB's *car, opens backseat door, puts toolbox on seat, slams door, opens driver's-side door and gets in.*

PISANGER (*Continued*): Here goes, sugar.

PISANGER *turns the key, the engine revs. Car jolts forward, tires screeching.* SARGE *weaves in, steadies himself on his carrying barrel and sees* PISANGER *driving Off.*

SARGE (*Waving computer read-out that* PISANGER *found*): Sudden! Is this important or not? You left it on the dash!

SARGE *inhales, hoists the loaded barrel to his shoulder, takes one step and doubles under—one leg gives way,* HE *drops to one knee, falls sideways. Glass breaks, garbage leaps out of his barrel.*

Sound of squealing tires. PHIL COBB's *car pulls back in,* PISANGER *jams the stick into park, kicks open his door.*

PISANGER: Sarge! (HE *dives out of car, straddles* SARGE)

SARGE: Be good to the little boy in you. Good seed, Sudden, your boy, Lomar.

PISANGER (*Taking computer read-out from* SARGE): Don't talk.

SARGE: Call Alma.

PISANGER: Shuttup.

SARGE: Don't die in jail, Sudden.

SARGE *blinks out.* PISANGER *pounds on* SARGE's *chest slow motion. Papers clutched in* PISANGER's *fist bunch up and scatter as* HE *beats on* SARGE's *heart like a drum.*

As light fades around SARGE *and* PISANGER, *the sound of a car door, ignition, engine revving, clutch popping, rubber rip across asphalt.* PISANGER *throws a look over his shoulder.*

Blackout. Sound of acceleration through three gears, two high-speed corners and gradual fade-out as the car leaves reach of the senses.

END OF ACT ONE

ACT TWO

Scene 1

INDUSTRIAL REFUGE, INC. PHIL COBB's *office. Late afternoon.*

BUTCH (*On phone*): Come on, Freddy, answer the goddam phone!

On far side of stage, FREDDY THE COP *ignores radio beeper in his car as* HE *focuses in on unseen parties through binoculars.*

BUTCH (*Continued; on phone*): Dammit Freddy!

FREDDY THE COP: Beep beep beep beep beep beep beep—goddammit! (*Answering car radio*) Mobile nine.

BUTCH (*Into phone*): Put your pants on, Freddy!

FREDDY THE COP (*Into radio*): My pants are on.

BUTCH: Well, pull them up and get over here.

FREDDY THE COP: What's the occasion, Butch? You set your truck on fire again?

BUTCH: No Freddy—

FREDDY THE COP: You have to dump another hot load in the middle of O Street I'm gonna have to help you clean up?

BUTCH: No Freddy, this is bigger than that. This is an emergency.

FREDDY THE COP: When King Dollar puts out ashes, you hose them down first, Butch, I told you. You don't have to haul their ashes.

BUTCH: Somebody stole my car.

FREDDY THE COP: Call the fire department.

BUTCH: Somebody stole my car, Freddy!!

FREDDY THE COP: Who'd want your car?

BUTCH: A twenty-three-thousand–dollar Lincoln Continental!

FREDDY THE COP: Phil's car! Hell that's different! Hold your horses! I'm coming! (HE *jumps into his car and screeches Off*)

At TRAILERHOUSE, PISANGER *sits on front stoop, poring over the computer read-out* HE *got back from* SARGE, *lips moving as* HE *reads with effort.* LEATHA *comes out of the trailerhouse, empties wastebasket in garbage can.*

LEATHA: Lomar's gone.

PISANGER: Sarge is dead.

LEATHA: He's dead?

PISANGER: Where'd she go?

LEATHA: In jail?

PISANGER: He got out of jail this morning. He worked the route today. Dropped dead an hour ago. Where'd she go?

LEATHA: I don't know. I came back from Weightwatchers wasn't nobody here. Then the kid came back from the dump. He said Lomar's still there.

PISANGER: With Running Joke?

LEATHA: I guess.

PISANGER *reads.*

LEATHA (*Continued*): Aren't you going to do something? She knows she's not supposed to be there or with him or leave the kid.

PISANGER (*Stands, enters trailerhouse*): Every light's on in this place. The CB, the TV—it's six o'clock in the middle of July and every goddam light is on!

LEATHA (*Follows* PISANGER *in*): It was like this when I got here. I told her a million times.

PISANGER *paces, punching off lights, the CB, the TV.*

PISANGER: Jesus Christ, the stereo!

LEATHA: Why won't you go get her?

PISANGER: 'Cause I just got home, I been up since five, hauled garbage, fixed the jimmy—

LEATHA: He's got her diggin' in the trash. God knows what else.

PISANGER: —came home, couldn't sleep, went back out there, greased six more trucks and Sarge is dead.

LEATHA: Sarge was an alcoholic. Their throats explode.

PISANGER: He worked too hard.

LEATHA: He drank too much.

PISANGER: His whole damn life.

LEATHA: So do you.

PISANGER: I haven't had a drink in three months!

LEATHA: You *work* too hard I said.

PISANGER (*Amused*): Sarge still owes Phil money. Four or five hundred dollars. Phil'd say don't worry, I'll get it out of you. He didn't this time.

LEATHA: He got enough out it killed the man.

PISANGER: His heart popped out of his mouth.

LEATHA: Go get Lomar.

PISANGER (*Stands, peels off his shirt*): I'm gonna take a shower.

LEATHA: You watch the kid, then, 'cause I'm going to get her.

PISANGER: You take the kid.

LEATHA *exits.* PISANGER *moves into bedroom, sheds clothes.* FREDDY THE COP *pulls up in his car, honks, gets out, slams door, speaks through a portable bullhorn.*

FREDDY THE COP (*Through bullhorn*): SUDDEN PISANGER!

PISANGER (*Appearing at trailerhouse door, wrapped in towel*): How long you known me, Freddy?

FREDDY THE COP (*Through bullhorn*): ALL YOUR LIFE.

PISANGER: What do you want? I'm taking a shower.

FREDDY THE COP (*Tossing bullhorn into front seat of car*): Not right now you're not. Right now you're gonna answer some questions.

PISANGER: I don't know nothing.

FREDDY THE COP: About what?

PISANGER: Anything you'd be interested in.

FREDDY THE COP: Oh, I'm interested, Pisanger. I'm real interested. Fact is I always have taken an unnatural interest in your growth and development. Knocking over tombstones out to Wyuka, hauling you home comatose countless times, watching you throw up out my back window in the rearview mirror—

Crow caws overhead. FREDDY THE COP *draws his .38.*

FREDDY THE COP (*Continued*): Salt and battery, destructing property—(HE *fires over* PISANGER's *head*)

PISANGER: Put that thing away!

FREDDY THE COP: —resisting arrest, DWI.

PISANGER: How far back in history you wanna go, Fred?

FREDDY THE COP (*Putting .38 back into holster*): So don't sell yourself short, Pisanger. We're real interested.

PISANGER: In what?

FREDDY THE COP: Like where's that foster kid of yours?

PISANGER: Lomar's my adopted daughter.

FREDDY THE COP: She's your foster kid. The County pays you to watch her.

PISANGER: So what?

FREDDY THE COP: So. You been watching her?

PISANGER: Yeh.

FREDDY THE COP: How good? Someone said they seen her with Running Joke. Fact, she's been seen with him quite a lot lately, here and there, off and on, up and down, in and out.

PISANGER: Like where?

FREDDY THE COP: Like coming out of Tebo's chicken shed on their hands and knees all covered with chicken shit grinning like coyotes.

PISANGER: That's a lie.

FREDDY THE COP: Then there's a lot of liars. Where is she?

PISANGER: With the kid.

FREDDY THE COP: Leatha's got the kid, I seen them when I drove up. Lomar wasn't with them. Fact, Leatha told me to ask you where she is.

PISANGER: What do you want from her?

FREDDY THE COP: Answers.

PISANGER: About what?

FREDDY THE COP: About where her boyfriend is. Running Joke just stole Phil Cobb's car.

PISANGER *cracks up laughing.*

FREDDY THE COP (*Continued*): You think that's funny? Grand theft auto's five years.

PISANGER (*Suddenly sober*): Three, I thought.

FREDDY THE COP: He'll get the max. And when we get his prints in the computer, no telling who wants him for what. Indians all got records. They got more violations against them then they got names.

PISANGER: She ain't here.

FREDDY THE COP: I'll take a look.

PISANGER *blocks* FREDDY THE COP's *path at trailerhouse door.*

FREDDY THE COP (*Continued*): You gonna force me to get a warrant? After all these years?

PISANGER (*Stepping aside*): She ain't here. I told you.

FREDDY THE COP (*Entering trailerhouse*): I'll remember you said that.

FREDDY THE COP *starts his search in the bedroom, going through drawers, sniffing laundry.* PISANGER *moves into the living room as* LOMAR *comes in the back door.*

LOMAR: *Sudden!*

PISANGER: Shhh!

LOMAR: Call me your bitch, Sudden.

PISANGER: Don't do that!

LOMAR (*Up against him*): You think Freddy'd find it funny walking in on me sucking your dick?

PISANGER: Goddammit!

FREDDY THE COP (*From bedroom*): PISANGER!

PISANGER: Jesus Christ! What?

PISANGER *shoves* LOMAR *into the armchair and sits down on her lap, attempting to hide her.* FREDDY THE COP *enters living room with the 12-inch rubber dildo.*

FREDDY THE COP: Now don't tell me you don't know this here is three inches longer than legal. (*Laughs at own joke*) Belongs over here. (HE *props the dildo on the TV like an antenna*) Help bring in the picture.

FREDDY THE COP *chuckles, moves into the kitchen, takes a look out the back door. Satisfied,* HE *turns to* PISANGER, *who is trying his best to mask* LOMAR.

FREDDY THE COP (*Continued*): All right! She's not here. But when she comes back, you call me first thing. Got that? You don't, your ass is grass.

PISANGER: Sure, Freddy. Let me take my shower.

FREDDY THE COP (*Finger to nose*): You should.

FREDDY THE COP *exits trailerhouse.* PISANGER *jumps up off* LOMAR.

LOMAR: Call me your bitch.

PISANGER: I shoulda given you to him.

LOMAR: I knew you wouldn't.

FREDDY THE COP (*From the car, on bullhorn*): SUDDEN! ONE MORE THING! WHEN YOU GONNA HAUL MY WOOD OUT FROM IN FRONT OF MY HOUSE?

PISANGER (*Shouting from the trailerhouse door*): That trash!

FREDDY THE COP: My tree limbs.

PISANGER (*Charging for the car, pounding on its hood*): When you cut them down into three-foot lengths like the law says, now get the hell outta here!

FREDDY THE COP *pops the clutch, the car lurches forward,* PISANGER *leaps back.*

FREDDY THE COP (*Backing up*): Sorry, Sudden.

Exit FREDDY THE COP. PISANGER, *back inside, starts pulling on his clothes.*

PISANGER: I was better off an alcoholic.

LOMAR: That was before I got here.

PISANGER: That's what I mean.

LOMAR (*Zipping up* PISANGER'*s fly*): So I wouldn't know.

PISANGER: Never home. Just working and drinking. I didn't have time to get into trouble.

LOMAR (*Fastening* PISANGER'*s belt buckle*): I'd swallow it, Sudden.

PISANGER: I sober up and get into this.

LOMAR: Shit, here comes Leatha!

LOMAR *shoots Offstage, back door slams.* LEATHA'*s coming up the drive with* SON. PISANGER *goes to meet them.*

LEATHA: What did Freddy want?

PISANGER *whispers in* LEATHA'*s ear.*

LEATHA (*Continued; swatting* PISANGER): Don't use that word in front of this kid.

SON *throws* PISANGER *a football.* PISANGER *returns it.*

LEATHA (*Continued*): Lomar wasn't at the dump. Just the guard.

> PISANGER *and* SON *drift Upstage, tossing the football.* LEATHA *goes into trailerhouse.*

SON: Do you love Mom?
PISANGER: Sure I love your mom.
SON: Do you love Lomar?
PISANGER: Yeh. I care about her. We take care of her.
SON: Do you love her?
PISANGER: Do you love me?
SON: Yeh.
PISANGER: Then go out for a long one.

> SON *backs off.* PISANGER *throws him a pass.* SON *fumbles, ball bounces,* SON *retrieves it.* THEY *walk back toward the trailerhouse.*

SON: You didn't answer my question, Dad.

> PISANGER *playfully cuffs his son, rubs* SON's *head. A patch of the boy's hair lifts in a powdery gust.* SON *goes inside.* PISANGER, *shaken, holds hair in his hand and drops to his knees.*

PISANGER: Jesus, his hair, Jesus.

> PISANGER *pulls out a handkerchief with his free hand, spreads it out and delicately transfers each and every hair from his palm into the handkerchief in front of him. Upstage, at* THE TANKS, *headlights blink on, off.* PISANGER *folds the handkerchief, puts it in his back pocket, exits.*

Scene 2

> THE TANKS. RUNNING JOKE *drinks from a 12-inch sewer pipe with a ladle. Ears prick. Someone coming.* HE *moves to an iron skillet which sits on the open end of a five-inch pipe coming out of the ground.* PISANGER *enters.*

RUNNING JOKE: Sudden.
PISANGER (*Eyeing skillet*): What's that?
RUNNING JOKE: Dinner. You hungry?
PISANGER: That rabbit's got two heads.
RUNNING JOKE: Lot of them hopping around like that.
PISANGER: Where at?
RUNNING JOKE: Some have three ears.

PISANGER: Down at the dump?

RUNNING JOKE (*Nods*): By the pond.

PISANGER: You call that a pond?

RUNNING JOKE: Swamp.

PISANGER: Toilet. The catfish are blind. Albino frogs.

RUNNING JOKE: The frogs won't fry. They're full of thirty-weight oil. They just lay there and bubble. The rabbits are better.

PISANGER: Two-headed rabbits.

RUNNING JOKE: I don't eat the heads. Do you?

PISANGER: Where's Lomar?

RUNNING JOKE: I haven't seen her.

PISANGER: This place stinks.

RUNNING JOKE: Like knowledge.

PISANGER: Like the dump.

RUNNING JOKE (*Pointing to separated piles*): Copper, aluminum, brass, lead, plastic, cardboard, kitchen slop and manure—dog, cat, chicken, cow—

PISANGER: You *are* a running joke.

RUNNING JOKE *smiles, shrugs.*

PISANGER (*Continued*): What kind of name is that?

RUNNING JOKE: Not mine. My name is Alex Slicing Lightning.

PISANGER: Who give you Running Joke?

RUNNING JOKE: The railroad. White culture. Actually, Butch Cobb gave it to me. But I aim to give it back.

PISANGER: You Indians really hang from your tits up there?

RUNNING JOKE: In the Sundance.

PISANGER: What is that?

RUNNING JOKE: It's a sacred ceremony of my people, the one Leonard holds.

PISANGER: Leonard Nimoy?

RUNNING JOKE: No. Your CIA taught SAVAK and the Shah of Iran how to piss into the mouths of their holy men over there. They tried that with us, too. One night on Rosebud they came down in helicopters, they broke up our meeting, scattered our fire, arrested the Roadman and Leonard and Grandmother. They didn't catch me. They won't. They paid. The wind swallowed up one copter and spit it out on the courthouse lawn in Valentine. Roadman and Grandmother were let go finally. Leonard's out now, too. Three years in the pen. They couldn't break him. The ones who did that, who still live, never stop hearing our drums. They turn on their CBs, breaker broke for a short stroke: all they get is drums. They turn on their radios for hog futures and the swapshop: drums. Five-point-eight to sixteen hundred, AM, FM. There is a power that you could not make no law for the power.

PISANGER: What they want you for?

RUNNING JOKE: Sentencing. Two hundred and eighty-five years. To life. (*Laughs*)

PISANGER: You are a crazy motherfucker.

RUNNING JOKE: I'm a running joke. But this here is the punch line. (HE *throws back a tarp to reveal* PHIL COBB's *car*)

PISANGER: You got even.

RUNNING JOKE: With who?

PISANGER: Phil.

RUNNING JOKE: I got nothing against Phil.

PISANGER: You stole his car.

RUNNING JOKE: From you. Not him.

PISANGER: What you got against me?

RUNNING JOKE: What were you going to do with this car? Drive Lomar over the state line? Sudden, I saved your ass.

PISANGER: Yeh? Who's gonna save yours when you try it? Lomar! (HE *opens car door, leans in*)

RUNNING JOKE: She's not here.

PISANGER: You told me. LOMAR!

RUNNING JOKE: I'm not taking Lomar anywhere.

PISANGER: Why'd you steal the car?

RUNNING JOKE: I'm going to clean the machine, get it running right.

PISANGER: Then where you going?

RUNNING JOKE: No place to go.

PISANGER: You stole Phil's car to give him a tune-up?

RUNNING JOKE: Something like that. You want to help?

PISANGER: I'm through helping Phil.

RUNNING JOKE: Why?

PISANGER: Phil killed Sarge.

RUNNING JOKE: Sarge never blamed Phil. Why should you?

PISANGER: 'Cause Phil's a greedy sonofabitch getting rich off me.

RUNNING JOKE: You agree to it.

PISANGER: I developed the habit of eating. So's my wife.

RUNNING JOKE: So you work for Phil. You make him your boss. He takes your time, he takes your money, you feel cheated so you hate him.

PISANGER: I don't exactly hate him.

RUNNING JOKE: No. Part of you loves him like a father. But he's not your father. You're not his son. And he's only your boss because you won't be your own boss.

PISANGER: I don't wanna be my own boss.

RUNNING JOKE: I know.

PISANGER: I wanna be *his* boss—

RUNNING JOKE: Sure. Boss him.

PISANGER: —boss him for a change. Make him work for me.

RUNNING JOKE: But you have to be your own boss first.

PISANGER: Why?

RUNNING JOKE: Because you have to know what you want. Do you know what you want?

PISANGER: Yeh.

RUNNING JOKE: What?

PISANGER: I used to want to just get out, quit, ditch Leatha, take off, steal a car—

RUNNING JOKE: Drive out West O at a hundred miles an hour and go sailing offa bridge?

PISANGER: Only I wouldn't get caught.

RUNNING JOKE: Or killed?

PISANGER: Hell what's the difference? I'm half dead now. I can't breathe, my joints swell up, get stiff, my whole left side is numb now. I can't think straight. I get headaches. Sometimes I have to just stop work and sit down I get so dizzy. The body don't last. I give mine to Phil. Just like Sarge did.

RUNNING JOKE: You used to want to take off.

PISANGER: Not so much since my boy was born I don't know.

RUNNING JOKE: What do you want now?

PISANGER *shakes his head.*

RUNNING JOKE (*Continued*): Phil knows exactly what he wants from you. And he knows how to get it. Did you bring your toolbox?

PISANGER: I'm not helping you.

RUNNING JOKE: Why not?

PISANGER: You can lose your job. You got no wife, no kids, no home. You got no responsibilities.

RUNNING JOKE: I have responsibilities. But not to Phil.

PISANGER: Not now.

RUNNING JOKE: Not even when I hauled for him. I like being my own boss.

PISANGER: You got the choice.

RUNNING JOKE: You choose not to choose, that's your choice.

PISANGER: You're not tied down.

RUNNING JOKE: I'm not locked up. I know what I want.

PISANGER: What do you want?

RUNNING JOKE: I want to modify Phil Cobb's car.

PISANGER: You know how?

RUNNING JOKE (*Eating from skillet*): No. That's why I need you.

PISANGER: How can you eat that shit?

RUNNING JOKE: I'm immune. I'm dead to damn near everything you give your life to, Sudden.

PISANGER: Fuck you.

RUNNING JOKE: Keep using your thumb as a hook. Keep hiding your tools.

PISANGER: They're mine!

RUNNING JOKE: So use them!

PISANGER: Look, Cochise, I gotta right to—

RUNNING JOKE: Die stupid?

PISANGER: I'm stupid!?

RUNNING JOKE: Do you know what you want?

PISANGER: And you're the smart one? You're the ancient idol? You're God's Head? Mr. Wisdom? Perfect jewels rush out your face? I usta drink with Indians couldn't stand up after a six-pack. We usta fuck a squaw named Pearl—three beers, she's flat on her back. You think you're something? You're nothing.

RUNNING JOKE: You think you're nothing? You're something.

PISANGER: What?

RUNNING JOKE: You think you're nothing, a machine. You think you deserve what you get, that you're no better than you are. You're more than that.

PISANGER: What am I?

RUNNING JOKE: You're a natural-born mechanic. And this is a mechanical problem.

Scene 3

INDUSTRIAL REFUGE, INC. *Outside* PHIL COBB's *office. Night.* LOMAR, *apparently alone, tosses pills into the air and catches them in her mouth like popcorn. Upstage, drunken* BOB *slowly struggles to his feet, ass first. Once up,* HE *finds balance on wide-spread legs and turns to see* LOMAR *Downstage—foggy, eyes cross to focus.* LOMAR *is startled and then accommodates* BOB *graciously with a perfectly executed curtsy fit for an Elizabethan court.* BOB *produces a mason jar half-filled with red fluid from behind his back and grins broadly.* LOMAR *whinnies, delighted.* THEY *drink. First* LOMAR, *then* BOB. LOMAR's *lip curls,* SHE *growls playfully.* BOB *growls back.* LOMAR *growls again and backs away, shifting weight from one foot to the other like an animal.*

BOB: Com'ere. I'll hit you with a stick.

LOMAR (*Straightening up*): That's ugly.

BOB: Oh, come on. I'll beat you with my hose, my rubber hose!

LOMAR (*Retracted*): Don't talk like that!

Dead to her feelings, BOB *grabs at* LOMAR.

LOMAR (*Continued*): Don't just grab at me.

BOB *reaches for her breast, pinches her nipple.*

BOB (*Pinching*): Honk honk.

Livid, LOMAR *shrieks and pulls away from him.*

LOMAR: Don't you *do* that! I am not your rubber ducky! (SHE *knocks* BOB *down*) I am not some pot to piss in! (SHE *kicks his groin*) Some public toilet you—!

BUTCH *is heard approaching.*

BUTCH (*Yelling*): I'll get it! I'll get it! Hang on!

Split wide at this point, BOB *put off and* LOMAR *fuming,* THEY BOTH *freeze as* BUTCH *answers an unringing phone in the office.* BOB *and* LOMAR *move up to eavesdrop.*

BUTCH (*Continued; into phone, drunk*): Industrial Refuge Incorporated. No. (*Second thought,* HE *replaces receiver*) R-r-r-i-i-n-n-g! R-r-r-i-i-n-n-g! (HE *answers*) Butch Cobb Unlimited. It's forty bucks a month twice a week on Tuesdays and Fridays and I want my money in advance! Where do you work? How much money you got? Hahahahahaha! (*Hangs up*) R-r-r-i-i-n-n-g! R-r-r-i-i-n-n-g! (HE *answers*) Butch Cobb Unlimited. Yes it is. Running who? No he doesn't. Not anymore he don't. No kikes, nips, niggers, dagos, spicks, slopes, slants, geeks, gooks, micks, mau maus, frogs, faggots, little girls or Indians. No. In fact, I tell you what we had to do with Running Joke. We had to shoot his balls off. Hahahahaha!

BOB *and* LOMAR *can't believe what* THEY*'re hearing.* THEY*'re cheek to cheek at a chink in the wall, listening to* BUTCH *rant.*

BUTCH (*Continued*): Yeh. It *was* a difficult shot. Little shriveled BBs—shriveled little shrunken blue peas, yeh.

Outside the office, BOB *and* LOMAR *are rolling in each other's arms, laughing and laughing. Inside,* BUTCH *is practicing a fast draw with the phone receiver, fanning it, fanning it. Finally,* HE *hangs up. Instantly, the phone rings.* BUTCH *nearly falls over.* HE *answers.*

BUTCH (*Continued; into phone*): Butch Cobb Unlimited—er—Industrial Refuge. Freddy? Yeh. Yeh, it's me. What about Running Joke? FBIA? Open season? Ten o'clock. Yeh. Yeh. I'm ready. I'm ready. (HE *hangs up. Sits, shotgun across lap*)

Scene 4

TRAILERHOUSE *bedroom. Before dawn. Slow motion,* LEATHA *pounds* PISANGER's *chest. His ribcage moans a slow percussion.* PISANGER *is beyond emotion.* LEATHA *pounds on him like a drum. Stops, rolls back onto the bed.* PISANGER *stands, starts to dress.*

PISANGER: Was that good for you?

LEATHA: Oh yeh. How 'bout you?

PISANGER: Yeh, great. What are you going to do today?

LEATHA: I got Weightwatchers at three.

PISANGER: You went yesterday.

LEATHA: He changed it.

PISANGER: I thought it was all women over there.

LEATHA: Yeh.

PISANGER: They still meet at the mall?

LEATHA (*Begins to cry*): Will you please hold me? Just hold me?

PISANGER: Why should I?

LEATHA: I need you to.

PISANGER: What about what I need?

LEATHA: You have to tell me what you need.

PISANGER *stands silent.*

LEATHA (*Continued*): What do you need?

PISANGER: Will you work on my back? (*Sits on bed*)

LEATHA (*Starting in on his back*): Where at?

PISANGER: Yeh.

LEATHA: Does that feel good.

PISANGER: Yeh.

LEATHA: This rash is getting worse.

PISANGER: Sarge is dead.

LEATHA: It's too bad.

PISANGER: Lomar's gone.

LEATHA: Again.

PISANGER: I'm forty years old, body falling apart, shit jobs all my life, nine dollars in the bank—

LEATHA: We got five dollars in the bank. King Dollar wouldn't take food stamps for the bottled water.

PISANGER: Great.

LEATHA (*Embracing his rigid body*): I love you, Sudden.

PISANGER: Bullshit. (*Stands*)

LEATHA: It's not bullshit. I love you.

PISANGER: You say that.

LEATHA: You want me to dance it? I will.

PISANGER: Leatha, you say you love me, you cry, you get mad, you show your emotions. I'm numb. You're there crying and I'm way over here. Behind glass. I don't feel a thing.

LEATHA: You don't love me?

PISANGER: I don't believe you.

LEATHA: You don't believe I love you?

PISANGER: Not like I love our son. I never loved anything like I love him. When he popped out I knew what love is. It's blood.

LEATHA: I love you like you love our son.

PISANGER: Is that why you go to the Terminal Hotel?!

Headlights sweep the trailerhouse. Honk-honk. PISANGER *leaves for work.*

LEATHA: Yes. (SHE *rises out of bed, dresses quickly, follows* PISANGER *out trailerhouse door*)

LOMAR *and* BOB *enter through back yard.* LOMAR *moves toward trailerhouse, swatting at* BOB *who moves backwards, blocking her path, talking nonstop.*

BOB: Motors! Lasers! Computers! Radar! Microwave! Macrowave—

LOMAR: Get away from me! Get offa me!

BOB: Missile-tracking video games. Traffic signals. Pacemakers. Price scanners in supermarkets. Seeing-eye doors. Hearing aids. Look around—headlights. . . . Anything with a plug hanging out of it I'll know how to fix!

LOMAR: When you grow up?

BOB: I'll take the static out of your CB.

LOMAR: When Francine lets you.

BOB: Francine's got nothing to do with it.

LOMAR: Bob, you're pussy-whipped.

BOB: How many strands in a standard-stranded cable?

LOMAR: She's had her foot on your throat since before I came.

BOB: Nineteen.

LOMAR: Always probably.

BOB: What's the resistance of a three-six–kilowatt heater wired one-twenty? Do you know? Do you know what a rheostat is?

LOMAR *breaks away, dashing into the trailerhouse through the back door.*

BOB (*Continued; chasing after* LOMAR): Or a polyphase-induction squirrel cage?

LOMAR *dives into the armchair in the living room.* BOB *corners her.*

BOB (Continued): If a four-pole two-twenty–volt sixty-cycle induction motor has a slip of five percent, what's the speed of the shaft? Do you know?

LOMAR: Who gives a shit!

BOB: Do you think Sudden could even say it? Let alone know what it means? Or Butch? Or Running Joke? Running Joke, hell, I'll blow his goddam doors off. Even Phil'd get lost in this. But not me, see. I don't breathe this air. I think my thoughts. I got a plan. I got a future. And the long-range picture is good for me, too, see, 'cause war goes on and the military'll always need electrical engineers—

LOMAR (Pulling out from under BOB): Cow blood my ass!

BOB: I didn't say it was cow blood. I never said what it was.

PISANGER storms across stage from one garbage can to the next, emptying them into his barrel, banging cans, slamming lids.

LOMAR (Swinging at BOB): Goddam tomato juice!

BOB: Lomar I didn't mean anything!

LOMAR: Goddam V-8! Shit fulla celery! Git away from me! Git away from me! Git! Git!

Hearing the commotion, PISANGER rages into the trailerhouse.

PISANGER: Leatha! Leatha!

LOMAR: Sudden!

PISANGER: Where you been?

LOMAR: Looking everywhere for you.

PISANGER: Last night where were you?

LOMAR: Out to the garage. Don't look at Bob like that. Nothing happened.

BOB: They want Running Joke, Sudden. Not her. We told them where to find him.

PISANGER: Told who?

LOMAR: We seen them on the road.

PISANGER: Who?

BOB: Freddy the Cop, Butch, and some Indian from the Bureau of Indian Affairs.

LOMAR: Wearing a suit.

BOB: Yeh, a three-piece suit.

LOMAR: And a flat-top.

BOB: Yeh, but he showed me his badge.

PISANGER: Where's Leatha?

LOMAR: I don't know.

PISANGER storms out the front door, lifts loaded carrying barrel to his shoulder.

LOMAR (*Continued; at trailerhouse door*): Sudden! Where are you going? Where are you going?! What'll I tell Leatha? What'll I tell Leatha?!

PISANGER: Tell her the truth.

LOMAR: I'll tell her everything!

PISANGER: You don't know everything.

LOMAR (*Blocking* PISANGER's *path*): I'll tell the cops! I'll tell the County!

PISANGER (*Knocks* LOMAR *down*): Bitch.

LOMAR: I'll spill my guts.

PISANGER *stomps Off.*

LOMAR (*Continued; yelling out after* PISANGER): What you promised me you wouldn't do and you said was okay and I knew better but was too weak to stop you out behind the Washout that one time or Robber's Cave or Trax Gas or the Cornhusker Hotel!

LOMAR, *livid, chugs back into the trailerhouse living room and throws herself onto* BOB, *kissing and hugging.*

CB (*Voice of* BOB's *wife Francine*): Breaker one nine, breaker one nine. Queen Bee, you copy?

LOMAR *pulls her shirt open and struggles with* BOB's *belt.*

CB (*Continued*): Breaker one nine, this is Cotton Candy looking for the Queen Bee, come on.

LEATHA *enters, sees* LOMAR *and* BOB *on the couch.*

LEATHA: Go 'head, Cotton Candy. Queen Bee here.

CB: Leatha, you feel awful? You must. Lomar still gone? Any sign of her? Over.

LEATHA: No, Francine. I don't know where she is. Over.

CB: I hate to trouble you, Leatha, but Bob's gone off. You see him? Come on.

LEATHA: Negatory. You call the garage?

CB: I couldn't get a straight answer. Everybody's on the warpath after Running Joke out there.

LEATHA: Ten four.

CB: You see my Bob or hear anything, you give me a buzz, ten four? Threes to you.

LEATHA *cradles the receiver.*

LEATHA: Bob.

BOB *extracts himself from* LOMAR's *grip and stumbles out the door, hitching up his pants.*

BOB: Thanks, Leatha.
LEATHA: You shit.

BOB *exits.*

Upstage, at THE TANKS, RUNNING JOKE *and* SON *are sorting garbage.*

RUNNING JOKE (*To* SON): What you got there?
SON (*Handing it to* RUNNING JOKE): Doorknob.
RUNNING JOKE (*Pointing to swim-flipper on* SON's *belt*): Big frog.
SON: This is my holster.
RUNNING JOKE: Where's your gun?
SON: It broke. Couldn't fix it. It was a piece of shit.

Dialogue at THE TANKS *continues as* LOMAR *sits up in* TRAILERHOUSE *living room, flushed, eyes flaming, limbs pounding.* SHE *races out the back door, Offstage.* LEATHA *heaves a rattling sigh which brings phlegm up.* SHE *clears her throat, coughs into a kleenex and moves out the front door.* SHE *sits down on an overturned garbage can.*

SON (*Continued; to* RUNNING JOKE): This is not strictly a holster.
RUNNING JOKE (*Fiddling with the doorknob and a caster*): No.
SON: I carry all kinds of stuff.
RUNNING JOKE (*Holding up the reconstructed doorknob*): Do you have room for this?
SON (*Accepting it*): What is it?
RUNNING JOKE: I don't know what you'd call it, but it looks like it might last.

SON *draws bone flute from swim-flipper. Holds it a moment.* RUNNING JOKE *starts to move away.*

SON: Hey.

SON *hands flute to* RUNNING JOKE. RUNNING JOKE *accepts it.* SON *moves Downstage into the* TRAILERHOUSE *back yard, throwing clods.* RUNNING JOKE *moves into the front yard where* HE *hunkers down 12 feet from* LEATHA.

LEATHA: Running Joke.
RUNNING JOKE: How are you, Leatha?
LEATHA: Sick to death of that goddam dump.

RUNNING JOKE: Hard living downwind. Maybe you should move.

LEATHA: Where? Up on the hill?

RUNNING JOKE: Better view.

LEATHA: Same dump.

RUNNING JOKE: I have something for you.

LEATHA: We ain't got the money to live here. Let alone leave.

RUNNING JOKE: Something I found.

LEATHA: I don't need more garbage.

> RUNNING JOKE *hands* LEATHA *three balls of twisted paper.* SHE *unfolds them.* RUNNING JOKE *turns from her, starts picking up toys scattered in the front yard.*

RUNNING JOKE: They're poems Lomar wrote and threw away.

> LEATHA *reads one, then the next. Finished,* SHE *looks up at* RUNNING JOKE, *who has piled most of the scattered toys into a wagon. A rubber doll* HE *cradles in his arms and, as* LEATHA *looks into his face for help,* RUNNING JOKE *slowly rocks the baby.*

LEATHA: You better get out of here. Everybody's looking for you.

> RUNNING JOKE *places the rubber doll in the wagon.* LEATHA *looks away.* RUNNING JOKE *exits.* LEATHA *puts the poems in her housecoat pocket and turns to go back inside.* PISANGER *enters, fuming, grabs* LEATHA *before* SHE *hits the door.*

PISANGER: Leatha!

LEATHA: I gotta go in.

PISANGER: Wait a minute, wait. I want to talk to you. I just come back from the Terminal Hotel. Room 309. I kicked the goddam door in.

LEATHA: Congratulations.

PISANGER: And there he was. Sitting with his legs crossed, smoking a woman's cigarette. What's his name?

LEATHA: Herman Splat.

PISANGER: Splat, yeh. You should have seen the look on his face when his door caved in.

LEATHA: Why didn't you just turn the knob?

PISANGER: Why didn't you tell me you were seeing a shrink?

LEATHA: I was afraid of what you'd do.

PISANGER: What would I do?

LEATHA: What you just did, I guess. Maybe to me.

PISANGER: I haven't hit you since I quit drinking.

LEATHA: I know.

PISANGER: And I been going to work every day.

LEATHA: I need to talk to somebody, Sudden.

PISANGER: Well, I give him something to talk about.

LEATHA: You are not the center of the universe.

PISANGER: What do you talk about—sex?

LEATHA: Yeh.

PISANGER: About how you hate sex?

LEATHA: I don't hate it. I just can't make it work.

PISANGER: It ain't work. It's fun.

LEATHA: For you it's fun. For me it's never been.

PISANGER (*Turning from* LEATHA): Oh shit, not this again!

LEATHA *hurries into the trailerhouse.*

PISANGER (*Continued; wheeling around*): You tell him that! You tell him I can't satisfy you! You pay him my money to agree with you that I'm no good, that it's my fucking fault!? What's this costing me! (HE *stomps off towards* GARBAGE TRUCK, *raging*) What's this costing me! What's this costing me!

At GARBAGE TRUCK, PISANGER *flips the switch in back. The blade lurches, gears grind.* RUNNING JOKE *approaches unseen from behind, grabs* PISANGER *and throws him into the hopper. The blade comes down, engages.* PISANGER *is pushed up into the compacted garbage. Blade stops at the top of the hopper. Power take-off shuts off. Truck idles. Dogs bark. Unseen cats screw. Expanding metal ticks. The truck groans.*

PISANGER *pulls himself up over the top of the blade and squeezes through, drops into the hopper, shaken, bleeding, smoke rising from his battered limbs, shirt shredded, hanging in ribbons.* HE *drops out of the truck onto the pavement, down on one knee, up again,* HE *stumbles. Weaving like a drunkard,* HE *drifts Offstage.*

At TRAILERHOUSE, BUTCH *enters through back door, places shotgun on table, mumbles to* SON, *who is in living room setting up a chessboard on the coffee table, and opens the refrigerator.* LEATHA *enters from bedroom.*

BUTCH: Got any beer, Leatha?

LEATHA: We don't drink in this house.

BUTCH: Lomar does.

LEATHA: Not in this house she doesn't.

BUTCH: It don't matter. (HE *crosses to the living-room couch, sits, heaves his foot-cast up on the coffee table and pulls on his pocket flask*) Ahhh . . . I'm gonna find that sonofabitch, Leatha.

LEATHA (*Picking up in the kitchen*): Running Joke?

BUTCH: You're goddam right. And when I do, I'm gonna take him down and shove gravel up his nose. Then I'm gonna shove a road flare in his ear. Then I'm gonna shove another road flare up his ass! (*Laughing*)

LEATHA: Don't you talk like that in my house.

BUTCH: I'll dry him out like a buffalo skin. You watch.

LEATHA: You hate him that much?

BUTCH: He's a lazy poaching sonofabitch never did a day's work in his life living off the sweat and toil of other people, Leatha.

LEATHA: Sounds like what they say about you, Butch.

BUTCH: If he wants to dress up in torn flags and sit in the garbage ripping open bags looking for whatever Indian arty-facts he thinks he's lost, he can do that till shit turns to gold as far as I'm concerned. And if it don't bother you what he's doing with Lomar, she ain't my concern. But that truck cost thirty-seven hundred dollars to fix, Leatha. That's three months of a man's wages lost and it ain't easy living off half what you're used to—

LEATHA: Phil's taking that out of your pay?

BUTCH: Who said that?

LEATHA: Well thirty-seven hundred's a lot more than three months of what Sudden makes.

BUTCH: Doesn't matter whose it is. It's hard enough in any business. Man like Dad demands you do good. Man that great makes you *want* to do good even if you can't, you love him so much.

LEATHA: Butch, you hate your father.

BUTCH: Dad's right. Make profit, not mistakes. Running Joke is a dog-eating cannibal's asshole but he is a human being and I knew he'd finally fuck up. He stole Dad's car. He's no damn good now, Leatha, and he's met his match. I'll chase him down whatever stinking hellhole he's hiding in and rip out his tongue and eat it.

LEATHA: You hate him so much you want his tongue in your mouth.

SON: You should have looked out front two minutes ago, Butch. He was standing in the front yard. Yeh. Talking to Mom.

BUTCH: Oh no. He's gotta be smarter than that.

SON: Depends on who's chasing him. You ready, Mom?

LEATHA: Not now, son.

SON: You promised.

BUTCH: I'll play you, son. I'm good at checkers.

SON: Chess.

BUTCH: You can't be that good.

SON: Mom!

BUTCH: You got anything to eat, Leatha?

LEATHA: Feed me, flatter me, fuck me, put up with me, clean up after me! God, I'm sick of men. You're all such babies.

BUTCH: Babies?

LEATHA: Yeh, babies.

BUTCH: Too bad about us, Leatha.

LEATHA: Yeh, it ever happened.

BUTCH: Too bad it had to end.

SON: Check.

BUTCH: Why don't you feed me, flatter me or fuck me?

LEATHA (*Pulling away*): Leave, Butch.

BUTCH (*Looking around*): You ever notice a garbage odor down here, Leatha?

LEATHA: Only when I breathe.

BUTCH: Hah hah hah! Only when I breathe! That's good.

SON: Butch—last week Buddy came home covered with black stuff from swimming in your pond. He couldn't pee. He just walked around with his leg up and nothing. Next day his fur fell off. Day after that his teeth fell out. Two days later his lungs blew up.

LEATHA: Yeh, Butch. Something stinks.

BUTCH (*Pulls out an aerosol can*): This here will take care of that. (HE *sprays*)

LEATHA: You selling Airwick?

BUTCH: I brought this back from the convention in Louisville. Not only does it cover up the odor. It's got something extra in there that disintensifies your nose. What's the word? Desensifies? It'll put your nose to sleep so you won't be bothered by the smell.

LEATHA: I don't want to be put to sleep, Butch. I want your ass out of my house. And take your plastered foot with you!

BUTCH: That's the thanks I get for taking a shot in the foot that coulda hit Lomar.

LEATHA: You shooting, it coulda hit anybody.

LOMAR *appears in the doorway, eyes red.* LEATHA *sees her.* BUTCH *doesn't.*

BUTCH: You don't know what happened.

LEATHA: I got a pretty good idea. Get out.

SON: Checkmate.

BUTCH: All right. I ain't stupid. I don't need a road map. You draw the line. I see it. You're all on that side. I'm over here. (*Collects shotgun*) But I got some irons in the fire nobody knows about that when I pull 'em out you'll see how bright I shine. (HE *exits*)

LOMAR: Leatha, I gotta talk to you.

SON: Mom! You promised you'd play me.

LEATHA: I will, sweetheart. Later.

SON: SHIT! (HE *upends the chessboard, sending pieces flying, stomps out front and scatters wagonload of toys* RUNNING JOKE *put in order, charges Offstage*)

LEATHA: I'm listening, Lomar.

LOMAR: It's about Sudden. It's about Running Joke. I love them both and they love me.

LEATHA: Of course you do. Well, maybe not Running Joke.

LOMAR: Yes, Running Joke. *And* Sudden. They love me. They both want me. Not like a father wants you either. They want to fuck me. They want to marry me. They want to run off with me, take me anywhere I want to go—

Cuba, Ceylon, Zaire, Kansas. It don't matter to them, it's whatever I want. That's why they stole Phil's car.

LEATHA: Who stole Phil's car?

LOMAR: Sudden stole it first I made him. Then Running Joke stole it from Sudden. They're both crazy about me. And super-jealous. They both want me so bad I'm afraid what they might do. I'm scared they'll kill each other maybe over me. You gotta do somethng!

LOMAR *charges* LEATHA, *buries her head in* LEATHA's *lap.* LEATHA *withdraws, arms in the air, can't give* LOMAR *what* SHE *needs.* LOMAR *bolts. Grabbing* LEATHA's *bottle of pills from the CB on the counter,* SHE *shoots out the trailerhouse door, runs Offstage.*

Scene 5

THE TANKS. RUNNING JOKE *uses ladle to drink from sewer pipe draining ochre sludge.* HE *hangs up the ladle and turns back to work on* PHIL COBB's *car, hood up, worklight hung under hood.* PISANGER *approaches. Chatter of geiger counter.* RUNNING JOKE *fiddles. Chatter grows louder.* PISANGER *jumps* RUNNING JOKE. THEY *fight—like animals of the strongest kind, splattering junk, kicking and punching, scattering ordered piles of garbage, rolling like logs until* THEY BOTH *nearly drop dead from exhaustion.*

PISANGER *gets to his feet.* RUNNING JOKE *rolls over.* PISANGER *turns to sewer pipe, takes ladle.*

RUNNING JOKE: Don't drink that. It'll kill you.

PISANGER *palms a bottle, sitting on an oil drum.*

PISANGER: What's this? (HE *catches a whiff of the brew, recoils, throws the bottle Offstage. It explodes. Silent thud in a ripple of soundwaves*)

RUNNING JOKE: Oxygen will blow it up.

PISANGER: What kind of shit is this!

RUNNING JOKE: That was chicken shit. Burns good, but it's dirty. Here, look at this.

RUNNING JOKE *stumbles up and slides in behind the wheel of* PHIL COBB's *car, turns the key, revs it, gets out. The car idles.*

RUNNING JOKE (*Continued*): There's no gasoline in that car.

PISANGER: There was when I stole it.

RUNNING JOKE: I drained the tank. It's empty.

PISANGER: And it runs.

RUNNING JOKE: It runs.

PISANGER: Witchcraft.

RUNNING JOKE: Methane. Comes out of that pipe in the ground. Or I got it down now I can brew it in this barrel. Three buckets of shit. Airtight. Keep it at eighty degrees with this heater under here and two microbes inside'll eat each other. That makes gas. You put the gas in the bottle, feed it into the carburetor through this adapter and—

The car farts out, stops running.

RUNNING JOKE (*Continued*): I'm having trouble with the adapter.

PISANGER: Why'd you throw me in the garbage truck?

RUNNING JOKE: Somebody did it for me. Shook me up. It's faster than peyote.

PISANGER: I don't understand that.

RUNNING JOKE: You eat peyote, you eat earth. You're never the same, that inside you. But that takes time, work. This way, throwing you into the hopper is a shortcut.

PISANGER: A shortcut to where?

RUNNING JOKE: To wherever you can get from the shock of seeing yourself once, straight, from the outside. And this way there's no drums full of water, no morning meal, no sweat lodge, no little wind, no crosses, no messiah talk, no white-man paranoia. Just real fear and the face of your own death.

PISANGER: What gives you the right to mess with me?

RUNNING JOKE: It's more my job.

PISANGER: Throwing me in the hopper?

RUNNING JOKE: My aim.

PISANGER: Goddam killing me is your job?

RUNNING JOKE: If you don't get smarter, I can't get smarter. It's taken awhile, you gotta admit, you and me, working on this car finally.

PISANGER (*Sits down on his red toolbox*): It hasn't happened yet.

RUNNING JOKE: Sarge didn't convince you?

PISANGER: Sarge is dead.

RUNNING JOKE: What he tell you before he died?

PISANGER: That my kid was good and I should protect him.

RUNNING JOKE: Yeh.

PISANGER: You heard him.

RUNNING JOKE: He told you to get out of jail.

PISANGER: He told me not to die in jail.

RUNNING JOKE: Sarge's dying words. You going to piss on his grave?

PISANGER: Yeh. While you light a fart in his memory!

RUNNING JOKE *laughs.* PISANGER *tries not to laugh.*

PISANGER (*Continued*): That's all you're doing, making methane—

RUNNING JOKE: Right. And when you and I are finished here, Phil's car will run on his own shit. Not yours, not mine, not Sarge's, not Bob's—and no exhaust. It's good work, Sudden. You've had some bad jobs.

PISANGER: I've had nothing but bad jobs.

RUNNING JOKE: Slaughterhouse, garbage. You ever jump?

PISANGER: Off what?

RUNNING JOKE: Into a nuclear power generator. People who go down into that slop to clean that out they call jumpers. We called ourselves sponges, 'cause that's what you do, you soak up radiation. Waste agency hires people with no money or nothing to lose but their lives to jump down and clean them out. You get a badge to wear that tells you how much you've taken in. If you go the whole hog, they give you two hundred dollars extra. Yeh. I went in three times, took the bonus three times. I needed money. So I did it. My father died digging uranium and I did it anyway. Took in three times what the government says is okay. My toenails fell off. I broke out, couldn't breathe, shit blood. My hair fell out. I threw up for weeks.

PISANGER: Why'd you do it?

RUNNING JOKE: Mimimum wage. I bought a car I blew up ten days later. I paid for an abortion.

PISANGER: Now you glow in the dark.

RUNNING JOKE: I glow in the light. I can drink that water. I eat six-legged snakes. I should be dead. I don't know why I'm not. It'll come.

RUNNING JOKE *helps* PISANGER *to his feet.* THEY *stand shoulder to shoulder.*

PISANGER: What is a car-sin-no-gin?

RUNNING JOKE: Something that causes cancer.

PISANGER: Am I saying that right?

RUNNING JOKE: Yeh, carcinogen.

PISANGER: What's . . . (*Pulls out computer read-out from back pocket, reads*) what is ah . . . dimenthyl sulfoxide?

RUNNING JOKE: A carcinogen.

PISANGER: What is dibromochloropropane?

RUNNING JOKE: A carcinogen.

PISANGER: What is dioxin?

RUNNING JOKE: Agent orange. What have you got there?

PISANGER *hands read-out to* RUNNING JOKE *and carries his red toolbox across stage to* PHIL COBB's *car. As* RUNNING JOKE *reads,* PISANGER *leans in under the car hood to start work on the engine.*

Downstage in TRAILERHOUSE *front yard, fading light.* LOMAR *stumbles in, half dancing, eating pills like candy. Ground fog pours in.*

LOMAR (*Singing*):
> HOW HIGH'S THE WATER, MAMA?
> THREE FEET HIGH AND RISING.
> HOW HIGH'S THE WATER—
> PAPA! YOU HAD ME!
> BUT I NEVER HAD YOUUUUUU! I-I-I-I!
> (*Drops to her knees. Spits poem*)
> Clean up my bleeding streets!
> Make a park of night sweats!
> Some cure for continents of flesh!
> (SHE *falls sideways, rolls left, rolls right, rolls left—frantic—picks herself up and swirls like a dervish, around and around, freezes, arms up.* SHE *collapses*)

Up at THE TANKS, PISANGER *slams the hood of* PHIL COBB's *car.* PISANGER *and* RUNNING JOKE *get into car, start it up, drive Off. Slow fade to black.*

Scene 6

ALMA's BAR & GRILL. *Following morning.* ALMA, *in black, polishes a glass at the bar.* BOB *sits board-straight in a borrowed suit, black eye, bandaged forehead.* RUNNING JOKE *enters.*

ALMA: Alex.

RUNNING JOKE: Alma.

ALMA: Can I get you something?

RUNNING JOKE: An applejack, Alma.

BOB: Don't sit next to me.

RUNNING JOKE: You still mad at me, Bob?

BOB: Why'd you come here?

RUNNING JOKE: To pay my respects.

BOB: You showed your respects when you knocked Sarge off number twelve that time and crippled him for life.

RUNNING JOKE: Butch put me on that truck had no brakes, Bob. My first week working. Butch set me up. Ask Phil.

BOB: I was always going to kill you for that.

ALMA: Unbutton your jacket, Bob, relax.

RUNNING JOKE: I felt like killing Butch for a while. Let me buy you a drink.

BOB: I stopped.

RUNNING JOKE: Drinking?

BOB: After what it did to Sarge?

ALMA: After what Francine did to you last night.

RUNNING JOKE: Sarge worked too hard. You're in no kind of danger there.

BOB *stands, ready to fight.*

ALMA (*Laying change on the counter*): Oh play something, Bob.

BOB *crosses to the Wurlitzer jukebox.*

ALMA (*Continued; to* RUNNING JOKE): I usta sit on his lap and tell him Dugan, work together. Don't let Phil split you up like he does to exploit you. Bob wants to kill you. You want to kill Butch. Divide. Conquer. Phil gets rich and you get old.

BOB: Damn right.

ALMA: But what makes you so weak, Bob? Sarge was tired, he got old. But he wasn't weak. I never did see him back down into the crick like you do. And Sudden's no better.

BOB: Hell, he's worse.

ALMA: You boys been eating garbage so long you think you got it coming. You think you can't live without it. In this goddam town, on those goddam trucks, you need a union.

BOB (*At Wurlitzer, dropping a coin in slot, punching a button*): Here's to Sarge.

Wurlitzer plays Hank Williams' "May You Never Be Alone like Me."

VOICE OF HANK WILLIAMS (*On jukebox*):
LIKE A BIRD THAT'S LOST HIS MATE IN FLIGHT
I'M ALONE AND OH SO BLUE TONIGHT
LIKE A PIECE OF DRIFTWOOD ON THE SEA
MAY YOU NEVER BE ALONE LIKE ME—

ALMA: Bob—

BOB *kicks the Wurlitzer. Song cuts out.* RUNNING JOKE *produces bone flute from inside pocket.*

RUNNING JOKE (*To* ALMA): Remember this?

ALMA: A flute carved from the thigh bone of a human being. The sons do it— hollow out the leg bones of their fathers to make flutes.

RUNNING JOKE: It's so old. It's still here.

ALMA: He gave it to you.

BOB *drops another coin, punches another button. Wurlitzer doesn't play.* HE *kicks it. Wurlitzer plays Merle Haggard's "Everybody's Had the Blues."*

VOICE OF MERLE HAGGARD (*On jukebox*):
LOVE, HATE, A WANT, A WAIT
TILL MISERY FILLS YOUR MIND.
EVERYBODY KNOWS THE WAY I'M FEELING
'CAUSE EVERYBODY'S HAD THE BLUES—

ALMA *shakes her head at* BOB's *selection.* RUNNING JOKE *hands* ALMA *the flute, squeezes her arm with affection and crosses to the Wurlitzer.* HE *kicks it hard. The song cuts out and* BOB *jumps up ready to fight.* RUNNING JOKE *kicks the Wurlitzer a second time. Wurlitzer plays Aaron Neville's "Tell It Like It Is."*

VOICE OF AARON NEVILLE (*On jukebox*):
TELL IT LIKE IT IS!
DON'T BE ASHAMED!
LET YOUR CONSCIENCE BE YOUR GUIDE!

ALMA *puts the flute in its box and returns it to the shelf.*

Stage Right, at TRAILERHOUSE, LEATHA *discovers* LOMAR *collapsed in front yard.*

LEATHA: Lomar! Lomar! Lomar! (*Kneeling, trying to lift* LOMAR) Oh my God! Wake up! Wake up!

PISANGER, *in suit and tie, comes through trailerhouse into front yard.*

LEATHA (*Continued; slapping* LOMAR): How many did you take? (*Sees* PISANGER) Help me!
PISANGER: What happened? What happened!

PISANGER *lifts* LOMAR *in his arms and carries her into the trailerhouse bedroom, placing her on the bed.* LEATHA *follows, grabs the wastebasket.*

PISANGER (*Continued*): Talk to me, talk to me!

LEATHA *gently triggers the gag reflex by tickling* LOMAR's *tongue.* LOMAR, *on knees, vomits into wastebasket.*

LEATHA: Cough 'em up, Lomar. Cough 'em all up. Spit out the ugly ones. Get rid of the monsters, baby.

At ALMA's BAR & GRILL, PHIL *enters, in suit and tie, back from* SARGE's *funeral.*

PHIL: It was a beautiful funeral, wasn't it? Was I all right? What I said, my little statement? Was it—
LEATHA (*To* PISANGER): She's all right. She's all right. It's all right.

PISANGER, *nervous, jumpy, steps out onto the trailerhouse front stoop.*

ALMA (*To* PHIL): Except for that part about the Soviet threat. You lost me there.
BOB: You calling Sarge a Communist?

PHIL: No no no. Sarge was the kind of man that makes this system work, this nation great.

ALMA: What kinda man is that exactly?

PHIL: One hard worker. No complaints.

ALMA: What if he had complained?

PHIL: We'd have settled it.

ALMA: Out of court.

BOB: In a game of cards.

At TRAILERHOUSE, PISANGER *is pacing on the front stoop.* SON, *far Stage Left, throws football to* PISANGER. *It is a bullet pass, straight and hard. It nails* PISANGER.

PISANGER: Right between the eyes!

In the TRAILERHOUSE *bedroom, blue-green luminescence, yellow smoke.* LEATHA *cradles* LOMAR *in her arms on the bed.* LEATHA *gently rocking.*

PHIL (*To* BOB *and* ALMA): It's been awhile since I spoke in public. Public speaking is a difficult thing.

ALMA: It's hard to speak out both sides of your mouth at once.

PHIL: But I loved the man.

BOB: You showed it.

PHIL: Did I?

BOB: Yeh. When you picked up his tab at the hospital that time he broke his leg falling off your truck.

PHIL: Bob, how many bosses do you know of that pick up their workers and take them to work every morning? I never ask for gas money or anything else.

BOB: That's true.

PISANGER *and* SON *enter* ALMA'S BAR & GRILL.

PHIL: Sarge died singing my praises as far as I know. God, he was so happy to get work right out of jail this time. Lots of employers won't hire a convict.

PISANGER: What was he convicted of?

PHIL: It's the same for alcoholics. A lot of them cannot get hired.

ALMA: That's right, Phil. You even bought him drinks.

PHIL: True. See?

ALMA: And you bought him gloves and cigarettes and breakfast and gave him spending money.

PHIL: I'd forgotten all that. Yes. You're right.

ALMA: How much does Sarge still owe you, Phil?

PHIL: Five hundred and eleven dollars.

ALMA: You're sure?

PHIL (*Catching himself*): Roughly.

ALMA: Then that's what I owe you.

PHIL: No, Alma.

ALMA (*Opens register*): Sarge would have paid you back. He'd want me to.

PHIL: Call me sentimental, Alma. I feel like I owe Sarge that much.

ALMA: Phil.

PHIL: That's how I feel.

ALMA: You put five hundred dollars on the counter and I'll put five hundred next to it. That's a thousand dollars in Sarge's name for an insurance fund that'll cover your workers.

PHIL: Alma—

ALMA: How 'bout it, Phil?

PHIL: It's the end of the month.

ALMA: And a full moon.

PHIL: I'm not made of money.

ALMA: We know what you're made out of, Phil. We want to see what you're going to do with it.

PHIL: It can wait until after you've run the route. We'll talk about it then. I promise. If you get started now you can be done before dark.

NO ONE *moves*.

PHIL (*Continued*): Men, I gave you time off for the funeral. I didn't complain. But Sarge is planted now and this is a work day. There's no days off when it comes to trash on this planet, heh heh—

PISANGER: When it comes to trashing the planet?

PHIL: Only Christmas.

PISANGER: Trashing people on this planet?

BOB: You wasted Sarge sure as if you shot him down in the jungle, Phil.

PHIL: Let me buy you all drinks.

BOB: I stopped drinking.

PISANGER: I'm not starting.

PHIL: Look, men, this ain't Christmas.

PISANGER: We know. It's Easter.

PHIL: We *work* Easter!

PISANGER: I don't.

BOB: Me either. And I'm late for church.

PHIL: Wait. Think about your families. You've got to work.

PISANGER: Why?

PHIL: Because I don't know the route. Sarge is dead, Butch is out looking everywhere for Running Joke and—Running Joke. What are you doing here?

RUNNING JOKE: Paying attention.

PHIL: Where's my car?

RUNNING JOKE: Parked out back. (*Tosses* PHIL *the keys*) Start it up. See what you think.

PHIL *goes out.* EVERYBODY *stands at the window to watch* PHIL *start his car up, rev it.*

RUNNING JOKE (*Continued*): There you go, Bob, living proof. If you pack garbage tight enough for long enough and apply enough pressure you get power, heat, gold, light—
PISANGER: Phil's driving a shit-eating car!

THEY *laugh.* FREDDY THE COP *slams in from the back room, revolver drawn.*

FREDDY THE COP: FREEZE!

BOB, ALMA, PISANGER, SON *all dive for cover.* RUNNING JOKE *alone stands tall,* FREDDY THE COP's *target, moves to the Wurlitzer.* BUTCH *enters from the back room, shotgun pointed.* HE *moves past* FREDDY THE COP.

BUTCH: Party's over.

BLAM! The shotgun fires.

PISANGER: Jesus Christ!

RUNNING JOKE *sprawls half-standing against the Wurlitzer. Its neon facade blinks through a hole in his chest.* PHIL's *car horn blares.* PHIL *enters.*

PHIL: Butch!
BUTCH: He stole your car.
PHIL: He gave it back.
BUTCH: I'm pressing charges.
PHIL: It's not your car.
BUTCH: It will be.
PHIL: When I die, Butch. When I die you get the car and you take charge of the business. But that is when I die and I will not die until I know you *can* take charge of the business, that what I spent my life building up won't fall apart when you slam my lid!
RUNNING JOKE: How's the car, Phil?
PHIL: Not a scratch on it. Starts up real good. Idles kinda high, but—Butch, you dumb fuck. Look what you did!
BUTCH: I ain't sorry.
RUNNING JOKE: I forgive you, Butch.
FREDDY THE COP (*Transfixed*): Lookit that hole.
BUTCH: What are we going to do with the body? Throw it in the pond.
RUNNING JOKE: It won't sink. Not in that stool. But you got more problems there than disposing of my dead body.

PHIL *tilts an ear.*

RUNNING JOKE (*Continued*): What are you going to do about the EPA?

PHIL: What do you know about that?

RUNNING JOKE: Your dump is a municipal landfill. You got a permit to bury household garbage and that's it. You been running tanker trucks in and out of there dumping toxic chemicals and industrial waste for how many years? Dead Man's Run is tarred shut. Ted Kooser's trailerhouse exploded.

BOB: Ethel Benzene's got a brain tumor.

ALMA: Ethel's husband had his spleen removed.

RUNNING JOKE: Kids up and down that street are deaf and lame, Phil. Their dogs die.

SON: My dog died!

BUTCH: You got your facts wrong, Running Joke.

RUNNING JOKE: Alex Slicing Lightning.

BUTCH: We got some methane moving. That's natural. You said so yourself. But it's under legal limits. We ran tests.

BOB: Who ran tests?

BUTCH: Uncle Al. Didn't he, Dad?

RUNNING JOKE: Ask your Uncle Al what are the legal limits for benzene and chlorobenzene and dichlorobenzene and toluene and trichlorobenzene and chlordane and hexachlorobenzene. Asbestos. Vinyl chloride. Hexachlorocyclohexane. Kepone. Mirex. Cyanide. Carbon tetrachloride. Toxaphen. Strontium. Dieldrin. Diethyl ether. Heptachlor epoxide. Chromium. Nitroglycerin. Orthobenzyl parachlorophenol. Orthonitroaniline. Dimenthyl sulfoxide. Dibromochloropropane. Ethanol. Ethyl acetate. Sulphur dioxide. Hydrogen sulfide. Nitric acid. Nickel. Naphthalene. Lithium. Tritium. Xylene. Zirconium. Tetrachloroethylene. Trichlorophenol. Trichloroethane. Hexachlorocyclopentadiene.

SON: Tetrachlorodibenzoparadioxin.

RUNNING JOKE: That's in your land, Phil. In our water. In our air.

BUTCH: Says who?

PISANGER: In this here. (HE *holds up a twisted mass of paper, the computer read-out* HE's *pulled from an inside pocket*)

BUTCH (*Grabs read-out, throws a look at* PHIL): Give me that!

PHIL (*Grabs read-out from* BUTCH, *rips it*): Dammit, Butch!

BUTCH: I threw it out.

RUNNING JOKE: There's a copy in the bank. It's been recycled.

BOB: Freddy, you gonna arrest Butch?

FREDDY THE COP: What for?

BOB: For making that hole in Running Joke!

RUNNING JOKE: Freddy wants more evidence. (*Arms, wide, coughing*)

FREDDY THE COP *approaches* RUNNING JOKE *cautiously, revolver drawn. His hand disappears in* RUNNING JOKE's *chest.* HE *pulls out a blood-smeared letter which* HE *reads aloud, half dazed.*

FREDDY THE COP: ". . . a letter of confirmation in lieu of a contract regarding the agreement made between the Broken Bone Nuclear Power Plant and one Philip Cobb Junior. . . ." Butch!

BUTCH *smiles.*

FREDDY THE COP (*Continued*): "Regarding the proposed dumping of three-point-seven million cubic tons of nuclear waste in trenches four inches deep in the Cobb family landfill dump."

PHIL (*Broken*): Butch.

BUTCH: Hey, Dad—Initiative in the fifth. My own route. Something I did on my own. Something I finally did right all by myself. Dad, it'll mean a lot of money.

ALMA: It'll mean evacuating the town. Unless you weren't going to tell anybody. Which case it's more nausea, nosebleeds, lesions, stillbirths, paralysis, sterility and death.

PISANGER: Or we cap it.

RUNNING JOKE: We do what?

PISANGER: We cap the landfill. We spread broken brick and a layer of sand. Then clay mixed with—

RUNNING JOKE: Fly ash.

PISANGER: —and lime'll set like cement and stop the runoff into Dead Man's Run. We close the well—

RUNNING JOKE: We dredge the pond.

PISANGER: We can lower the water table ten feet with two pumps upslope. Change its direction out around the toxic shit and use the water up here to flush lechate into treatment beds. Eight-inch perforated clay-fired pipe in trenches eighteen feet deep backfilled with gravel the perimeter of the landfill. Then we build a slurry wall.

RUNNING JOKE: No.

PISANGER: A grout curtain! Above the dump. Below the pumps. Drill staggered double row of holes to bedrock. In. Ject. Four to seven percent by weight suspension Wyoming Bentonite—

RUNNING JOKE: In water.

PISANGER: —in water. Forms a gel, hardens, makes a wall. Then. We mine methane. Drop six-inch PVC to the bottom of the landfill every fifty feet. Each pipe vents into an exhaust header hooked to a manifold connected to a fan. Each branch take-off's got a butterfly valve and a flow-rate meter so we can check for head loss and vapor flux. May have to come down to four-inch PVC or put in a larger fan. Fewer elbows maybe. Molecular sieves'll separate out the methane. It'll upgrade. We can sweeten it to eight or nine hundred BTU through dehydration and nitrogen removal. Sell it like that or mix it with natural gas. It'll run a car. It'll heat your home. Lift a Lear jet right off the ground. . . . And then . . . what's left . . . we excavate! Incinerate! We wet-air oxidate, macrowave-plasma detoxify, solidify! I can turn that landfill into glass! Plastic! Asphalt! Concrete! I can change it into cinderblocks and build a hundred houses with it! Banks! Jails! Lawyers! Doctors! Presidents! Landlords! Kindergartens! Flying buses! Space shuttles! Bombs! Dogs! I can inject it fulla vinyl ester styrene and put it on a railgun and shoot it to the sun! (HE *pulls white handkerchief from back pocket and carefully unfolds it, holds patch of* SON's *hair in fingers*) I cannot put one hair back . . . in.

Lights pop out on Wurlitzer. RUNNING JOKE *collapses, dead, at* PISANGER's *feet. Blackout.*

END OF PLAY

Mensch Meier
A Play of Everyday Life

Franz Xaver Kroetz

translated by
Roger Downey

About Franz Xaver Kroetz

Playwright Franz Xaver Kroetz was born in Munich, West Germany, in 1946. He attended acting school and, between 1967 and 1970, worked in various alternative theatres there (including the late Rainer Werner Fassbinder's *antiteater*). During this period Kroetz made his first experiments in playwriting, influenced by the realistic, socially critical plays of ordinary life written in the 1920s and '30s by Ödön von Horvath (*Faith Hope Charity, Tales from the Vienna Woods, Kasimir and Caroline*) and Marieluise Fliesser (the *Ingolstadt* plays). In 1970 Kroetz received a stipend from the Suhrkamp publishing house and began writing plays full time.

Since then he has written more than 30 plays, radio scripts and television plays. His early play *Game Crossing* was filmed by Fassbinder (U.S. release title: *Jail Bait*). By 1974 he was Germany's most produced living playwright, but his first widespread popular and financial success was the family drama *Mensch Meier*, which had its world premiere in four simultaneous German productions in 1978. The television production of *Mensch Meier* in 1981, directed by and starring Kroetz himself, earned one of the highest audience shares for a dramatic broadcast ever recorded on German television. Kroetz's first novel *The Slave of Moonshine* was published by Suhrkamp in 1982 and was followed by a sequel in the fall of 1983.

About Roger Downey

Translator Roger Downey was born in 1937 in a small mining town in British Columbia, Canada. After neglecting his studies at the University of Chicago in favor of involvement in Chicago-style improvisatory theatre and street theatre, he entered the United States Army, spending two-and-a-half years in Frankfurt, Germany. After returning to civilian life in 1964, he studied political science and theatre at the University of Washington, where he was deeply influenced by the ideas of Duncan Ross and Arne Zaslove, founders of the Professional Actor Training Program there. Supporting himself as a journalist since 1968, Downey has also worked at The Empty Space theatre (founded in 1970 by UW classmate M. Burke Walker) as an actor, director, publicist, business manager, translator and dramaturg. His translations of Kroetz's *Through the Leaves* and Horvath's *Oktoberfest* received their premieres at the Space in 1983. *Through the Leaves* has also been produced by L.A. Theatre Works, and both it and *Mensch Meier* are scheduled for New York productions in 1984.

Production History

Mensch Meier was nominated for TCG's *Plays in Process* script circulation series by M. Burke Walker, artistic director of The Empty Space in Seattle. The American premiere production was presented there from March 10 through April 25, 1982. The production was assisted by a generous grant from Goethe House, New York.

M. Burke Walker directed. The set was designed by Scott Weldin, costumes by Michael Murphy, lighting by Michael Davidson and sound by Dennis Kambury. The cast was as follows:

Otto . . . . .John Aylward
Martha . . . . .Jean Marie Kinney
Ludwig . . . . .James Etue

The official world premiere of *Mensch Meier* took place at the Schauspielhaus, Düsseldorf, West Germany, on September 23, 1978, in a production by Rolf Stahl, with Hans Brenner as Otto, Ruth Drexel as Martha and Markus Völlenklee as Ludwig. An earlier English-language version, adapted to a contemporary British setting, was performed in 1980 at the Half Moon Theatre, London, under the title *Tom Fool*. Manhattan Theatre Club staged the New York premiere of the Downey translation in 1984.

Translator's Note

This translation was made from the 1979 Suhrkamp edition of *Mensch Meier*. None of the original text is cut. A few lines, set off by square brackets, have been added where, in my opinion, cultural or political matters require clarification for an American audience.

On the Title: In colloquial German, "Mensch Meier" is an ejaculation of surprise, not necessarily pleasant. The exact (but out-of-date) English equivalent would be "Great Scott!" Since the German word "Mensch" means "human being," there's a flavor of universality about the title as well: "Meier-kind," on analogy with "mankind."

On Dialect: On this subject Kroetz says: "The characters speak Bavarian dialect. It would be better that they speak High German, though, than a dopey imitation 'dialect' that only makes them seem absurd." For an American production, any urban white working-class accent would be suitable, but the author's stricture applies: Unless the accents are effortless, genuine and consistent, it would be better to do entirely without. Particularly to be avoided is the notion that Germans speak stiffly, formally, without emotive intonation. For what it's worth, I "hear" Kroetz's characters speaking the unhasty, lilting, faintly querulous American of South Philadelphia. In the places where he is "role-playing," Otto speaks with a much more cultivated, i.e., TV-announcer, accent.

On the Setting: American producers may be tempted to adapt the piece to an American setting. In my opinion, this temptation is to be avoided. The basic action of the play revolves around Ludwig's unemployed status and his relationship with his father. To make the former correspond to North American mores and legalities regarding child labor, school-leaving age, etc., Ludwig would have to be 18 years old at the very least, which in turn would make his dependent relationship with his parents highly implausible. If, on the other hand, Ludwig's age is maintained at 15 or 16, the character becomes a "dropout," rather than the well-behaved, obedient son Kroetz has in mind. Either way, the principal motivating situation in the play is seriously compromised.

Characters

MARTHA, the wife, average, about 40 years old, a little hefty but not unattractive; very honest and practical.

OTTO, the husband, also average and around 40, fairly big, lean, likes to smoke and drink, rather nervous, fidgety; in his best moments he comes across as almost elegant.

LUDWIG [Ludi], the son, a nice kid of about 15; looks more like his father than his mother, growing up fast, but shy and sparing with his words; listening a lot, talking little.

[CASHIER]

Time

The spring and summer of 1976.

Place

Munich or nearby, perhaps in one of the high-rise housing projects built at Neuhausen around 1950.

The Play

Mensch Meier

A Play of Everyday Life

ACT ONE

Scene 1
Lazybones

The living room. The sofa bed is open. LUDWIG *is in it, but invisible;* HE *has the covers pulled over his head. A faint sound of gentle, yearning English pop music comes from the bed. Around the bed, about three feet from it, is a little protective wall of personal treasures: a few cassettes, wallet, sunglasses, comb, a nice lighter, cigarettes, fairly fancy rocker-boots, jeans, short leather jacket, wristwatch, etc. Two or three posters on the walls.*

MARTHA (*Calling from kitchen*): Time to get up!

LUDWIG *doesn't respond.*

MARTHA (*Continued*): Early bird gets the worm! (*Pause.* SHE *comes into the living room*) It's nearly eight and you're still lying in bed. Good grief, how many times do I have to call you? Get up now and don't waste the day God gave you.
LUDWIG (*Under the covers*): Ten more minutes.
MARTHA: Not one minute more. Out I said, and straighten up. It's like a rat's nest in here. I want to clean.

LUDWIG (*Emerging*): Why do I have to get up?

MARTHA: Because I say so. Imagine, [nearly sixteen and] still lying in bed when his poppa's been on the job an hour already. Look at you! Now get a move on before I lose my temper. (SHE *goes out again*) Nothing but trouble from morning till night.

Pause. LUDWIG *listens to the music a little longer, then switches it off.* HE *puts the cassette recorder carefully aside, gets up and slowly gets dressed. Then* HE *begins tidying the room. Since* HE *does it daily,* HE *has a routine: first* HE *collects all his possessions in one place, then takes them to "his" drawer and stows everything in its place. Then* HE *tidies further, takes the posters down from the wall (making sure no dirt comes with them), rolls them carefully together, and puts them behind the dresser. Everything is clinically clean, only the bed remains. Then* HE *leaves the room, we hear him enter the bathroom, turn on the water, etc.*
   Pause.
   MARTHA *comes busily in, goes to the sofa bed, shakes out the comforter and pillows, folds them and makes them into a bundle, opens the bed's storage space and puts them in it, folds the bed up into a proper living-room couch again.* SHE *straightens a few more things, puts a spread and a few cushions on the couch, tidies up and is satisfied that all traces of the night have vanished, that everything's tidy.* SHE *returns to the kitchen.*

MARTHA (*Continued; calling out*): Hurry up, the coffee won't stay warm forever!

LUDWIG (*From the bathroom*): Coming!

Scene 2
Company

Saturday, mid-day; EVERYBODY *is watching television in the living room.*

LUDWIG: I saw somewhere [he's so dumb] he can't even write his own name. (HE *laughs*)

MARTHA (*Angry*): What kind of paper would say a thing like that? That man is a king!

OTTO: [They don't care what they say just so long as they're talking about "The Royal Wedding." That's all we had in the papers for a solid month.]

LUDWIG: [Or on TV.]

Pause.

OTTO: Just give me a tenth of the money he's got, I could get along just fine without writing my name.

MARTHA (*Nods*): It's only people who are jealous say things like that anyway.

Pause.

OTTO: You think she's still a virgin? [Your magazines say anything about that?] I mean, a girl who's going to be a queen ought to be . . .

MARTHA (*Definitely*): Of course not, at her age. Imagine, just an ordinary middle-class girl doing so well for herself.

LUDWIG: Who cares?

MARTHA: And a German girl at that! (*Nods*) "Germany's Golden Girl," even the King of Sweden couldn't resist her! (*Nods. Pause*) Our wedding was nice, too. (*Pause*) There, he said it: (*With pleasure*) Sylvia Renate Sommerlatt—imagine how she feels when she hears her name like that? (*Pause*) Now they've said "I do." (*Smiles and nods*) Now they exchange the rings.

OTTO: What do you think all this stuff cost, the whole circus?

MARTHA: Listen, she's whispering, so nobody else can hear her. (*Short pause. Firmly*) Very beautiful.

OTTO: She's got fat hands on her.

MARTHA: Don't be so silly. Oh, now they're going to sing. Men's voices are beautiful.

OTTO: Not these, they're not.

MARTHA: Well, they're only like cardinals, not real singers. We had a harmonium play at our wedding, remember?

OTTO *looks;* HE *doesn't remember.*

MARTHA (*Continued*): What was it he played? "The Lovely Galatea" by Von Suppe! (*Nods*) You see, I remember and you don't.

OTTO: Sure.

Pause.

MARTHA: All the royalty and famous people in the world are there.

LUDWIG: Who *cares?*

MARTHA: Because you have no notion what's beautiful. . . . How many kings are there left in the world? You can count them on the fingers of one hand. A person ought to be thankful just to see it, an event like this.

OTTO (*Orotund*): *Ep*-och-making. (*In his normal tone*) Course, they don't amount to anything anymore, your "crowned heads."

MARTHA: She's supposed to be very intelligent, Sylvia is.

OTTO: Not him, though. This one's got that right, anyway. (*Referring to* LUDWIG) Just the same, you get to where he is and his money, then you can talk, not before.

MARTHA: Be quiet, this is where they become man and wife. (*Laughs*) She keeps peeking up at him, see?

OTTO (*Laughing*): Poor SOB! She's got him now. "No, no, you're not going nowhere, little fella," that's what she's thinking.

MARTHA (*Has to laugh*): Oh, you men!

OTTO: Wham, the trap closes! (*Laughs, nods*)

Pause.

MARTHA: You hear that? "What is happiness? To forget yourself, and live for others."

OTTO: Easy for them to say.

MARTHA: What's beautiful about it and what I like, it's a real love-match. He saw her at the Olympics and said, "She's the one I want, whoever she is." That's the way a king ought to be!

OTTO *laughs.*

LUDWIG: 'M hungry!

MARTHA: Wait till they're finished, can't you?

OTTO (*Looking at* LUDWIG, *unemotional*): I wouldn't mind having your life!

LUDWIG *just looks at him.*

MARTHA: Everybody takes it easy on Saturday. Nearly everybody.

OTTO: Yeah? So what'd he do yesterday?

LUDWIG (*Looks at him, nervous*): Nothing.

OTTO: Exactly. You could learn something from them there. (*Points at TV*) Te-le-vision!

MARTHA: So. That was nice. (*Emphatically*) Very, very nice. (*Nods. Pause*) Recognize them?

OTTO: Who?

MARTHA: The man doesn't see a thing! Queen Fabiola and King Bauduin! There's [our] President Scheel too and his wife.

OTTO: She looks like a hippo.

MARTHA (*Extenuatingly*): Well, she's five-foot-eleven. . . . (*Pause*) Did you hear, she can speak six languages, Sylvia. Respect! That's worth more than all the gold in China. . . . And the King has four sisters! Busy, busy!

OTTO (*Gives* LUDWIG *a friendly punch*): Get yourself one of them and you won't have nothing to worry about!

LUDWIG *shows his gratitude by laughing too hard.*

MARTHA: Man proposes, God disposes. (*Means the wedding*) Now it's really over and they're going out of the church. Look at how they strut along. Imagine if you tripped, you'd wish you were dead! (*Laughs. Pause*) He's really nice, though, the King, look how he's always smiling! That's not easy.

OTTO: Sst! (*Points at screen. Pause*) The Reds don't like it. (*Nods*)

MARTHA: That's no way to act at a wedding, what's it got to do with politics, what it stands for.

OTTO: Sweden.

MARTHA: That's right.

LUDWIG: 'M hungry.

MARTHA: Listen to him talk, like he's the one who brings the money home to feed us. I want to watch the rest!

OTTO: Earn something, then you can give the orders. Right?

LUDWIG: OK.

Pause.

MARTHA: The nicest thing about it, she's German.

OTTO: Suppose he married a black girl, what then?

MARTHA (*Fast, dismissive*): Kings don't do things like that.

OTTO: Sure.

Pause.

MARTHA: Everybody's standing up and cheering them! (*Short pause*) A real fairy-tale wedding. (*Nods and smiles*)

LUDWIG (*Provoking her*): Aren't we gonna eat at *all* today?

MARTHA (*Snapping back at him*): Lazy loafers don't need to eat.

OTTO: I'm getting hungry too.

MARTHA (*Irritably*): Ten more minutes! Men, they can't leave you in peace for a minute!

LUDWIG: Big deal.

OTTO (*Weakly complaining*): Never going to amount to anything, always got to be out of step.

MARTHA: He's still young.

OTTO: Not much longer.

MARTHA: Young and silly.

THEY *go back to watching. After a little* LUDWIG *gets up, takes something out of "his" drawer and leaves. We hear a doorlatch snap shut.* OTTO *and* MARTHA *don't notice.*

MARTHA (*Continued*): Look at [the banner on] that housefront: "Juan Carlos, Murderer, Franco the Second."

OTTO: They shouldn't ought to allow that.

MARTHA: I hope *he* didn't notice. He's a king too, [just like Juan Carlos,] it could spoil the happiest day of his life.

OTTO: They didn't read it.

MARTHA: Well, I hope not, because it'd be a shame when they're so happy.

OTTO: You got to let people have their happiness.

MARTHA: Sylvia Sommerlatt, Queen of Sweden, from now on.

OTTO: 'M *hungry.*

MARTHA: Earn some money, you can go stuff yourself at Humpelmeyer's for all I care!

OTTO (*Thinks* SHE's *talking to him*): What the hell way to talk is that?

MARTHA: What?

OTTO: That's what I ought to be asking!

MARTHA: Where did he go?

OTTO: Out somewhere.

MARTHA: Well, I'm going to watch it to the end and that's that! (*Pause*) White orchids for a bouquet! Look at how she keeps waving it around all the time, that's not right, somebody ought to tell her, people are sure to talk.

OTTO: They'll never know in Sweden.

MARTHA: Think so?

Scene 3
Coitus Interruptus

In the bedroom: furniture from Neckermann's, nice. OTTO *and* MARTHA *are going at it.*

MARTHA: What are you thinking about?

OTTO: Nothing.

Pause. THEY *do it.*

MARTHA: You got something else on your mind.

OTTO: Hmmmh—!

MARTHA: No.

Pause. THEY *keep at it.*

MARTHA (*Continued*): I want to know what you're thinking about!

OTTO: What'd I say?

MARTHA: When you're in bed with me and thinking about something else, a woman's got a right to put a stop to it. (SHE *does*) Completely inconsiderate!

OTTO: No, really, it's OK. No, hey . . .

MARTHA: What is it then? (SHE *has pulled free of him*)

OTTO: I didn't say anything . . .

MARTHA: Exactly.

OTTO: No, but. . . . It's embarrassing.

MARTHA: Well, thank you very much! The kind of things a woman has to put up with!

OTTO: No, you got the wrong idea. What it is, [this supervisor,] he borrowed my ballpoint, it must have been two weeks ago, it cost me twenty-eight seventy. (*Short pause*) And forgot to give it back. (HE *turns over abruptly in bed. Pause*) I been thinking about it for a long time already, how I could lead up to asking for it back without getting him angry. Whether I should just go in and say "Excuse me, Chief, but you borrowed a ballpoint off me, please could I have it back?" Or maybe not "please," just "You think I could get it back?" Then he might just smile and say, "Sure, sorry about that." (*Laughs*) Then just reach in his pocket. . . . (*Short pause. Meaningfully*) If he still *got* it!

Pause. MARTHA *hasn't really been listening, but since* HE's *talking to her like a wife now* SHE *gradually manages to listen to him, but doesn't really understand the point yet since* SHE *was expecting something different.*

OTTO (*Continued*): What if he doesn't have it anymore? So he goes, "What did it look like?," and then I have to describe it, right? And then he looks around on his desk, and if he doesn't find it, then it could get embarrassing. "Are you sure it was me that borrowed it?" "Yes." "When was that?" "Oh, two weeks ago." "So why didn't you mention it before now?" (*Short pause*) What do I say then? (*Pause*) What I'm afraid of. . . . (*Short pause*) What I think is, he didn't even hold onto it.

Nods, looks at MARTHA, *who doesn't understand any of this.*

OTTO (*Continued*): He probably left it laying around the top floor somewhere that same day.

Long pause. MARTHA *nods sympathetically.*

OTTO (*Continued*): It's hopeless. (*Pause.* HE *smiles and nods*)
MARTHA (*Looking at him*): Well, it's easy to do, I mean, a ballpoint, you just stick it in your pocket and don't think what you're doing.
OTTO (*Fast*): Even if you see it cost something, it's worth something?

MARTHA *looks at him.*

OTTO (*Continued*): Does the boss see things like that, that's the question, he probably takes expensive stuff for granted. You know? I even thought, what about I put a notice up on the bulletin board? "Lost ballpoint"—you know, diplomatic—"gunmetal gray, retractable point, red enamel cap, clearly marked, no Jap imitation: Pelikan Mercator Super model. Reward for return." (*Looks at his wife*) Five marks maybe. Since it cost twenty-eight. (*Looks at her*)

MARTHA: That won't help if the boss's got it.

OTTO: That's exactly my point, 'cause the boss don't have any reason to look at the bulletin board. And anybody else isn't going to give it back, not when they see what a nice piece of goods it is. He's going to stick it away and keep it for himself. (*Nods*) That's only human, it feels great in your hand and writes beautiful.

Long pause.

MARTHA (*Thinking about it*): You should have gone right in and asked before he forgot about it.

OTTO (*Looks at her irritably*): Listen to her! (*Pause*) He come in with a delegation, maybe twenty men, every one a section chief at least, most of them supervisors, brings them in personally, that was a special situation right there we thought, and he wanted to explain something and needed a ballpoint! (HE *nods. Pause: a serious problem*) He asked me personally for it, which was kind of special too, explained the problem and then went on with the tour, (*Formally*) forgetting that he happens to have my pen. You think I'm going to stop them, the whole delegation, practically grab the boss by the elbow and make him give my pen back? (*Pause*) Impossible. (*Looks at his wife*)

MARTHA: Then you should have gone over to the office as soon as they were finished.

OTTO: As soon as they were finished they all went over to the Casino for a banquet to celebrate getting a thirty-million–mark contract. (*Emphatically*) Impossible.

MARTHA: What about the next day?

OTTO: He was in Brussels.

MARTHA: How do you know?

OTTO (*Quietly*): Because I am not stupid and was planning to go over and checked beforehand to find out if he was there. Negative.

Pause.

MARTHA: So why didn't you do it the day after?

Pause.

OTTO: I didn't have the nerve.

MARTHA (*Sniffs*): Well, for pity's sake, if at first you don't succeed, you know what they say.

OTTO: Well, it was too late then.

Pause.

MARTHA: Then there's nothing to do, it's just bad luck.

OTTO: Yep. I'll just have to forget my Mercator. (*Pause*) But catch me buying another one that expensive. The cheap ones write good enough and you don't have to worry about them.

MARTHA (*Laughs*): You go ahead and buy another good one!

OTTO *laughs, pleasantly surprised.*

MARTHA (*Continued*): But if the boss or someone comes around again, you just put it away quick, or always have a cheap one in your pocket you can give him if you have to.

OTTO: If I got another Mercator I wouldn't even take it to work, I'd keep it at home where nothing can happen to it.

MARTHA (*Nodding*): Let things out of your sight and they're gone. . . .

OTTO: But you got to admit I take care of my stuff, don't I? It's been a long time since I've lost anything. I've had that gold cigarette lighter six years.

MARTHA: Well, but what about that silver money clip I gave you, I haven't seen it for a long time?

OTTO: 'Cause I don't carry it, 'cause it's broken, and anyway it's not my style. But I got it right in the night table, I could reach it from here.

MARTHA: That's all right, then.

OTTO: I still got everything I ever had that's worth something.

Pause.

MARTHA (*Nods*): And there's no way you could know the boss was going to walk up and borrow your ballpoint.

OTTO: I had a funny feeling as soon as he said, "Do you happen to have something to write with?," and boom, it's gone.

Pause.

MARTHA (*With a sidelong look at him*): Go to sleep now and forget about it. (*Pause*) Sleep tight.

OTTO: Thanks, you too. And I'll forget about the ballpoint.

MARTHA: That's right.

Scene 4
World Champion

OTTO *sits in a very, very small room. No window. It seems to be a closet of sorts which* OTTO *has turned into a hobby room.* HE's *working on a model plane, which is complicated by the fact that the plane's wingspan (between two and four meters, after all!) makes it hard to deal with. After working for a long time,* HE *suddenly begins to speak [with a TV-announcer accent].*

OTTO: "I know it's not customary to disturb a contestant just before a race, (*Artificial laugh*) but Otto, if you could just take time to answer a few questions for our viewers."

Sure, go ahead!

"Your career in sports could be called nothing short of meteoric. You began participating actively in model airplane competition just two years ago, and in that time astonishing as it seems you've taken the national championships for both short- and middle-distances. And now you're on the trail of the European Title as a steppingstone, so to speak, to the Championship of the World. Will you win today? (HE *gives the fake laugh again*) When you think of all the titles you've pulled down in just the last few months already, it wouldn't surprise our audience too much if you did it again today. How does a man learn to fly like that?"

Well, I think you've got to have an understanding of how the atmosphere works to start with, and a real love of flying, and of course a lot of luck.

"How long have you been flying model planes?"

I started fifteen years ago, if you go back all the way to the beginning. But of course the techniques were completely different back then.

"Let me break in here for just one question: you fly only models you've built with your own hands?"

Yes.

"The experts tell me that's another big reason for your success. One writer for a model magazine called it, and I quote, 'a kind of genius for aero-engineering.' Do you agree?"

Well, you shouldn't blow your own horn, but of course you got to have some natural ability, because models you see are all pretty much state-of-the-art already. And the big manufacturers have a lot of advantages. Like I don't have my own wind tunnel, for example.

"And you used to be, you don't mind my asking this I'm sure, a worker on a assembly line?"

Yes, I was.

"But today the hobby has grown into a full-time occupation, what with your model airplane factory and all."

You could put it that way.

"Mr. Meier, all of us and I'm sure all our viewers at home wish you the very best of luck in the European Title trials here in Rome, and hope that the name of the next holder of the European Long-Distance Model Airplane Championship will be Otto Meier of Germany."

Thank you!

"And now ladies and gentlemen we return you to ZDF Sports Central."

OTTO *sniffs.* HE *looks up a little and almost looks around to see if* HE'*s been overheard. Then, still "in character,"* HE *labors grimly away at the greatest model airplane in the world.*

Scene 5
Next Stop: Freedom

In a department store. OTTO *is trying on a "leisure suit."* MARTHA *is considering the result.*

MARTHA: I don't know. (*Shakes her head;* SHE *doesn't like it*)
OTTO: Me neither.
MARTHA (*Nodding*): It looks kind of cheap.
OTTO: Well, it *is* cheap.
MARTHA: Exactly. The other one is better.
OTTO: It ought to, it costs enough.
MARTHA: But this one really does look cheap.
OTTO: You shouldn't be able to tell just by looking that I'm some guy off the line with a couple weeks' vacation coming.
MARTHA: That's just what this looks like! The other one's more (*Smiling*) I don't know . . . international.
OTTO: Man of leisure. (*Laughs*)
MARTHA: Because it really is a leisure suit. In this one anybody can see you don't get much time off. Not so much with the other one; it's more . . . casual.
OTTO: Because it costs almost twice as much.
MARTHA: Quality has its price. (*Short pause*) Get the other one. (*Nods*)

Scene 6
Happiness

OTTO *and* MARTHA *at home in the little kitchen eating dinner.* OTTO *laughs; eats; looks to see if* MARTHA *has reacted to his laugh.* SHE *hasn't. Pause.* OTTO *takes something out of his pocket.*

OTTO: Know what that is?

MARTHA (*Looks*): It's a ballpoint, what about it?

OTTO (*Shaking his head*): Some memory you got! It's my Pelikan Mercator Super; the same one! (*Laughs*)

MARTHA: The one you lost?

OTTO: What else? There she is. Ta-dah!

MARTHA (*Looking*): There, and you were so sure it was gone for good.

OTTO: Like we talked, I decided to forget all about it, you know? (*Laughs*) But I put up a notice on the bulletin board anyway.

MARTHA: And the boss saw it?

OTTO: No, course not, it was just like we thought: he left it lying around somewhere and someone else picked it up.

MARTHA: And gave it back?

OTTO (*Nods*): And you know who it was? (*Looks*) One of them I would have sworn on the Bible would never give it back.

MARTHA: You can't tell a book by its cover.*

OTTO (*Laughs*): How's that for luck?

Scene 7
Life

In a beer garden. OTTO, MARTHA *and* LUDWIG. *Beautiful warm day.*

OTTO: You got to take the time sometimes just to enjoy life.

MARTHA: Beautiful Sunday weather. It was a good idea coming out here.

OTTO: Looks like the lord and master's enjoying himself too.

LUDWIG: 'S that mean I can have another beer?

OTTO: Request granted. (*Laughs*)

LUDWIG: A stein this time!

OTTO: A glass is all. Don't get big ideas.

Scene 8
Pipedreams

Morning in the kitchen. MARTHA *and* LUDWIG.

MARTHA: Look at him sit there the whole morning like he hasn't got a thing to do.

---

*[NOTE: The script does not spell it out, but the implication is that the fellow worker who returned the pen is a Turkish or South Italian *Gastarbeiter* and hence by nature dishonest. Martha's final line actually reads, "To err is human." The change brings the racial motif a little closer to the surface. If desired, Otto's "One of them. . ." can be made explicit: "One of them Turks/Eyetyes/Greasers/Darkies/ etc."]

LUDWIG: What am I supposed to do?

MARTHA: Decent people always have something to do.

LUDWIG: You want me to go shopping for you?

MARTHA: That's my job.

Pause.

LUDWIG: At the employment office they said they'd let me know when I was supposed to come in again. Anyway, I was there last week and I'm going in next week whether they call me or not.

MARTHA: You have to stay on the ball.

LUDWIG: Oh sure. But if you go in too often without them asking then the counselor gets mad at you, I already noticed that, then I *really* won't get anything.

MARTHA: Other boys have jobs already, only you.

LUDWIG: Well, what do you want me to do, Momma, tell me.

MARTHA: What do I know about it, I don't know anything. You have to be up and doing, show some initiative, that's what you have to do. Look around. Keep your ears open for where they need people.

LUDWIG: I ought to just go down to the post office and get the business directory and call up all the big companies [and say, "Hello, this is Ludwig Meier, I got a seventy-eight in my school finals, send a limo round for me right away."]

MARTHA: [Fine way to talk, young man.] Frittering good money away on the telephone.

LUDWIG: Well? [What then?]

Pause.

MARTHA: To get along in this world you have to play by the rules.

LUDWIG: No.

MARTHA (*Quickly*): Don't talk that way!

LUDWIG *grins and nods.*

MARTHA (*Continued*): You're a good boy. But with you sitting around like this all the time, it makes me nervous and I just get furious.

LUDWIG: But I don't know what to do, Momma. (*Short pause*) I can't just go sit on a bench like the old people. (*Pause.* HE *looks at her and laughs*) If you want I can hang myself, then I'll *really* be out of the way. . . .

MARTHA: You could do that to your parents, that's the thanks we get! (*Pause. Firmly, stubbornly*) Dental technician, loan officer, tax agent. (*Pause*) Shine your poppa's shoes, there's a good boy, it makes him happy to see that you want to do the right thing, then he won't be after you all night when he gets home.

LUDWIG *goes into the entry hall and gets to work polishing shoes. Pause.*

LUDWIG: Anyway, it doesn't matter how you make your money just as long as you have some.

MARTHA (*From the kitchen*): What?

LUDWIG: I said it doesn't matter how you make your money, just so long as it's an honest job.

MARTHA: That's enough of that.

Pause.

LUDWIG: But if you and Poppa think I'm going to get a good apprenticeship like what you're talking about, that's not going to happen. You're just dreaming.

MARTHA (*Loudly*): We are no such thing. You have a right to job training, that's the law, that's why we pay our taxes to the government, so our son doesn't have to be a common laborer.

LUDWIG: I'm not talking about common labor. But bricklayer . . .

MARTHA (*Quickly*): You think bricklayers are happy?

LUDWIG: What?

MARTHA: Look at your father, that's no way to live.

LUDWIG: He's not a bricklayer . . .

MARTHA: It's the same thing, a laborer is a laborer.

LUDWIG: Well, so? If there weren't any laborers . . .

MARTHA: Now that's enough, I said. I'd like to know where you got this nonsense, not around here, that's for sure. (*Pause*) It's as plain as the nose on your face. They'll take anybody as a laborer, [look at the kind of people you see working on those jobs,] it doesn't take anything special.

LUDWIG: But they're taking apprentices in the building trades, they told me at the employment office.

MARTHA: Oh, I can believe that, because they can't find enough [German] boys dumb enough to take jobs like that. You have to get ahead in life. Even in a family [, from one generation to the next]. Your poppa is [just] a laborer, never mind the money's not bad. It's too late to change that. But you (*Formal*) have to climb the next rung of the ladder, otherwise nothing we've done for you makes any sense.

LUDWIG *is silent.* MARTHA *comes to him in the hall.*

MARTHA (*Continued*): You'll see, when you have a son of your own . . .

LUDWIG: He's going to have to be president, at least.

MARTHA: Idiot. (*Pause*) Time is fleeting.

LUDWIG: I know it. In July more kids will be getting out of school and they'll need jobs too and some of them are going to have better diplomas than I do.

MARTHA: Because you didn't study hard enough. There's nothing wrong with your brains, no one can tell me that.

LUDWIG: I passed my exams.

MARTHA: By the skin of your teeth.

LUDWIG: Other guys didn't.

MARTHA: All right, and that's why you're going to be a dental technician and not a bricklayer.

LUDWIG: Keep dreaming, Momma.

MARTHA: Don't be smart when someone only wants what's best for you.

LUDWIG: I've been sitting around for eight months . . .

MARTHA (*Furiously*): You talk like it's our fault you're out of work!

LUDWIG: If I'd apprenticed as a bricklayer right away I'd almost be in my second year now.

MARTHA: And someone asks, "What's your son doing now?" "Oh, he's a bricklayer's helper . . ."

LUDWIG: What's the matter with that?

MARTHA: . . . [As if you were no better than some of these foreigners!] That's what I'd have to tell them. I'd rather say . . .

LUDWIG: "My son? Oh, he's dead."

MARTHA: That's an awful thing to say. (*Pause*) You don't have the slightest understanding of what your parents want for you. That's what it is.

LUDWIG: You don't understand either.

MARTHA: He can say that, sit there and do nothing and just let himself slide.

LUDWIG: Right, because around here everybody's living in a dream world, that's why!

MARTHA: We've been too good to you. If we got strict with you, then you'd see soon enough. (*Pause*) It's easy enough to say, "Go on, earn some money. Go into the factory or into construction or where you like, just bring something home." But honey, you mustn't get used to living like that, or you'll never get away. (*Pause*) You're all we've got, if I could only make you understand.

LUDWIG *looks at her.*

Scene 9
Recollections

At dinner in the kitchen. MARTHA *and* OTTO.

OTTO: You know, I just about decided I been screwed.

MARTHA: When?

OTTO: Last week when we went to the Lowenbraukeller, don't you remember?

MARTHA: Of course I do, it was beautiful.

OTTO: I paid sixty-six marks twenty including tip; call it sixty-seven marks.

MARTHA: That's a lot, but it was really nice.

OTTO: Monday I was standing on the line and was thinking back about what a good weekend it was, and you know what hit me?

MARTHA: Nothing sensible, I'm sure.

OTTO: I suddenly realized the waiter must have screwed me, because what we had, that couldn't have cost any sixty-six twenty.

MARTHA: Really, even with the pickled pork?

OTTO: Twenty-six marks.

MARTHA: That's a lot, but when you think how all three of us picked it over, it looked like more than there was, but we all got some.

OTTO: It was pretty dry, just the same.

MARTHA: Then you had three beers.

OTTO: Four twenty each, already figured in: twelve sixty.

MARTHA: And I had . . . [(*Trying to recall*)]

OTTO: I remember if you don't. You had two glasses of wine and an ale before that.

MARTHA: I forgot all about the ale.

OTTO: But I didn't. The wine cost nine twenty-five. And there's something funny about that too; how can two times anything come out with a five on the end?

MARTHA: The waiter must have made a mistake.

OTTO: How?

MARTHA: It couldn't amount to much anyway, because I remember I didn't want the Bernkastler, even at three sixty, and then there were only two others on the menu and one was too expensive, over five marks a glass it was . . .

OTTO: Ridiculous.

MARTHA: . . . so there was only the one in between, that was the May wine, and it was four marks . . . four fifty, I think.

OTTO: All right, so that doesn't matter. Twenty-six for the pork, three beers twelve sixty, plus wine . . .

MARTHA: And the ale.

OTTO: How much was that?

MARTHA: I don't know.

OTTO: Why not?

MARTHA: Well, for goodness' sake, you don't look at the price before you order a glass of ale, do you?

OTTO: I know what everything I ordered for me and the kid cost, because I studied the menu, the prices, before I ordered. (*Pause*) Over to the Ratskeller they charge one sixty for a glass of ale.

MARTHA *stares at him.*

OTTO (*Continued*): Just for comparison. Call it another mark, because the Lowenbraukeller is so well-known and popular.

MARTHA *nods.*

OTTO (*Continued*): Thirty-eight sixty plus two seventy is forty-one thirty, plus the wine, nine (*With emphasis*) twenty-five, that comes to fifty fifty-five.

MARTHA: Fifty marks.

OTTO: No, let's do this right. Ludi had a half-glass of wine to start with and then a glass of beer . . .

MARTHA: He wanted a stein, remember?

OTTO: Let him earn his own money and he can have a gallon as far as I'm concerned. I never got beer at all when I was his age. Now we're getting down to it, because I know for a fact that Ludi's wine cost two ninety and the beer was two thirty. That's interesting; a stein costs four twenty and it's twice as big, so anybody who orders a glass is paying a penalty.

MARTHA: Oh, for goodness' sake . . .

OTTO: All right, let's total up. Fifty fifty-five plus two ninety is fifty-three forty-five and two thirty is fifty-five seventy-five. (*Pause*) And that's the problem; where did the other ten marks go? Funny business? Maybe the waiter made a little mistake on purpose when he was adding up the bill. That could be what happened. It makes me so mad I can't tell you. I haven't been able to enjoy anything since.

MARTHA: Well, that's not a very nice thing to do, screw someone out of ten marks.

OTTO: It sure isn't, if. . . . Oh, boy! (*Laughs. Pause*) I'll give you a hint. Pretzels!* Off the menu!

MARTHA: Well, of course!

OTTO (*Nods*): That's what it was. We even had a big discussion about it, remember? The pretzel girl came to the table with those big pretzels, and we got three, because everybody wanted one, and it was right before we were going to leave, too. And I was going to pay for them with a hundred, and the pretzel girl said she couldn't change a hundred, pay her later when she had change. And then she didn't come back. And then when I was paying the waiter I told him, "Wait a minute, we had three of those big pretzels too and we didn't pay the girl for them yet, let me pay you and you settle up with her. . . ."

MARTHA: Do you suppose he did?

OTTO: Would he cheat someone he works with? That's the missing ten fifty, all right. Three fifty each. It all comes out even. (*Pause*) When I thought of the pretzels, it was like a weight falling off me.

*[NOTE: The forgotten items in Otto's accounting are actually "Radi," the giant white radishes that many Bavarians relish with their beer. In order to avoid distracting an American audience with folkloric irrelevancies, "the radish-seller" has become "the pretzel girl."]

MARTHA: When you get cheated it makes you feel that way.

OTTO: But it's all right now. (*Pause*) We got to the bottom of it. (*Nods;* HE *is exhausted*) I'm really tired.

MARTHA: Well, it's late.

Scene 10
Going for the Top

OTTO *alone on a little hill.* HE's *wearing the leisure suit.* HE *has a gadget in his hand and is staring up into the sky at his toy plane.*

OTTO: There's no place for fear in this business. (*Laughs*) Of course, it's not easy to get life insurance when you're a test pilot, but (*Laughs, shrugs*) you can die just as easily in bed. (*Pause*) Jesus, if anybody heard me. . . . (*Looks around, sees no one, smiles*) And when you're up there . . . you're free! (*Laughs, nods*)

END OF ACT ONE

ACT TWO

Scene 1
Shadowplay

It is evening in the little apartment kitchen. OTTO *is nursing a beer—it must be after dinner—and staring into space, smoking.* LUDWIG *is reading an auto magazine.* MARTHA *laboriously repairs* LUDWIG's *leather jacket. Pause.* OTTO *looks around, almost says something but suppresses it. Pause.*

OTTO: What are you doing there, (*Emphatically formal*) so late in the night and all?
MARTHA: You can see perfectly well what I'm doing.
OTTO: You should let him fix his own trash, he's got plenty of time.
MARTHA (*Calm, but you can tell something's up*): Leather is harder to fix than anything else. He can't do it.
OTTO: And I'm going around with holes in my socks.
MARTHA (*Looks at him angrily*): What's that?

OTTO *doesn't answer.*

MARTHA (*Continued*): What's eating you? Hmm? And why are you taking it out on us?
OTTO: Nothing.
MARTHA: Then just be quiet.
OTTO: He's got money for that junk, anyway. (*Meaning* LUDWIG's *magazine*)
MARTHA: He can buy whatever he wants with his allowance.

LUDWIG *is about to say something, decides not to.*

OTTO: As long as I earn it for him, he can. (*Short pause*) Does the young gentleman have any prospects for employment?

LUDWIG *shakes his head.* OTTO *laughs.*

OTTO (*Continued*): Everybody in the world has to work, while young Mister Meier sits there and reads his magazine. Pretty soft situation, I'd say.
MARTHA: Leave him alone!
OTTO: Always defending our little prince.

Pause. LUDWIG *gets a packet of cigarettes out of his shirt-pocket and lights up;* HE's *nervous.*

OTTO (*Continued; looking at him*): Yes sir, he's going to end up just fine.

Pause.

MARTHA: Otto, what's bothering you? (*Pause*) Otto?

OTTO: Silly question, nothing. Just looking at him sitting there drives me up the wall.

LUDWIG: If you give me fifty marks for the rock festival, you wouldn't have to look at me for three days.

OTTO: Earn some money, then you can go to Paris if you feel like it.

MARTHA *watches, keeps on with her mending.*

LUDWIG: As an advance on my allowance!

OTTO: An advance on his allowance, listen to your little prince. That's rich. He acts like he was hired to waste his time and do nothing around here, so naturally he wants an advance on his pay.

LUDWIG: Then forget it.

Pause.

MARTHA: I can't give it to him out of the household budget. But if he was away over the holiday you wouldn't have to look at him and it might be better. Out of sight, out of mind.

OTTO: I never got something for nothing in my life.

MARTHA: Who ever said you did?

OTTO: Kuno Gruschke lost his job.

MARTHA: What?

OTTO: Forty-seven men laid off. Fourteen Italians, eight Turks, the Iranian, fifteen women and nine (*Formal*) "senior employees." Kuno was one of them.

MARTHA (*Looking at him*): Be glad it wasn't you.

OTTO: Yeah, well what if he was my friend? Just about the only one.

MARTHA: It's too bad.

OTTO: Everything just keeps rolling along just the same as if he never been there. Just gone. Nothing slowed down, no problems. "Redisposition of Resources." I've got two more screws to put in, a couple of other guys too. Up ahead there's a kid does the door handle, he's new. Five of the nine were off my line. From farther up, don't even know what they did. The foreman was already there with the new breakdowns. Five men, just like the earth opened up and swallowed them.

MARTHA: You have to go along with the way things are. They're picking out the older ones. You're not one of them.

OTTO: You're right there, forty-two's not old.

MARTHA: The best years of your life.

OTTO: If only it hadn't of been Kuno. The union council went along with it. "It's in the contract." "You can't argue with facts." Cutting out the fat, they call it. "You have to stay flexible to keep up with the times." The way things are you can forget about finding a job when you're fifty-eight. (*Softly*) "Early retirement!"

MARTHA: He'll have time to enjoy life.

OTTO (*Loud*): He doesn't want to enjoy life, he wants to work! (*Points at* LUDWIG; *softly*) Will you look at him there?

MARTHA: This is no reason to bully him. This isn't the first time people have been laid off. You never got worked up like this before.

OTTO: It's like an epidemic. First twenty-five, then thirty-one, another thirty-one, now forty-seven. When they get to forty-eight, it's mass layoffs, that's in the contract.

MARTHA: What does that mean?

OTTO: It means they can't pretty it up anymore, they're running out of time and got to do something fast. It means that this isn't the end, it's just the beginning. (*Pause*) I don't have anything to worry about, these are my best years, I'm good at my job. Some of the men tried to argue, they turned down the new plan to work around the vacancies. The foreman just looked at them. I knew what he felt like saying.

MARTHA: What about you?

OTTO: I said fine, sure, swell, nothing to it, and he slapped me on the shoulder and said, "Good for you!" I know what that means, too. (*Short pause*) It means security, thank God. (HE *is perspiring*)

MARTHA: Is it easy to do the extra work?

OTTO: I got to screw down the housing for the left wing-window, put in one more Gruschke used to do. Somebody sixty feet back had the wing-window, I never knew him. (*Nods*) Everything's split-up different. (*Pause*) They slow the line down a couple days till you got the new moves into your hands. Then it's rolling again, (*Sniffs*) and when it speeds up you got to stay on top of it and not let your mind wander, like the foreman says.

MARTHA: If you do your best, it'll be all right.

OTTO *nods, sweating as if after heavy labor; sniffs, smokes, sips his beer. Pause.* LUDWIG *looks at his father.*

OTTO: What are you looking at?

LUDWIG: Nothing. (HE *reads on, that is to say buries his nose in the magazine*)

OTTO: Good thing. You're not going to be around here to look at me much longer, anyway. You can go find yourself somebody else to stare at.

LUDWIG: Can I have the fifty marks?

OTTO: No.

LUDWIG *looks at him. Pause.*

Scene 2
Worldly Wisdom

[OTTO *and* LUDWIG.] *Saturday morning, the hallway. With shoes.*

OTTO: When you got as much time as you got, you can get it perfect.
LUDWIG: Uh-huh.
OTTO: You make yourself useful, nobody notices you. Look here, (*Takes a shoe*) in between the sole and the leather, that's the critical point, you can't get in there with the brush, you don't even touch the dirt, so it builds up.
LUDWIG: Uh-huh.
OTTO: Now here's the trick. (*Takes a piece of cord out of his pocket*) You take care of the problem with this. (*Laughs*) You get in there and clean right down to the bottom.

OTTO *takes the shoe between his knees, holds it there, and scours with the cord, which* HE *holds in both hands and tugs rapidly back and forth in the recalcitrant crack between sole and upper.* LUDWIG *watches.*

OTTO (*Continued; holding up the string*): The proof! Look how much darker it is, see the dirt?
LUDWIG: Uh-huh.
OTTO: OK, you try it.

LUDWIG *looks at him.*

OTTO (*Continued*): You ought to be glad, somebody shows you how to do something.

LUDWIG *imitates his movements and cleans a shoe.*

OTTO (*Continued*): When you're finished call me, I'll inspect it.
LUDWIG: OK.
OTTO: You can come out flying this afternoon.
LUDWIG: I was planning to do something else.
OTTO: What's that?

LUDWIG *looks at him, doesn't answer.*

OTTO (*Continued*): Well, that's nice, a person offers to take you along to break in the new model. A test flight.
LUDWIG: I don't care about your old test flight.
OTTO: Well, I do. I care a lot about it.
LUDWIG: I know.

OTTO: The conquest of nature.

LUDWIG: I know.

OTTO: When you're not up there, when you're on the ground steering, it's harder than if you were sitting right in the plane. That's what the experts say. (*Pause*) It's the eye that does it, you got to be able to read the wind. (*Laughs*)

LUDWIG *nods.*

OTTO (*Continued*): You'll never get the hang of it, flying. (*Looks at* LUDWIG *awhile, then goes into the kitchen*)

MARTHA: Let's go shopping now, it's Saturday and the store's going to be crowded if we don't hurry.

LUDWIG: Bring me a pack of cigarettes back?

MARTHA: Sure. That's your pay.

LUDWIG *polishes shoes.* OTTO *and* MARTHA *put their coats on and go out.*

Scene 3
Market Crash

At the checkstand of a supermarket. MARTHA *and* OTTO *have made a fairly large purchase; both, especially* OTTO, *are peeking into the market baskets of other customers in the check-out line.*

OTTO (*To* MARTHA, *softly*): Look.

MARTHA: What?

OTTO: Them up there.

OTTO *indicates with a guilty tilt of the head.* MARTHA *looks.*

OTTO (*Continued*): Look what they got in that basket.

MARTHA *nods ["So what?"].*

OTTO (*Continued*): With tomorrow Sunday! Two packages of soup mix, a pickle, two bottles of beer and a loaf of bread. Understand? That's for a whole family, those two kids are with them.

MARTHA: Maybe they did most of their shopping yesterday and just forgot a few things.

OTTO: Fat chance! Two packages of Maggi, a pickle, bread and two bottles of beer? (*Nods, laughs knowingly*) He's out of work, that's what it is.

MARTHA: How can you tell?

OTTO: You got eyes in your head you can tell.

BOTH *look.*

MARTHA: Our turn!

MARTHA *unloads the groceries onto the little conveyor belt of the checkstand while the* CASHIER *totals them and puts them into another cart.*

CASHIER: Seventy-three ninety-four.

MARTHA *is poking around in her purse.*

CASHIER (*Continued*): Seventy-three ninety-four.

MARTHA (*Nods, blushing furiously; to* OTTO): Do you have any money? I don't have enough.

OTTO *goes red too, looks around at the people watching.* HE *speaks loudly, to shift the embarrassment off himself.*

OTTO: It's not my problem you come out without money!

MARTHA: I had a hundred marks in here and now there's only fifty!

CASHIER: What's the problem? It comes to seventy-three marks ninety-four pfennig [*pronounced "fennig"*].

MARTHA (*In total confusion*): We'll have to put back everything that comes to more than fifty-four marks.

CASHIER: But I already rung it up!

MARTHA: I'm sorry.

OTTO (*Audibly*): Will you look what I married. Let me through, miss, (*To the* CASHIER) this has nothing to do with me, she gets eight hundred fifty a month for housekeeping.

MARTHA: Be quiet!

OTTO *pushes past the checkstand and runs out.*

MARTHA (*Continued; to the* CASHIER): I'm Mrs. Meier, you certainly must know me by now, don't you?

Scene 4
Nightwatch

In the kitchen. MARTHA *is crying.* OTTO *stares at his son.*

OTTO: You're going to pay for this.

MARTHA *looks up.* OTTO *nods.*

MARTHA: Think how humiliated we were. It was horrible.
OTTO (*Nods*): You do a thing like that to your parents.

OTTO *gives* LUDWIG *a clout on the head.* LUDWIG *takes it, stares straight ahead, doesn't react.*

OTTO (*Continued; unmoved*): I want an answer. Where did you hide the fifty marks you stole?

LUDWIG *stares, says nothing.*

MARTHA: Give it back, you've got to give it back when you steal something or it only makes it worse.

LUDWIG *stares.*

OTTO: And this is supposed to be my son, now I've got a better idea what my son is.

No reaction from LUDWIG.

OTTO (*Continued*): Next we'll have my son the convicted criminal.

OTTO *jumps up, runs into the living room, goes to the sofa bed where* LUDWIG *sleeps, yanks it open, and tears the bedclothes apart.* HE *finds nothing, comes back.*

OTTO (*Continued*): Give me the fifty marks or there's going to be trouble.
MARTHA: Otto!
OTTO: You know what your son is? He's an animal. (*Nods*) That's why nobody will hire him, they could see it even if we couldn't. Personnel managers are trained, they see it right away: this young man is a thief! I'm going to count to three, now, and when I'm finished the fifty marks better be on the table. One. Two. Three.

OTTO *looks at* LUDWIG. LUDWIG *doesn't react.* OTTO *jumps up again and runs back into the living room, pulls out* LUDWIG's *drawer, throws everything out of it, rummages through it, tears up the posters; looks, finds nothing, comes back, looks at his son.*

MARTHA: Give the fifty marks back, Ludi, don't push Poppa too far.

LUDWIG *looks.*

OTTO: You hear what your momma said? He doesn't hear. He's tough. You're not tough enough for me. I'm going to finish you off once and for all if that's what it takes.

OTTO *and* LUDWIG *stare at each other. No reaction from* LUDWIG.

OTTO (*Continued*): Down with your pants.

LUDWIG *looks at him.*

OTTO (*Continued*): Put the money on the table, wherever you've got it.

LUDWIG *looks at him.*

OTTO (*Continued*): Down with your pants, I said. You want me to help you?

Pause. At first LUDWIG *doesn't react, then* HE *removes his jeans.* OTTO *grabs them and rifles them, finds nothing.*

OTTO (*Continued*): Keep going.

LUDWIG *looks at him, then pulls off his leather jacket.* OTTO *searches it, finds nothing.* LUDWIG *looks at him.*

OTTO (*Continued; wildly*): Give me the fifty marks, don't push me too far, I warn you. (*Screaming*) Give me my fifty marks!

LUDWIG *stares.*

OTTO (*Continued*): Where did you hide it, just tell me.

LUDWIG *remains silent.*

OTTO (*Continued*): The rest of the clothes, come on, quickly, that's an order.

LUDWIG *abruptly begins crying uncontrollably. The tears run down his cheeks as* HE *takes off the rest of his clothes garment by garment until* HE *is naked.* OTTO *stares at him, frozen; there's no trace of the fifty marks. Long pause.*

OTTO (*Continued; suddenly light, forgiving*): There's no need to be ashamed in front of your parents, we saw you when you were a little boy. (*Nods*)

Pause. MARTHA *turns her face away,* SHE *doesn't want to see* LUDWIG *naked.*

OTTO (*Continued*): You're proud, aren't you? Because you're sly, you won't give the secret away. (*Nods*) I can see that. (*Short pause*) You'll never amount to anything, I guarantee you, you can count on it. I know the way the world is, it hasn't got any use for your kind, as sure as God made Adam. You're not our kind at all.

LUDWIG (*Looking at his father, quiet, still crying*): I'd rather be dead than be like you.

OTTO's *control almost snaps.* HE *looks at his son.*

OTTO (*To* MARTHA): You hear that?

MARTHA (*Still crying*): What?

Long pause.

OTTO: That's how I feel. Just the same.

OTTO *looks at* LUDWIG *one more time, then suddenly oblivious of the others, goes uncertainly into his workroom. Long pause.*

MARTHA: Put something on, you'll catch cold.

LUDWIG *gathers his things up quickly, goes into the living room and gets dressed there.*

MARTHA (*Continued; to herself*): It's not so terrible, there are a lot worse things. (*Nods some spirit back into herself*)

LUDWIG *has gotten dressed; now* HE *puts his things away, sorrowing over the torn posters, etc. Then* HE *gets a suitcase, packs what* HE *needs and wants to take with him into it, gets his toilet articles out of the bathroom. When* HE's *packed* HE *comes back into the kitchen.* MARTHA *watches.* LUDWIG *reaches under a stack of saucers in the kitchen cabinet and takes out the fifty marks.*

MARTHA (*Continued; watching*): Take care of yourself and don't get into trouble. Come back soon.

LUDWIG *nods, sticks the money in his pocket and leaves the apartment.* MARTHA *watches him go. A very long pause.* OTTO *comes out of his workroom into the kitchen.*

OTTO: He gone?

MARTHA *nods. Pause.* OTTO *sits down on the left side of the table, looks at* MARTHA. *Long pause.*

MARTHA (*Very calmly*): Otto, I'll never forgive you for this.
OTTO (*Looks at her*): Why?

Long pause.

Scene 5
Count Down*

OTTO *and* MARTHA *are watching television late at night in the living room.*

OTTO *drinks a sip of beer.*

MARTHA *looks accusingly at him.*

OTTO *does not react.*

Pause. THEY *watch television.*

OTTO *pours out more beer, drinks.*

Pause.

MARTHA *gets up, goes into the kitchen, looks to see if* SHE *has taken the chicken off the stove, waits in the kitchen, comes back, sits down again.*

Pause.

MARTHA *looks at* OTTO.

OTTO *drinks some more beer.*

The TV plays on. It is a Western. Pause.

*[NOTE: Scene title in English in original.]

OTTO *pours more beer, dropping a little inadvertently on the carpet.*

MARTHA *notices, jumps up, runs into the kitchen, gets a towel, dampens it with hot water from the water heater by the sink, runs back into the living room, kneels down and virtuously wipes up the spot.*

OTTO *is disturbed, has to move his feet out of the way.*

MARTHA *gives him a reproachful look and wipes away.*

OTTO *watches* MARTHA *as* SHE *cleans by his feet, then takes the bottle and deliberately shakes a tiny drop onto the rug beside his wife where* SHE *kneels at his feet.*

MARTHA *notices, but only stares at* OTTO.

OTTO *puts the beer bottle down again.*

MARTHA *sniffs with careful audibility, then cleans up the new spot with ceremonious fussiness.*

OTTO *drinks off the last of his glass, watching.*

MARTHA *looks him reproachfully right in the eye, then goes on cleaning.*

OTTO *watches, sniffs, starts to pour another glass.*

MARTHA *looks at him accusingly.*

OTTO *smashes the bottle on the living-room table without warning.*

MARTHA *jumps up, screams.*

OTTO *gets up.*

MARTHA *thinks* SHE's *in danger, screams even louder.*

OTTO *goes to the TV set and wipes it off the buffet with one shove.*

MARTHA *stares, too scared now to scream.*

OTTO *destroys everything that comes to hand, smashing vases on the wall, overturning furniture, throwing chairs against the wall, pulling up the carpet; this goes on for a long time.*

MARTHA *runs from one corner to the other to avoid being hurt.*

OTTO *runs into his workshop and smashes everything to pieces, takes an almost finished model and gives it special treatment, throwing it several times against the wall until it is in fragments; then* HE *starts for the kitchen.*

MARTHA *leaps to meet him like a Fury incarnate, stands in the kitchen door, ready for anything.*

MARTHA: You come in here over my dead body, you understand me?

OTTO *looks at his wife, then turns away, stands a little while like a passenger at a train station waiting for his connection, looks around, sees the mess* HE's *made. Suddenly a tremor goes through him;* HE *flings himself with all the force in him at the wall, bangs his head against it as hard as* HE *can;* HE *yowls, but does it again, trying to smash through the wall with his head.*

Pause.

OTTO *suddenly goes into the bathroom and washes his hands very thoroughly with soap.* HE *stares into the mirror.*

MARTHA (*Continued; fast*): A broken mirror's seven years' bad luck, that's what they say. (*Nods*)

OTTO *looks at himself attentively in the mirror. Pause.*

Scene 6
Silence

The next day, Sunday, MARTHA *and* OTTO. *A very long, painful scene. It consists of* THE TWO *bringing "order" back to things.* OTTO *tries to save what can be saved (tries to fix a chair, etc.) while* MARTHA *mainly cleans. This goes on for a long time.*

Scene 7
On the Moon

It is evening. OTTO *and* MARTHA *are sitting in the living room, brought back to some semblance of order. Pause.*

MARTHA: That's all we needed. (*Nods*) If the picture tube is cracked, you can just throw the whole set right out. I figure the damage amounts to a thousand marks at least— (*Emphatic*) not including the color TV of course.

OTTO *looks at her. Pause.* SHE *goes on, trying to cheer herself up.*

MARTHA (*Continued*): My God, the way other people act in situations like this sometimes. Kill their whole family! (*Looks at her husband*) I wish I had a movie I could show you, just the same: if you could have *seen* yourself.

OTTO *nods. Pause.*

MARTHA (*Continued*): Well, the leopard can't change his spots, they say.
OTTO (*Nods*): You could dive all the way down to the bottom in me like it was the ocean, go as deep as you can, you won't find any great white shark down there, you know that, don't you? (*Pause*) You think he'll come back?
MARTHA: He has the money so he's at the rock festival. When that's gone he'll get hungry and come back.

OTTO *looks disbelievingly at* MARTHA. *Pause.*

MARTHA (*Continued*): Of course he'll come back, why shouldn't he? (*Pause*) This is his home.
OTTO: When I was little, we were out walking, and we saw this man on a horse, not a cop, a real rider. And he came toward us, my momma and me, and when he came even with us he slowed down, in case the horse kicked I guess. And he looked at us and said "Howdydo" and laughed and went on by. And then my momma told me, "That man is the son of a king!," and took my hand and we went on. (*Short pause*) Before you even get going it's all over. (*Short pause*) Sometimes I feel like they're switching me off.

MARTHA *looks at him.* OTTO *nods.*

OTTO (*Continued*): Work's the only thing that's still going. Because the line keeps going. But when there's a break they switch us off. They switch us on at seven so we can work till a quarter to nine. They don't switch us off between quarter to nine and nine, they let us stand around and talk to each other and grab a snack, make plans. Then from nine till a quarter to twelve it goes again. Quarter to twelve to one they let us go to the canteen 'cause it's still part of the plant.
MARTHA: You're off your head . . .
OTTO: Then it goes on again till five, or seven if there's overtime. Right before the weekend they finally switch us off, like the electric typewriters, slip a cover over us so we don't get dusty. Then we just sit there in the hall. Three hundred fifty men. If you got a chair, you sit on it, otherwise whatever, or sleep standing up like a horse. There's this one guy in central control who takes over from the others and plugs all our brains into the same circuit, so inside our heads, we see ourselves driving home in our own car to our families and our kids, our nice apartment, where everything's just

fine and it's the weekend, just like we've been looking forward to all week: and it keeps on going that way, because now we're switched on to home we can switch on the TV. (HE *laughs at the thought*) And then maybe somebody on the TV switches on the TV, eh? (*Laughs again*)

MARTHA: What are you talking about?

OTTO: "A man, a wife, and baby too,
  They all went down to see the zoo,
  They went to where the monkeys are,
  And when they peeked between the bars—
    What'd 'you think they saw?
  A man, a wife, and baby too. . ."

MARTHA: "They all went down to see the zoo . . ." (*Laughs*) Idiot!

OTTO: Monday morning at seven, off come the dust covers, everything's back to normal, and nobody notices a thing. (*Looks at* MARTHA) Did you know that?

MARTHA: No I didn't, because it's all nonsense, that's why.

OTTO (*Nods*): Because you don't go out to work like I do.

MARTHA (*Sour*): I have enough to do taking care of the house.

OTTO (*Nods*): That's imaginary, too. They just don't tell you 'cause you'd only get upset.

MARTHA: You have a screw loose, that's what I think.

OTTO: Well, what if it was true? How can you tell unless you work it out for yourself? Fourteen screws for the wing-windows, two new ones to put into the side panels, a couple of days excitement on the line because the brains upstairs know they got to allow us a little leeway while we're learning our new trick. (*Pause*) When we get old enough, they put us all together in an old empty warehouse and seal it up. And then they show a two-hour movie about ten years of happy retirement. . . . That's how it ends. (*Short pause*) If I could just get back behind it [where it's real] . . .

MARTHA: You got behind it all right this time! The things you smashed up were real enough, take my word for it!

OTTO: You trying to keep my ideas out? You can't, you haven't cut the wire.

MARTHA: Oh, fine, more . . .

OTTO: At first I thought that when I grew up I'd be free. But then we got to know each other and got married.

MARTHA: Thank you very much!

OTTO (*Softly*): Sometimes I buy a magazine and beat off, instead of coming to you.

MARTHA (*Stares*): Well, I can't compete with that.

OTTO: No.

Pause.

MARTHA: Do I disgust you? You can just tell me, it's all right.

Pause.

OTTO (*Shakes his head "No"*): How about me?

MARTHA: No.

OTTO: Sometimes, when I've (*Very softly*) got it in my hand, I think, "It's shrinking!" And then I feel like a little kid again, and I really go at it hard.

MARTHA: It's not shrinking, you can take my word for it. (*Short pause*) You're the one that's shrinking, not it.

OTTO (*Looks at her; pause*): Everything's all balled up. I reach for anything, it's stuck. And inside me everything's oversize and falling apart.

MARTHA: Maybe you're the one falling apart.

OTTO: Like a freeway, everything just roars on through.

MARTHA: What about me?

OTTO: Yeah, you too.

MARTHA (*After a short pause*): After all the trouble you take.

OTTO: It's not your fault, I've got rubber gloves on, like what you wash the dishes in.

MARTHA: You have to take them off, then.

OTTO: When I was a kid I liked to sleep with a wool cap on, even in summer, 'cause it came down over my ears, and I always thought that somebody would sneak up on me at night and cut them off with a scissors. Momma used to take it off me when she caught me.

Pause of three minutes duration.

MARTHA: Is that it for the true confessions?

OTTO *looks at her.* MARTHA *goes out of the room and gets a suitcase.*

OTTO: What're you doing?

MARTHA: I'm going away, Otto, I'm leaving . . .

OTTO: Why?

MARTHA: Like I'm an animal or something, not a human being.

OTTO *watches her pack.*

Scene 8
Rebellion

MARTHA *is alone in a small room.* SHE *has just come in. Her things are lying all over the place.* SHE *is in the midst of putting things away.* SHE *stops while* SHE *makes herself some coffee, but it takes her a long time because* SHE'*s not used to the new stove. You can see that* SHE *is annoyed by her inability to cope with the stove. When* SHE *finishes* SHE *sits, fighting to keep her composure.* SHE *sips her coffee, crying quietly. Pause.*

END OF ACT TWO

ACT THREE

Scene 1
Demolition License

In MARTHA's *lodging, very simply furnished.* OTTO *sits in his coat on the only chair.* MARTHA *sits on the bed, looking at* OTTO. *Pause.*

OTTO: You come home with me if I take you?

MARTHA *shakes her head.*

OTTO (*Continued*): I shouldn't ought to take you back anyhow. Not now.
MARTHA: No. (*Pause*) Are you doing all right?
OTTO: Yep.
MARTHA: How about Ludi?
OTTO: Him too.

Pause. MARTHA *looks at* OTTO, *smiles.*

MARTHA: You still have the apartment?
OTTO: I'll hold on to that no matter what.

MARTHA *smiles.*

OTTO (*Continued*): I'll never go into a rooming house, never.

MARTHA *nods.*

OTTO (*Continued*): You're not here a lot, right?
MARTHA: No, but it does for me.
OTTO (*Looks at her. Pause*): I'm not home much either. (*Pause*) I'm not seeing anybody, understand. But soon maybe! (*Pause*) Come home with me, I for-give you and we can . . . start over. (*Pause*) OK, we won't, then. (*Gets up to leave*)
MARTHA: Just the same as ever?
OTTO: Thank God for that.
MARTHA: Haven't changed at all?
OTTO: Maybe; none of your business.
MARTHA: That's true.
OTTO (*Actually at the door now*): You're still my wife. If I wanted to make you do your duty, you'd have to do it.
MARTHA: You wouldn't do that.
OTTO: No. (*Pause*) Can I come around again sometime?
MARTHA: When you're in the neighborhood.

OTTO: Right. See how you're doing. Well, so long.
MARTHA: See you soon, Otto.

OTTO *leaves.* MARTHA *looks in the mirror.*

Scene 2
Concrete

At the door of a barracks, a lodging for workmen in the compound of a construction firm. Inside one can hear [Turkish] voices, music, card-playing, drinking, etc. OTTO *in his coat, his son.*

OTTO: I come to get you, we're going home.

LUDWIG *looks at him. Pause.*

OTTO (*Continued*): Your momma's coming back too.

OTTO *and* LUDWIG *look at each other. Pause.*

OTTO (*Continued*): This is no kind of life, here.
LUDWIG: If I like it . . .
OTTO: Living in a barracks, a place to sleep and that's it, this is what my son wants to be. You ought to be ashamed, you been brought up for something better.

LUDWIG *nods. Pause.*

OTTO (*Continued*): You're not of age yet, I can make you come along with me if I want to.
LUDWIG: I guess so.
OTTO: Suppose I do that? (*Looks at* LUDWIG. *Pause*) I won't though. If a person's determined to be miserable, that's his business. (*Short pause.* HE *looks at* LUDWIG) It's more comfortable at home this way anyhow, I don't have to climb over the sofa to get to the bathroom. And the thumbtacks in the walls, no matter how many times you were told.
LUDWIG: That's right. (*Pause*)
OTTO: Come on home, you've made your point.
LUDWIG: Uh-uh.
OTTO (*Feels* HE*'s been caught out*): Only kidding. A little trap. (*Pause*)
LUDWIG: You doing all right?
OTTO: See for yourself.

LUDWIG: How about Momma?

OTTO: She's OK too.

LUDWIG: You see her?

OTTO: Course I do, she's coming back, isn't she?

LUDWIG: Right.

Pause.

OTTO: This is an awful place.

LUDWIG: But I got a job. I'm earning a living.

OTTO (*Laughs. Pause*): Can't take much pride in saying "My son the bricklayer." Better not even mention you.

LUDWIG: Or don't start talking in the first place.

OTTO: You getting smart with me?

LUDWIG *shakes his head.*

OTTO (*Continued*): That's a good thing, because the law says I'm still your father, no one can take that away from me. (*Short pause*) So, I think we've talked enough: pack your bag if you've got one and then we go. I'll give you five minutes.

LUDWIG: I'm not going.

OTTO: Then I'm going to clip you one and take you along anyway.

LUDWIG: If you hit me I'll call the others.

OTTO: You'd let them gang up on your own father?

LUDWIG: If you start anything.

OTTO: Then I guess I'll have to get a cop to help me. (*Pause*) You can have the living room to yourself, your own room, do what you like there, no questions. I'll leave the TV in there. Your territory; the bedroom and my workroom is all I need. We can share the kitchen, nobody gives any orders there. We can put it all down in writing and swear to it.

LUDWIG: What about Momma?

OTTO: To hell with her. (*Pause*) You can't leave your old dad in the lurch like this, you'll be sorry you did when I'm gone, you know that.

LUDWIG: You're not going anywhere. But I'll come and see you if you like.

OTTO: I don't need any visits from you, spare yourself the trouble. (*Leaves*)

LUDWIG *watches, uncertain, but goes back into the barracks.*

Scene 3
The Little Mirror

In the apartment. The change is extraordinary: it's squeaky-clean but unoccupied. OTTO *has arranged it to suit himself. Since* HE *couldn't cope with the whole apartment alone,* HE *has moved everything* HE *needs into one room: the kitchen. It is obvious that this is the only place life continues.* HE *sleeps here,* HE'*s moved the TV in—everything. And the kitchen is still too large.* OTTO *really only occupies the kitchen couch, where* HE *sleeps. And it's only a place to sleep: everything else is far away, untouched, grand.*

OTTO *sits watching the Bavarian version of "What's My Line" on TV.* HE *talks doggedly to himself as* HE *watches. So far as possible* HE *should look thinner, also as if* HE'*s been to the barber.*

OTTO: "[And now it's time for Bavaria's favorite panel show,] 'Jolly Jobs,' with Robert Lembke!"

"[Good evening, good evening, all. Let's see if our first contestant can puzzle our panel and 'fill the piggy'!* Would you please give our panel their first clue?]"

I Am An Asshole.

"Excuse me, what was that again?"

I am an asshole.

"Amateur or professional?"

Hard to say: see, I studied how to be an upholsterer, [but of course there wasn't any jobs, so I went on job training,] and now I work for BMW and screw sixteen screws into the Model Five-Twenty-Five.

"You are an auto builder?"

Yep: an autoscrewinstallationist . . . a screwscrewer . . . screwologist . . . screwster.

"Are you perhaps . . . a *screwdriver?*"

How's that again?

"Mr. Lembke, is the contestant a screwdriver?"

"Yes, panel, the contestant *is* a screwdriver."

"Mr. Meier, if you'd be good enough to show the panel your hands?"

Sure, glad to. . . .

"Now let's let our viewing audience at home see a fully developed pair of screwdriver hands, this one with three fingers and the other with just two. This modification is the result of breeding. The fingers that are left are twice the size of ordinary fingers and are optimally suited to their function. Mr. Meier, I wonder if you'd be kind enough to run through the typical hand-movements related to your job?"

*[NOTE: In this passage Otto uses various "voices" for the moderator and panelists. *Heitere Berufraten* (literally, "Amusing Job-Guessing") uses "coins" in a piggy-bank to indicate a contestant's score instead of flip-cards a la *What's My Line:* hence "fill the piggy."]

OTTO *cripples up his hands and mimics screwing in the screws.*

"Thank you so much. Even though he didn't 'fill the piggy,' let's have a wonderful round of applause for our screwscrewing contestant!"

OTTO *applauds himself. Pause.* HE *speaks normally to himself.*

I'm a worker. W-o-r-k-e-r! Not a doctor, not a lawyer, not an accountant, not a cabinet minister, not a factory owner. (*Pause*) I can't get any line on myself. Funny. Whether I try to or not.

Scene 4
Showing Off

OTTO *and* MARTHA *in a little cafe.*

MARTHA: It's nice of you to come by.
OTTO: I wanted to see how you were doing, it's been two weeks since anybody's seen you, who knows what might have happened. I almost didn't have the nerve.
MARTHA: Why?
OTTO: What if I'd run into your other guy.

MARTHA *looks.*

OTTO (*Continued*): You like your work?
MARTHA: No, it's not much of a job, but I'll get something better when there's an opening. Selling house slippers isn't very interesting.

Pause.

OTTO: If I said come back, right now, everything will be just the same as it was, you probably still wouldn't do it, huh?
MARTHA: No.
OTTO: But if you don't like working. . . . You don't have to work when you're with me.

MARTHA *smiles.*

OTTO (*Continued*): You don't want to change back again.
MARTHA: No.

Pause.

OTTO: You grown since we been apart and I've shrunk up. That's what's rotten. I used to be a happy man. Now I sit around at home all night and think about all kinds of things, get these crazy thoughts.

MARTHA: Why's that?

OTTO: Like for example, I convince myself I'm going blind.

MARTHA: Why should you be going blind?

OTTO (*Very dramatically*): That's what I say, but I imagine it. Then I think how it would be if I was alone in a mountain cabin, somewhere lonely way high up, and suddenly I wake up one morning and notice I'm blind, like the Count of Monte Cristo, from the shit from the eagle nest he got into his eyes, and there's nobody around and no telephone where I could tell someone what's happened to me. (*Laughs at the vision* HE's *creating*) I can find my way around the cabin, by touch, see, but I got to get out and down, 'cause I only have food for two days. And how am I going to find my way down to the valley if I'm blind? It's certain death somewhere in the wilderness, 'cause I'll lose the path, wander off, fall off a cliff, and no one will hear me. But if I stay in the cabin, it's just as hopeless. . . . (HE *laughs; short pause*) It's bad with you away.

MARTHA *gazes at him.*

OTTO (*Continued*): You think we could ever . . .? I know you got another guy, but. . . . It doesn't have to be right now, just sometime maybe. . . . I went to a whore. It cost fifty marks and I couldn't do a thing. I asked her would she give me half the money back. But she said no and didn't give me nothing.

MARTHA: Too bad about the money.

OTTO *nods.*

MARTHA (*Continued*): Masturbating's cheaper.

OTTO (*Looks at her, gets her point*): Yes. (*Pause*) Suppose we just start over from the beginning.

MARTHA: Go ahead, start.

OTTO: I mean together.

MARTHA: That's crazy and you know it.

OTTO: Just because a guy smashes up an apartment once in his life doesn't mean we got to break up.

MARTHA: No.

Pause.

OTTO: You still enjoy the work?

MARTHA: I haven't enjoyed it yet. But it's better than back home. Only sometimes at night my feet feel like overshoes full of water.

OTTO: Don't you ever think about coming back?

MARTHA: I bought a little radio, and I feel better already.

OTTO: Never even think about it?

MARTHA: Don't ask stupid questions if you can't guess the answers.

OTTO: Who is he?

MARTHA: Who?

OTTO: The one you have, the other guy, I mean.

MARTHA: A lot like you. (*Laughs*)

OTTO: I don't believe it.

MARTHA: It's true.

OTTO: Couldn't you do better than that?

MARTHA: He's married, just like me, only he didn't tell his wife what I told you.

OTTO: Where'd you meet him.

MARTHA: At work. I thought, if I'm really going to do this, I'm going to need help, or I'll go back for sure, and I was determined not to. So I made friends with him.

OTTO: You never used to talk like that.

MARTHA: That was then, now is now. Ah, yes. (*Looks at him*) If somebody spits on you, you can't do much about it, Otto. But they only get one chance.

OTTO: You bitch.

MARTHA *looks at him.*

Scene 5
Myself

OTTO *in the kitchen, evening.* HE *is reading.*

OTTO (*To himself*): If there was some way I could know that you could still love me, Martha . . . if there was some way you could know the way I really am, then I could at least give it a try. Well, but, what *are* you? Like for instance when I try to sit down and try to do some reading I get all confused. I want to read because I'm lonely, right, and I know I'm not going to get anything straight, OK, unless I try to, like, read more, but the longer I read the more confused I get. How people can spend years at universities, study foreign languages. . . . Are you coming back? No.

OTTO *goes to the door, stands uncertain, looks out the peephole, opens the door quickly. Pause. There's nobody there.* HE *closes the door again.*

Just go to bed, now, like a good boy.

Scene 6
Who Is Who?*

Sunday afternoon. OTTO *has put the living room to rights.* HE *sits there with* LUDWIG. THEY're *drinking coffee and schnaps.*

OTTO: Glad you could find your way over here for once.
LUDWIG: Well, I said I'd come.
OTTO: Unexpected pleasure. Cheers.
LUDWIG: Cheers.

THEY *drink. Pause.*

OTTO: You still planning on being a bricklayer?
LUDWIG: Yes, Poppa.
OTTO: You have any idea what that means, a lifetime of that?
LUDWIG: Work.
OTTO (*Looking at him*): I sure would rather have seen you at the bank.
LUDWIG: Bricklayers make more than bank messengers.
OTTO: But when you're a workman, you're *nothing*. Get filthy, morning to night. You go into a tavern, the barmaid can tell just by looking at your hands, this guy don't amount to much.
LUDWIG: But you're a worker, Poppa. You didn't even go to trade school.
OTTO: So much the worse for me. You remember what you said: better dead than like me?

LUDWIG *nods. Pause.*

OTTO (*Continued*): Well, why do you think you said that?
LUDWIG: I didn't mean it.
OTTO: Because I'm nobody. I'm nothing to look up to.

Short pause.

LUDWIG: But . . . you don't want to be any different than you are, do you?
OTTO: I would have jumped right out of my skin and run away long ago if there was any way I could. (*Pause*) I'm not making excuses. I feel like I'm standing in a hole, and I want to climb out to where it's light, about thirty feet over my head. But there's nothing to get a grip on, it's all slick. (*Laughs*) When I've had a little too much to drink I feel like taking a razor-blade and cutting myself open top to bottom, and it's as if somebody else would come climbing out of my skin, somebody who I've been all along only he's had no way to get out.

*[NOTE: Scene title in English in original.]

LUDWIG: Like the frog-prince.

OTTO: Are you making fun of your father?

LUDWIG: No.

OTTO: It doesn't matter. I just wish you didn't have to go through that. A man needs something he can recognize himself by, something to be proud of. (*Pause*) The Average Man.

LUDWIG [(*Nervously joking*)]: You're not average, Poppa; you're smaller than average.

OTTO [(*Taking the remark seriously*)]: Maybe 'cause I didn't grow to where I was supposed to.

LUDWIG: What's that supposed to mean?

OTTO: If all you are's a bricklayer, Ludi, I wish you the very best, but you're going to find out you're no different from me and you'll remember what I said. Sometime you're going to look around and see just what a bricklayer amounts to in this world, and that's nothing, and that there are so many other things in the world! (*Nods*) And then you're going to be exactly like I am now, I guarantee you.

LUDWIG: No I won't.

OTTO *smiles*.

LUDWIG (*Continued*): Poppa, I don't just want to be a bricklayer, I want to be a human being.

Pause.

OTTO: Maybe so.

Pause.

LUDWIG: What's holding you back from being who you want to be, if you're not satisfied the way things are?

OTTO: Dreams.

LUDWIG: Right. Poor Poppa.

OTTO: You know about that, do you? About having conversations with yourself?

LUDWIG: No.

OTTO: I do. I think things up that way. (*Laughs*)

LUDWIG: Like, you pretend you're rich?

OTTO: Not so much rich as recognized . . . successful.

LUDWIG: But if you had your weight in gold . . .

OTTO (*Laughs*): Like the Aga Khan . . .

LUDWIG: . . . you'd still be the same person.

OTTO: But money makes a difference!

LUDWIG *looks at his father.*

OTTO (*Continued*): You know, I often thought that I'd trade all the years I got
    left for just one, if . . .
LUDWIG: What would you do?
OTTO: God . . . just to be four or five inches taller, and handsome, have all the
    women checking me out, and if I liked one all I'd have to do is smile at her
    and off she'd go with me, love me; and lots of friends, because I'm rich and
    throw my money around, take trips around the world and if anyone wants
    to come along, they're welcome; no grief, no loneliness, no trouble—just
    freedom.
LUDWIG: And what happens when the year's over?
OTTO: It'd be a long year. (*Short pause*) I went to a whore a while back. I
    shouldn't tell you something like that, but now it doesn't matter.
LUDWIG: That's disgusting.
OTTO (*Laughs*): Your momma doesn't want me anymore. A person's got to look
    out for himself. She's got herself another man, your mother has.
LUDWIG: What if you went to see her?
OTTO: She boots me out.
LUDWIG: Have you been there already?
OTTO: Yeah. Before I lost my nerve . . .
LUDWIG: How come?
OTTO: 'Cause he's always there.

Pause.

LUDWIG: I got to go now.

OTTO *looks at him.* LUDWIG *stands up.*

OTTO: You can stay ten more minutes.

Scene 7
Farewell

In MARTHA's *room. After sex,* OTTO *and* MARTHA *both in bed.* THEY *talk very
softly.*

OTTO: You got two men now. (*Short pause*) But I don't have two women.
MARTHA: Find yourself another.
OTTO: None of 'em'll have me except you.
MARTHA: Likely story.
OTTO: Cross my heart.

MARTHA: They don't know what's good for them.

OTTO: I'm stuck with you. 'S awful.

MARTHA: Idiot.

Pause.

OTTO: Does he know that I come around here?

MARTHA: Of course, I told him.

OTTO: What'd he say?

MARTHA: What could he say, he's married too, I already told you that.

Pause.

OTTO: How does he do it?

MARTHA: Do what?

OTTO: From behind, or . . .

MARTHA: Don't talk that way, Otto.

OTTO: Like me, or sophisticated?

MARTHA: Stop it.

OTTO: Like me?

MARTHA: *Yes.*

OTTO: Bitch.

MARTHA: What?

OTTO: Bitch.

Pause.

MARTHA: You haven't changed the least little bit.

OTTO: You protected me; now I'm naked.

MARTHA: Unfortunately.

OTTO: And now it's too late.

MARTHA: Let's talk about something else. How's everything at the plant?

OTTO: Bad, just like always.

MARTHA: You always look at the dark side of everything.

OTTO: What I'd really like is to crawl right up inside you and never come out. Like a baby, you know?

MARTHA *laughs.*

OTTO (*Continued*): You just pull me in right in there and I'm gone.

MARTHA *laughs.*

OTTO (*Continued*): So how's it been with you?

MARTHA: Next month I get transferred to another department.

OTTO: Not a brain in her head. That's not the kind of thing I mean!

MARTHA: Well, it's important to me!

OTTO: You never feel like you want to come back home?

MARTHA: Of course I do, sometimes.

OTTO: I need you.

MARTHA: Oh, nonsense. You're a tidy man and don't need much picking up after. And Ludi, toward the end he was like a little mouse, he would have washed his own underwear if I'd've let him. But when nobody's at home, housework is stupid.

OTTO: You've got a bad conscience, haven't you, woman?

MARTHA: Wouldn't that just suit you. There used to be whole mornings when I sat down and howled like a barnyard dog. Not *about* anything; there wasn't anything to cry about; but just the same I'd finish the housework, sit down at the kitchen table and wait for the tears to come: can you understand that? (*Laughs*) It'd really give them something to talk about at the store if I sat down and started bawling. But I don't need to anymore, because I have a living to earn.

OTTO: There isn't any sweetness left in you. You talk like a man.

MARTHA: Then find yourself a woman to talk to.

OTTO: Don't you have any respect for me anymore? No, because the other one, he's better than me, isn't he?

MARTHA: If you go on talking like that, Otto, I promise you this is the last time you'll ever lie in my bed.

OTTO *laughs. Pause.*

OTTO: Suppose I changed so much you'd never know me?

MARTHA *looks at him.*

OTTO (*Continued*): You'd like that, wouldn't you?

MARTHA: I'm getting up now.

SHE *does.* OTTO *watches her.*

Scene 8
Man

OTTO *alone in the kitchen, late at night.* HE *has had too much to drink, looks sloppy besides.* HE *has a book in one hand, his finger marking his place.*

OTTO (*To himself*): I have this longing, Martha. I see myself from a long way off.

My skin is tanned, I'm doing heavy work and I'm sweating. Suddenly you come running, you're looking for me. When you see me you come up to me, you want to say something. Then you suddenly jump back like you're frightened. My eyes are calm, I got a handsome face, not stupid or afraid. But it's me, all right.

When OTTO *stops talking, his expression is strange and vacant.* HE *pages through the book a little. Then* HE *opens his trousers and starts to masturbate, weakly and without pleasure. After a little while tears begin to run down his face.* HE *cries.*

Scene 9
The End

In MARTHA's *rooming-house room [a different one].* MARTHA *and* LUDWIG *are hugging each other.*

MARTHA: Did your poppa send you?

LUDWIG *shakes his head "No."*

MARTHA (*Continued*): I haven't seen you for so long.
LUDWIG: Because you went underground.
MARTHA (*Laughs*): I had to move, your father wouldn't leave me alone for five minutes.
LUDWIG: Don't you ever go home?

MARTHA *shakes her head "No."*

LUDWIG (*Continued*): Me either. (*Pause.* HE *looks around*)
MARTHA: It's not the kind of life you dream about, is it? But an old lady like me . . .
LUDWIG: Who says you're an old lady?
MARTHA: The employment office, that's who: an old lady with no training and no experience. If the department store hadn't taken me on in the shoe department . . .

LUDWIG *laughs.*

MARTHA (*Continued*): All day long I sell house slippers, can you imagine? I have my own table that I'm responsible for. They don't let me near the cash register yet. But that'll come when I've shown I can do the work. (*Pause*) Sometimes I feel like dropping everything and just going home.
LUDWIG: If you did I'd go too.

MARTHA (*Nods*): When I'm at the end of my strength because I don't seem able to do something or other. (*Laughs*) It's not as if it's hard work. All I have is my one table to stand behind, fuss with the merchandise so it looks tidy; "salesworthy" the manager says. When somebody asks me something I answer them, when they buy something I wrap it and take it to the cashier. If I sell a lot I go to the basement and bring up more. Once a month they give me new styles . . . (SHE *starts to cry*)

LUDWIG: Go home, Momma.

MARTHA: People like me should stay where they're put. I didn't realize that. Sometimes I stand there and just shake from head to foot. (*Pause*) I'm not used to it. That's what it is. It ought to be so simple. Not even sizes are a problem, not with house slippers; half a size bigger than your street shoe, that's all. (*Smiles*) And in the evening I sit here as if I've been running a marathon all day. (*Pause*) And then your father comes and wants to argue for hours when I'm dead tired and have other things to think about. Not now, because he doesn't have my new address yet. (*Smiles*) And if you give it to him, you'll be sorry, young man. . . .

LUDWIG *shakes his head "I won't."*

MARTHA (*Continued*): I even told him I have another beau, just so he'd leave me in peace. (*Smiles*)

LUDWIG: Is it true?

MARTHA: Don't be silly, you think I'd get involved again so fast?

LUDWIG *laughs, relieved.*

MARTHA (*Continued*): And what about you, are you satisfied?

LUDWIG: Better than before, anyhow.

MARTHA *smiles, nods.*

LUDWIG (*Continued*): Didn't you ever love Poppa?

MARTHA: Oh, honey, what does that mean? I put up with him, those last few years. That's perfectly normal.

LUDWIG: But not love.

MARTHA: Who knows. . . . Let's talk about something else. (*Laughs*) You know I can't stand to look at a pair of slippers? Not even the pair I brought from home and . . .

LUDWIG: And didn't steal from the store? (*Laughs*)

MARTHA: Idiot. (*Pause*) If everything goes right, I'm supposed to be transferred to another department, that's what they promised me. To housewares. That's what I'm hoping for, because I think I'll feel better where things are more interesting.

LUDWIG: My work is interesting already.

MARTHA: Because you're learning something. That's the difference. (*Pause.* SHE *wipes away the tears of earlier*)

LUDWIG: Don't, Momma . . .

MARTHA (*Nods*): I won't. Sorry to be so mushy. (*Pause*) Just yesterday I went to the movies. The first time. And do you know what happened? After the show, while I was looking at the pictures in the lobby, a man my own age came up to me and asked me if I'd like a bite to eat! (*Smiles*) Of course I didn't say a word and walked right away . . .

LUDWIG: Good thing you did.

MARTHA: He was very nice-looking.

LUDWIG: Let's move in together.

MARTHA *smiles.*

LUDWIG (*Continued*): I can't stay where I am now. The company's supposed to keep it for foreign workers, and you got to be eighteen for them to make an exception.

MARTHA: You've got courage, that's a good thing.

LUDWIG: Hold out your hand.

MARTHA *does.* LUDWIG *squeezes it hard.*

MARTHA: Ow!

LUDWIG (*Laughs*): That's right. (*Pause*) Either we move in together or I give your new address to Poppa. (*Laughs*)

MARTHA: Blackmailer. (*Pause*) Maybe in a few more months, when we've all found out how to stand on our own feet. I can't bother myself about you right now, Ludi. I have to think about myself first, and I'm not used to that.

LUDWIG: What about Poppa?

MARTHA (*Shrugs her shoulders, calmly*): He has to do the same.

LUDWIG: What?

MARTHA: Just the same as us. He has to learn.

END OF PLAY

Buck
Ronald Ribman

About Ronald Ribman

Ronald Ribman is a native New Yorker and was educated at the University of Pittsburgh, where he received a Ph.D. in English literature. He is the author of *Cold Storage*, winner of the 1976–77 Hull-Warriner Award of the Dramatists Guild, and the Obie-Award–winning *Journey of the Fifth Horse*, which starred Dustin Hoffman. In addition to *Buck*, these and three other plays, *Harry, Noon and Night*, *The Ceremony of Innocence* and *Fingernails Blue as Flowers*, were initially presented at The American Place Theatre. Ribman is also the author of *Passing Through from Exotic Places*, produced at the Sheridan Square Playhouse, *A Break in the Skin*, staged by Yale Repertory Theatre, and *The Poison Tree*, produced on Broadway at the Ambassador Theatre during the 1976 season.

Avon Books published *Five Plays by Ronald Ribman* in 1978. *Journey of the Fifth Horse* and *The Ceremony of Innocence* have been seen on PBS, and *Ceremony* was subsequently presented by Britain's Granada Television. A Canadian production of *Cold Storage* has been shown on cable's Entertainment Channel. In 1967 Ribman's teleplay *The Final War of Olly Winter* was produced by Fred Coe for CBS, receiving five Emmy nominations, including Best Drama. Ribman has been a fellow of the Rockefeller Foundation, the Guggenheim Foundation and the National Endowment for the Arts. In 1975 he received a Rockefeller Foundation award "in recognition of his sustained contribution to American theatre."

Production History

Buck was nominated for TCG's *Plays in Process* script circulation series by Wynn Handman, director of The American Place Theatre in New York City, which coproduced the play with Playwrights Horizons. It was presented at American Place from February 24 through March 13, 1983.

Elinor Renfield directed. The set was designed by John Arnone, lighting by Frances Aronson, costumes by David C. Woolard and sound by Paul Garrity. The cast was as follows:

Buck Halloran . . . . .Alan Rosenberg
Charlie Corvanni . . . . .Robert Silver
Fred Milly . . . . .Morgan Freeman
Professor Pipe-in-the-Mouth (Frank) .Jack Davidson
Mr. Lollipop. . . . . .Bernie Passeltiner
Mr. Hawaiian Shirt. . . . . .Ted Sod
Joy (Shirley) . . . . .Priscilla Lopez
Salesman . . . . .Michael Lipton
Mr. Heegan . . . . .Richard Leighton
Vendor . . . . .Jimmy Smits
Woman with Turban . . . . .Madeleine le Roux
Milton Berman . . . . .Bernie Passeltiner
Mr. Goglas. . . . . .Ted Sod
Vincente . . . . .Jimmy Smits
Madame . . . . .Madeleine le Roux
Mr. Nathan. . . . . .Joseph Leon
Stagehands . . . . .Mitchell Gossett, Nick Iacovino, Charles Kindl,
Michael Linden, Kenneth Lodge, Richard Mandel,
Michael O'Boyll, Jason O'Malley, David Sennett

Characters

BUCK HALLORAN

CHARLIE CORVANNI

FRED MILLY

PROFESSOR PIPE-IN-THE-MOUTH/FRANK

MR. LOLLIPOP

MR. HAWAIIAN SHIRT

JOY BONNARD/SHIRLEY

SALESMAN

MR. HEEGAN

VENDOR

WOMAN WITH TURBAN

MILTON BERMAN/DERELICT

MR. GOGLAS/RAMON LUIS CARPIO DE LA BARCA

VINCENTE/A YOUNG ACTOR

MADAM/A MIDDLE-AGED ACTRESS

MR. NATHAN

STAGEHANDS (non-speaking)

Time

The present.

Place

The Play

Buck

ACT ONE

Scene 1

A cable television studio. The studio is in the cavernous, windowless basement of an old building. Beyond Stage Left and Stage Right is a darkness, the end of which cannot be seen. Upstage Left, several steps above the basement floor, is a large freight elevator. Downstage Left on the basement floor is a large worktable with several chairs behind it. The worktable is littered with papers, ashtrays, pens, pencils, a Silex of coffee, cups, an open box of jelly donuts and a phone. Nearby can be seen a portable television camera resting on a tripod, and some television monitoring equipment on a stand. Upstage Right, near the rear wall of the basement, is a movable platform used as a production set. The set, at the moment, is that of a rather rundown-looking apartment, the apartment suggested mostly by the few pieces of furniture in it: a small sofa; an end table with a half-finished sweater lying on top of it, knitting needles poking through; a linen-shaded floor lamp; a small liquor cabinet; a phony wooden fireplace. Because the platform has been turned around to face the Upstage wall and is unlit, nothing can be seen of the apartment except the outside scrim walls. A number of television cables, feeding out of a Downstage Right outlet, run across the entire rim of the stage.

A cone of light illuminates BUCK HALLORAN *as* HE *sits behind the worktable, staring blankly forward.* BUCK *is a man in his middle to late 30s; his eyes are dark and tired. As the cone of light expands to reveal another man,* CHARLIE COR-

VANNI, *seated behind the table,* BUCK *shuts his eyes, pressing the tips of his fingers against them.* CHARLIE, *close in age to* BUCK, *is intently interested, at the moment, in selecting a good jelly donut for himself. The one he has just bitten into has brought a sour expression to his face. He looks at the donut, sticks his tongue out in disgust, and then putting the donut aside, reaches into the box for a new one. The new one is as much a loser as the first, as far as* CHARLIE *is concerned.* CHARLIE, *in despair, lowers the second donut to the table. The cone of light continues to expand, illuminating the entire Stage Left side of the basement to the elevator.*

CHARLIE: What kind of jelly donut did you get, Buck?

BUCK: I got a blueberry one, Charlie.

CHARLIE: Boy, they're the best ones, aren't they? They got the most powdered sugar on them and everything.

BUCK: That's right, Charlie.

CHARLIE: I mean even on the inside they're the best because they got whole pieces of berries, while the others just got jam or something.

BUCK: You better believe it, Charlie.

CHARLIE: Boy, this one I'm eating now tastes like it was filled with mushrooms or something.

BUCK, *his eyes still closed, has begun massaging his temples with his fingertips.*

CHARLIE (*Continued*): I don't know what it is with me. I always reach for the ones with the most powdered sugar on them because I know the ones with the most powdered sugar on them are the blueberry ones, but I always end up with the ones that taste like mushroom. (*Grabs another donut out of the box, bites into it, makes a sour face, and puts it down*) You always get the best. (*Pause*) I guess all I can do is keep trying, huh, Buck?

BUCK: That's right, Charlie. All you can do is keep trying.

Suddenly the elevator snaps into life with a shrill whine, its descent marked by a pulsing red lightbulb above the elevator door. BUCK's *eyes pop open.* CHARLIE *jumps to his feet, in his fright knocking over a stack of paper coffee cups.* HE *scrambles about the floor, trying to collect them before whoever it is in the elevator arrives.*

CHARLIE: Oh, shit . . . oh, shit.

The elevator door suddenly opens, an almost blinding white light pouring out. The object of their trepidation, FRED MILLY, *stands motionless in the elevator for a few moments.* MILLY *is a large black man with an awesome-looking club foot.* HE *is impeccably dressed in an expensive business suit, his fingers displaying several gold and diamond rings.* MILLY *enjoys his joviality and his smile, though it is the all too evident unnerving smile of a cobra.*

MILLY: How you boys doing?

CHARLIE (*As eager to please as a fawning dog*): Great, Mr. Milly. Just great. Can I get you a cup of coffee?

As MILLY *steps forward, the elevator door snaps shut behind him.*

MILLY: I like what you do with your camera, Charlie. You do nice work.

CHARLIE: Thanks a lot, Mr. Milly. I appreciate that coming from you.

MILLY (*Beginning his awkward clubfooted descent down the three steps into the basement*): But you never call me Fred. I tell you to call me Fred, but you never call me Fred.

CHARLIE: Can I get you a cup of coffee, Fred?

MILLY: Sure. You get me a black cup of coffee. That's what I like . . . just black.

MILLY *laughs loudly at his own private joke as* CHARLIE *pours him a cup of coffee.*

BUCK: I'll have these cost figures for you in a second, Fred.

MILLY: How come you don't call me Mr. Milly?

BUCK: Whatever you say, Mr. Milly.

MILLY: Sure. That's good. I like that, too. You call me Mr. Milly. Charlie calls me Fred. Everybody calls me something different.

MILLY *laughs loudly again as* CHARLIE *comes forward, the coffee in his outstretched hand.*

MILLY (*Continued*): How's your two little girls, Charlie?

CHARLIE: They ain't so little anymore, Fred. They're in Junior High School.

CHARLIE *continues to hold the cup of coffee out to* MILLY, *who makes no movement to take it.*

MILLY: Junior High School, is that a fact?

CHARLIE: Yes, sir, that's right.

MILLY: Well, that's wonderful, Charlie. Just wonderful. All those wonderful Junior High School dances and basketball games to go to. Wonderful time in a young girl's life . . . especially if she's pretty. Your girls pretty, Charlie?

CHARLIE (*Lowering his arm*): They do okay in that department, Fred.

MILLY *finally holds out his hand to take the coffee, forcing* CHARLIE *to hold the cup out again.*

MILLY: I bet they do.

MILLY *laughs again, nudging* CHARLIE, *as if the two of them were sharing some kind of private dirty joke.* CHARLIE *nervously joins in the laughter.*

MILLY (*Continued*): Pretty girls never have any trouble getting themselves all the dates they want, do they, Charlie? Phones ringing all the time, boys with hot pants sitting around outside in their cars, honking their horns, jiggling their hands around in their pockets, waiting to take them to all those wonderful Junior High School dances and basketball games. Show me a picture of them, Charlie.

CHARLIE, *uncertain, hesitates for a moment, and then, slightly turning away from* MILLY, *reaches into his back pocket for his wallet.*

MILLY (*Continued*): It's absolutely incredible what people try to hide away in their wallets and purses: old photos, torn ticket stubs, little pieces of lint and cellophane, tinfoil prophylactics waiting so long to get used they make ringworms in the leather.

MILLY *takes the photo* CHARLIE *has produced and looks at it.*

MILLY (*Continued*): Pretty, Charlie, pretty. (*Holding the picture up and rhapsodizing into a few lines of Sapphic verse*)
"Like the sweet apple ripening atop the topmost bough,
Atop the topmost limb, which the pluckers forgot—
Forgot it not, nay, but got it not!
For none could get it till now."
(*Handing* CHARLIE *back his photo*) Don't let the boys get them too soon, Charlie.

CHARLIE *puts the photo away and sits down at the worktable.*

MILLY (*Continued*): The boys always want to pluck our sweet apples too soon.
CHARLIE: Don't worry, Fred, I can always hear a plucker coming a mile away.

For a moment a small smile plays on MILLY's *face and then* HE *lifts up his club foot and crashes it down on the table.*

MILLY: Now I remember when I was back in Junior High School. Tried out for the baseball team, but I couldn't make it out of the locker room in time. Tried out for the football team, but I couldn't get my foot through the leggings in time. Tried out for the track team, but I accidently crushed another runner's foot in the relay. I guess the only thing I got to on time was the graduation prom. That was a wonderful night, so wonderful. Dancing and dancing under the Alabama stars, whirling down the white colonnades with all those pretty Alabama girls in their perfumed corsages and crinoline dresses, sneaking in a little kiss from their pouty little red mouths, crushing their starchy skirts into my genitals till they exploded like jellied gasoline. (*Laughing heartily at his memories*)

CHARLIE: Boy, you sure can't buy memories like that. (*Pause*) Why don't you sit down, Fred? Take a load off your foot.

The smile on MILLY's *face drains away as* HE *slowly draws his club foot off the table. Opening a folder lying on the table in front of* CHARLIE, MILLY *suddenly jabs his finger into the middle of one of the pages.*

MILLY: What's this thing for twenty-four dollars?

CHARLIE: A vibrator I had to buy for the show.

MILLY: Twenty-four dollars?

CHARLIE: That's what it cost.

MILLY: Twenty-four dollars?

CHARLIE: We needed a good sound to pick up on the audio equipment!

MILLY (*Picking up a pencil and applying greater and greater pressure against it as his voice rises in intensity*): Twenty-four dollars!

CHARLIE (*Turning to* BUCK *for help*): Isn't that right, Buck? We needed a good sound to pick up on the audio equipment?

BUCK: Twenty-four dollars!

CHARLIE: We followed the police reports! It was the same vibrator the girl was using when she was killed! Isn't that right, Buck? Buck!

MILLY: Twenty-four dollars! Twenty-four dollars!

The pencil snaps in MILLY's *hand as* CHARLIE *cracks under the strain and blurts out his confession.*

CHARLIE: Seventeen dollars! I only paid seventeen dollars, Fred.

MILLY: Why don't you call me Mr. Milly, Charlie? (*Becoming gently paternalistic*) Oh, Charlie, what a world we live in. Greed, avarice, corruption, nobody satisfied with what they got, always wanting more. If I could give you one word of advice, one word that would sum up everything I've learned about life, it would be this—be sincere. (*Placing his club foot on top of* CHARLIE's *toes and gradually increasing the pressure*) How does that song go? "I'd like to teach the world to sing in perfect harmony. I'd like to buy the world a Coke and keep it company. That's the real thing."

While MILLY's *foot presses down on* CHARLIE's *toes in time to the song,* CHARLIE *does everything* HE *can to withstand the crushing pain, including a kind of silent singalong with* MILLY.

MILLY (*Continued*): Well, Charlie, that's what sincerity is—the real thing.

CHARLIE: I've been as sincere with you as you've been with me, Fred! (*The attempt to continue calling* MILLY *by his first name fails as the pain becomes unbearable.* HE *screams out in agony*) Mr. Milly! Mr. Milly!

MILLY (*Lifting his club foot from* CHARLIE's *toes in total victory, and moving over to* BUCK): And you, Buck? Have you been as sincere with me as I've been with you?

BUCK: Sure, Mr. Milly.

MILLY: Just call me Fred, Buck. (*Sitting down next to* BUCK) I'm glad because I want you to know I never miss a chance telling the big boys upstairs what a hell of a job you're doing down here with your murder reenactments, and how I think you're ready to move up to major corporate responsibility. You believe me, Buck? You believe I'm doing these things for you?

BUCK: Sure, Fred.

MILLY: That's fine, Buck. Only I can't push you too hard. I push you too hard there's a chance they may cool off on you. So what I'm doing now, Buck, is working on them one at a time. I'm casting the old fishing plug out for Mr. Nathan right now. It may take a couple of months, maybe even a year, but once he snaps at your bait and I get the hook set deep in his mouth, I can reel him in and start trolling for Mr. Jacobs and Mr. Stein. Once we gaff 'em good, Buck, we can start dragging your meat in front of the big one— Mr. St. George. We get his salivary glands going for you, Buck, we get him thrashing and drooling in the water over your chitterlings, there ain't nothing gonna keep you outta that board room.

BUCK: Sure, Fred.

MILLY: Unless of course they was to get it in their head you've been dragging your feet on the Joy Bonnard murder reenactment . . . get it in their head you got problems taping the killing of that department store perfume counter whore by the college professor. . . . Why then who knows what could happen . . . they get something like that in their head.

BUCK: Sure, Fred.

MILLY (*Sliding back his chair and standing up*): Well, I gotta get on my horse. I can't tell you how much your faith in me means, Buck, and how much I look forward to these little visits with you in the basement.

As MILLY *heads toward the elevator,* BUCK *and* CHARLIE *begin visibly breathing with relief.* CHARLIE *has just stuffed a new jelly donut in his mouth as* MILLY *pauses for a moment on the steps.*

MILLY (*Continued*): Oh, by the way . . .

The donut literally drops out of CHARLIE's *mouth as both* HE *and* BUCK *turn simultaneously to look at* MILLY.

MILLY (*Continued*): I guess you heard about the funny thing that happened to Mr. Nathan when he came to work this morning. (HE *presses the elevator button and the door opens, flooding everything in front of it with its harsh white light*) It seems he saw an old crone of a woman setting up an applecart in the lobby. It threw him into a panic. He told Mr. Jacobs, and Mr. Jacobs told Mr. Stein, and Mr. Stein told Mr. St. George. The rumor now is that if she's still there tomorrow her applecart may trigger a depression in the entire industry. We may have to expect some layoffs from the bottom of the building up. (*Stepping into the elevator*) Well, trust me, Buck. Trust me. Nobody's in here more solid than you are.

MILLY *presses the button to shut the elevator door. The last sound we hear before the door shuts and the elevator begins its noisy ascent is* MILLY's *final laugh.* MILLY *has no sooner exited than the phone on the worktable begins to ring. It rings and rings,* BOTH MEN *obviously afraid to pick it up.* BUCK *finally reaches for it.*

BUCK: News reenactments. Buck Halloran speaking. (*Pause*) Good morning, Mr. Nathan. How are you this . . .

BUCK *never has a chance to finish, and the artificial smile* HE *has glued to his face disintegrates in an instant. When* HE *speaks now, his voice is a blur of fear. The stage lights begin contracting, until by the end of his conversation* BUCK *is left standing alone in a pool of light.*

BUCK (*Continued*): I never said anything like that to Mr. Milly, so I don't know why Mr. Milly would say anything like that to you, or how Mr. Milly could be standing in your office on the top floor right now when the elevator door just shut on Mr. Milly and the elevator is still rising! (*Pause*) I never never never said anything about being unhappy with my job and feeling that the expense of my divorce gave me the right to mark up the price of a vibrator to supplement my income. (*Pause*) I am not accusing Mr. Milly of being insincere! I realize his level of sincerity is higher than my own since he occupies a higher position of trust than I do, but I know that I am being sincere when I tell you that I am happy happy happy with my job and I would never do anything to jeopardize it by dragging my feet on the Joy Bonnard murder reenactment, or phonying up the expense sheet on the vibrator! (*Caller has hung up*) Mr. Nathan? (*Screaming into the phone*) Mr. Nathan!

BUCK *slams the phone down, and for a moment stands there panicked and struggling to catch his breath. The lights on the Upstage production set begin to come up, allowing us to see through the scrim walls into the apartment. The light comes from three sources: the yellow bulb of the floor lamp, the red glow of the phony logs "burning" in the phony fireplace, and a pair of sconces set up over the mantle. There are three men and a young woman (*JOY BONNARD*) in the apartment. The youngest man (*MR. HAWAIIAN SHIRT*), his hair slick and greasy, wears his loud shirt over his pants; the middle-aged man (*PROFESSOR PIPE-IN-THE-MOUTH/ FRANK*), distinguished-looking as* HE *sucks on his pipe, is dressed only in his briefs; the old man (*MR. LOLLIPOP*), sucking a lollipop, is in an undershirt, his baggy* *pants held up by suspenders. As* JOY, *dressed in a flowing white dressing gown, moves among them, the* MEN *reach out, grabbing at her, assaulting her. At the first sound,* BUCK *has whirled around to face the nightmarish events taking place in the apartment behind the scrim.*

PROFESSOR PIPE-IN-THE-MOUTH/FRANK: Come on over here, you witless bimbo! I want you to lie down next to me on the couch! I want you to pretend you've got something to offer a man besides your body!

MR. LOLLIPOP: Could we pretend we're sixteen years old and we live in a little house in the forest and the snow is coming down?

MR. HAWAIIAN SHIRT: Lick me all over! I wanna go around the world! Get off your goddam high horse, Miss Joy Bonnard, and gimme what I want!

MR. LOLLIPOP: I want you to put on a garter belt and a pair of black stockings! That's the only thing that gets me up anymore!

PROFESSOR PIPE-IN-THE-MOUTH/FRANK: You know what it's like for me facing four hundred morons in a lecture hall and trying to teach them something about Kierkegaard? Listen to me! They're eating me alive! They're sucking out my marrow and eating me alive!

MR. LOLLIPOP: I want to pretend with you! Joy? Joy!

MR. HAWAIIAN SHIRT: I want you to get down on the floor! I want you to spread your legs because I'm gonna do whatever I wanna do with you!

PROFESSOR PIPE-IN-THE-MOUTH/FRANK: You dumb whore! You moronic slut! You tell me what the salesgirl behind the department store perfume counter thinks anybody would be interested in hearing her talk about!

The scrim door to the apartment swings open and JOY *stands in the doorway confronting* BUCK. *There is a weariness to her face as* SHE *stares at him, as if* HE *might be just another exploiter.* HE *takes several steps towards her and then stops as the hands of the* MEN *behind her wind about her face and body like the slow-moving tentacles of an octopus.* BUCK *whirls forward, pressing the fingers of his hands against his skull as behind him* JOY *is slowly drawn back into the apartment. Lights dim and out.*

Scene 2

A department store. Sound of store chimes in the dark followed by a soft sensual female VOICE *over the loudspeaker.*

VOICE: Discover the fragrance of summer. Come meet Joy and sample the woodland scents of her summer collection: the crush of sweet grass on the forest floor, violets and sweet musk roses, woodbine and eglantine. Echoes of a time when all the world was young, and gentle knights with sword and lance took up the sacred quest to slay the dragon and right the wrong. Come to Joy now and let her cast your fragrance future with her new Lady Guinevere collection. With every purchase you'll receive a lovely lead crystal spray dispenser for just twelve fifty. It's happening now at La Parfumerie. Main floor. Fifth Avenue exit.

The lights come up first on the well-dressed SALESMAN *standing behind his counter in the sporting goods department. The light emanating up from the counter casts an odd, almost devilish, shine on the* SALESMAN's *smiling face. The counter light now fades away as the general lighting in the department store comes up.* BUCK *stands some yards away from the* SALESMAN. BUCK *has a hunting arrow in his hand, and stares down at it, totally absorbed. The* SALESMAN *watches him for some moments before speaking.*

SALESMAN: If you're going to hunt large game, you couldn't pick a better arrow.

BUCK (*Almost as if coming out of a trance*): I . . . I was on my way to the perfume counter.

SALESMAN: The perfume counter's over there. (*Gesturing Stage Left*) You've been standing here with that arrow for quite some time.

BUCK: Have I? I was thinking about something. There was a girl who worked at the perfume counter . . . Joy Bonnard. Did you know her?

SALESMAN: Afraid not.

BUCK: She got murdered a while back. (*Looking down at the arrow again*)

SALESMAN: It *is* a beautiful instrument, isn't it?

BUCK: Yes.

SALESMAN (*Walking over to* BUCK): Perfectly balanced, true in flight . . . one of the last few really beautiful things left in this world a man can rely on.

BUCK: It's not for target work, is it?

SALESMAN: No. It's for killing . . . just killing.

BUCK: Yes. You can see that just by looking at it. Does it have a name . . . if you were to ask for it . . . by name?

SALESMAN: It's a Rumsford razor point on a twenty-six–inch flexible aluminum shaft. It features a double blood groove and moisture-resistant New England turkey fletching.

BUCK: Fletching?

SALESMAN: Feathers.

BUCK: You could really kill something with this.

SALESMAN: Oh, yes. You could kill just about anything you wanted to with that.

BUCK: Yeah. I would like to kill something.

SALESMAN: Something specific in mind?

BUCK: I don't know. What would you suggest?

SALESMAN: Deer are nice. Wild boar, antelope.

BUCK: Something bigger, stronger.

SALESMAN: Elk, moose?

BUCK: Stronger, furrier. Something that would make a good rug. What's doing in the way of buffalo?

SALESMAN: African?

BUCK: American.

SALESMAN: The American buffalo is on the restricted game list. They're an endangered species, protected by law.

BUCK: Just suppose I found a way to get around all that legalistic crap and wanted to kill one of them. I could do it with this. Right?

SALESMAN: Right.

BUCK: One stick and it's over with. Hit the skull and the eyes pop out. Hit the lung and a thousand legal injunctions collapse in a bag of wind.

SALESMAN: Over the foreleg into the heart. That's actually the best place to stick it for a good kill.

BUCK: That's the kind of information I need.

SALESMAN: Ever hunt before?

BUCK: No. Does it count against me?

SALESMAN: Not if the desire is there.

BUCK: I've wanted to kill something for a long time. How does it actually do it? Sever an artery? And then these little things . . .

SALESMAN: The blood grooves.

BUCK: They would help, too, huh?

SALESMAN: Oh, yes.

BUCK: Sure. They would prevent the blood from clotting. The body would naturally want to clot, protect itself, but they would prevent it from doing that. They would just make sure the blood kept pouring out.

SALESMAN: You have a good instinct for the kill.

BUCK: You know it.

SALESMAN: Men with a good instinct for the kill always make the best hunters.

BUCK: How long does it take to kill something with this?

SALESMAN: A few minutes.

BUCK: From the time I first stick it into the rug, or the time it rolls over on the ground.

SALESMAN: The time it rolls over on the ground.

BUCK: And then what while I'm waiting for it to die? Smoke a cigarette? Stare at the sky? Clean the day's filth from the ends of my fingernails?

SALESMAN: Do whatever you want, or nothing. The hunter's only responsibility is a clean kill.

BUCK: But what do I do if it isn't a clean kill? If the rug doesn't die right away? If it just lies there on the ground writhing in agony, blood gushing out of its side? What do I do then? Cut its throat? Step forward with some penknife, kitchen knife . . .?

SALESMAN: No problem, sir. Our hunting department recommends the five-inch MacFadden dressing knife with bone handle, safety lock, and a high-tempered carbon steel blade.

BUCK (*Growing increasingly anguished*): And if it starts screaming when I slash its neck with the five-inch MacFadden! Bellowing in pain as the blade twists into the windpipe, severing cartilage and arteries, veins ... severing it from air and voice, the ability to breathe and cry, everything that made it what it was, a hundred million years that made it what it was pouring out through flayed skin: blood, serum, mucus, bile ...

SALESMAN: There's no need to go through that mess, sir. Many of our hunters prefer to have their game dressed at any one of a number of recommended butcher shops. I can give you a list of dressers that have served our clientele for many years. Six or a dozen, sir?

BUCK: What?

SALESMAN: Will that be six or a dozen, sir? The arrows are three ninety-eight each, twelve for forty-two dollars. You save the price of almost two arrows if you buy twelve.

BUCK: No. I don't want that many. I was just *looking* at this one.

BUCK *hands the arrow to the* SALESMAN.

SALESMAN: You can't count on getting a perfectly placed shot with one arrow.

BUCK: I was just passing by. I was just thinking.

Backing away from the SALESMAN, BUCK *almost knocks into a floor display consisting of several Cub Scout manikins gathered around a campfire in the forest. A number of toy archery sets are stacked up within the display.*

SALESMAN (*Approaching* BUCK): All right, sir. Just one it is then. Every sport has to have a beginning. I'm sure as soon as you use the Rumsford, you'll be back for more. That's the way it is with so many of our clients. One toe in the water at a time, and then they can't get enough. Will that be cash or charge?

Circling around the display as the SALESMAN *watches him,* BUCK *seems visibly distressed.*

BUCK: I don't have a charge card here, anymore. My wife used to.

SALESMAN: Might your wife be interested in hunting, too? We have a large selection of ...

BUCK: My wife and I are divorced.

SALESMAN: Oh, that's too bad. Were there little ones?

BUCK: I had a little boy. I don't see him very much anymore.

SALESMAN: Oh, that's too bad. Divorce is always hardest on the fathers.

BUCK (*Suddenly picking up one of the toy archery sets*): What's the story on this? This thing's got a price tag on it for four ninety-eight.

SALESMAN: That's right.

BUCK: What's it on sale, or what?

SALESMAN: No, that's the regular price.

BUCK: How can it be the regular price? You're charging me three ninety-eight for one lousy arrow, and this whole outfit here is only a buck more? For a buck more, I get three arrows, a bow, a three-colored target, and an entire Indian headdress with pigeon feathers? That doesn't make any sense.

SALESMAN: Of course it does, sir. This is a real arrow. That's just a toy.

BUCK (*Walking away from the* SALESMAN, *back to the counter*): Keep that arrow. I'm taking this. I'm not paying four dollars for one arrow when I can buy the whole ball of wax for a buck more!

SALESMAN: Look at those little arrows! They're fourteen-inch little arrows with rubber tips! (*Walking back to the counter*) You can't kill anything with them.

BUCK: You'd be surprised what you can do with suction tips. Once one of these babies sticks, it sticks!

SALESMAN: You can't hunt with that!

BUCK: Why? You think the animal's gonna know how much I spent on the equipment?

SALESMAN: But that's not the point, is it, sir? That's really not the point at all.

BUCK: Just give me this one.

SALESMAN (*Staring at* BUCK *for some moments before* HE *speaks*): Five forty with tax.

BUCK (*Putting some bills on the counter*): Keep the change. (*Starts to exit Stage Right, the toy archery set under his arm*)

SALESMAN: The perfume counter's the other way, bwana.

BUCK *changes his direction, backing away from the* SALESMAN, *before turning and hastening Off Stage Left.*

SALESMAN (*Continued; calling after* BUCK): Catch you next time, bwana, when you're ready for the real thing.

The SALESMAN *drops the arrow back into the display case alongside the counter, and then spotting a new customer, leans forward with his hands on the counter and a fresh smile on his face. Lights dim and out. In the dark we hear a pop love ballad from the 1950s being sung. The music segues into the next scene.*

Scene 3

A bar. The bar consists of a counter with a number of stools around it, a blue glass mirror behind the liquor bottles, and, inscribed above the mirror in stained glass letters, the names of the owners, "Boyle and Heegan." Downstage Right is a small table with a couple of chairs.

*Two customers are at the bar: one is a woman in a cheap-looking gaudy dress and a turban (*WOMAN WITH TURBAN*), the other a man with several layers of sweaters and a white apron, a* VENDOR *of some sort. As the bartender,* HEEGAN, *pours* BUCK *a drink at the table, the music fades out.*

HEEGAN: So I says to your Professor Pipe-in-the-Mouth, "No, it ain't July, it's December. Right around New Years. That's when all the jerkos make their move." I tell him about this particular jerko who comes in here to rob the place around Christmas time. The jerko's doing his Christmas shopping, right? Right outta my cash register. Only he ain't even got a real gun. It's a plastic Luger he got outta Woolworth. I see what it is right away, but I don't let on, see? I give him the money and then as he's walking out the door I ease out my thirty-eight Colt Diamondback and I give him three quick ones right in the back. Bam, bam, bam! Enough to kill a water buffalo, right? Only the jerko son-of-a-bitch don't go down. He turns around as nice as you please like someone just tapped him on the shoulder, aims the plastic Luger right at my head and pulls the trigger. Piss, piss, piss—water comin' outta it, right? So I let him have two more in the gut. Pieces of his belt buckle flying up in the air, but he still ain't down.

VENDOR: How about somebody else putting in some change in the jukebox?

HEEGAN (*Ignoring the* VENDOR): He's hopping out the door, bleeding like a stuck pig, but still moving. By the time I catch up with him he's twenty yards down the street, sitting on a garbage can. I'm about to administer the coup de grace when he pitches over. "You understand what I'm gettin' at?," I says to your Professor Pipe-in-the-Mouth. "The thirty-eight ain't worth a shit! It ain't got no stopping power. You're gonna defend yourself, you gotta get something with real knockdown power, something you give them one shot and they're blown away." You wanna see what I'm packing now? (*Starts to open his jacket to expose a gun in a shoulder holster*)

VENDOR: How about somebody else coming up with some change?

HEEGAN: How about shutting your mouth?

VENDOR: You got no call saying that to me. I'm the only one feeding that machine. I just want somebody else . . .

HEEGAN: You wanna feed the machine, feed it! Don't tell anybody else what to do with their money! (*To* BUCK) The less money they got, the bigger their mouth.

VENDOR: I wasn't telling anybody anything!

HEEGAN (*Opening his jacket again*): This is what I'm packing now.

WOMAN WITH TURBAN: I want a Chivas Regal on the rocks.

HEEGAN: We don't serve Chivas Regal here, lady. We serve bar whiskey and beer.

WOMAN WITH TURBAN: How about a frozen daiquiri? You got a frozen daiquiri?

HEEGAN: Do me a favor, lady. When you're finished with your beer, go back uptown to Maxwell's Plum or wherever it is you usually do your drinking.

WOMAN WITH TURBAN: What's the matter? You don't think I'm properly attired for this place? The man on 14th Street who sold me this dress said it was sleazy enough to get me in anywhere.

HEEGAN (*Taking the gun out and showing it to* BUCK): This is what I'm packing now. You know what this is?

WOMAN WITH TURBAN: Your wee-wee.

HEEGAN (*Ignoring the remark*): This is the most powerful handgun in the world. Forty-four caliber magnum. The heaviest load in the world. Five times the juice of the thirty-eight. This baby drops one load they're gonna have to pick up your spine with a vacuum cleaner.

WOMAN WITH TURBAN: When you're finished showing off your wee-wee, you can get me a pina colada.

HEEGAN (*Still ignoring the woman, pulling a bullet out of the chamber to show* BUCK): You see what I've done to this bullet? I've filed it down into a dum-dum. Every last bullet in this gun is a dum-dum.

WOMAN WITH TURBAN: Every last cell in your brain is a dum-dum.

HEEGAN: Listen, lady, why don't you just take a walk outta here? I'm trying to talk to this man. You know who this man is? This man's an important television producer. I'm trying to appraise him of a situation that happened here pertaining to a murder.

WOMAN WITH TURBAN: No shit!

HEEGAN: Look, lady, your beer's on the house. Just finish it up and take a walk outta here.

WOMAN WITH TURBAN: I'm waiting for my chauffeur.

BUCK (*To* HEEGAN): What else can you tell me about the professor?

HEEGAN: Not a hell of a lot more than I told your friend when he was in. He looked like a normal guy, you know, with a business suit. The only thing was he kept talking about some guy named Kierka something, and how he was going to be delivering a lecture on this guy, and the lecture had to be real good or they were going to eat him alive. I mean he was really concerned about that, like they were really going to eat him up.

WOMAN WITH TURBAN: You don't think I have a chauffeur? You imagine anyone using your facilities must be reduced to the same poverty of intellect and circumstances as yourself? Has it ever occurred to you that I may for reasons of my own prefer going around this way? Too much lipstick, too much face powder, a hideous dress of indisputable bad taste!

BUCK: What about the girl? Joy Bonnard.

HEEGAN: Yeah, she was different. She was a real sweetheart. I think she had a kid, but the kid died. You wanna find out about that you can ask them over in the department store across the street. She worked there in the perfume section.

BUCK: Yeah, I know. I already spoke to them. Go on.

HEEGAN: There's not much more I can tell ya. She'd come in three, four times a week, drink a couple of beers by herself, go on home. Always give you a smile on the way in, ask how you were, thank you whenever you brought over a drink. I guess she was kind of special now that I think about it. She kind of lit up the place. You could talk to her and she really listened. I just wish somewhere along the line I had said something to her about how nice she was.

VENDOR (*Flapping his apron up and down like a woman's skirt*): Hey, Heegan, you got a beer on the house for me, too?

HEEGAN (*To* BUCK): I just wish I knew what that pipe-smoking son-of-a-bitch was going to do to her. I woulda blown his fucking head off! Go figure it—a college professor, right? The elite! What the hell you got left when they start doing things like that?

BUCK: She pick up a lot of guys in here?

HEEGAN: Hey, look, she's dead. What's the point in it?

BUCK: I just wanna know.

HEEGAN: Yeah, all right, sometimes. Like with Professor Pipe-in-the-Mouth. He was sitting in here when she came in. He went over, bought her a couple of drinks, and left with her. She was easy that way, I guess.

BUCK: She take money?

HEEGAN: Why? Is that what he said to the police?

BUCK: Yeah. He said she came at him with a knitting needle when he wouldn't pay.

HEEGAN: Yeah, well he's a fucking liar, isn't he?

BUCK: How do you know?

HEEGAN: Because I knew her! You knew her you wouldn't even ask things like that! She was no hooker. She was just a lonely kid who came in here for a few beers, and if she found someone to pass the night with, what the hell's the difference? It's no fun being alone, and I never heard no complaints from anybody who walked outta here with her.

BUCK (*Downing what's left of his drink and tossing some bills on the table as* HE *starts to exit*): Appreciate your help, Mr. Heegan.

HEEGAN: Mr. Halloran?

BUCK *turns to look at him.*

HEEGAN (*Continued*): You ain't gonna fuck her, too, are you?

For a moment HEEGAN *and* BUCK *look at each other, and then* BUCK *turns and exits.* HEEGAN *stands motionless for a few seconds and then turns and angrily points a finger directly Downstage.*

HEEGAN (*Continued*): Hey, you! That ain't no public toilet! You don't drink in here, you don't piss in here! Get out!

Lights dim and out.

Scene 4

The studio. The reenactment production set of JOY BONNARD's *apartment has been brought Downstage and turned around to face the audience.*

In the dark we hear the sound of footsteps coming down a hall, laughter, and then the door to JOY's *apartment opens and the sconce lights over the fireplace mantle come on.* JOY *enters, followed by* PROFESSOR-PIPE-IN-THE-MOUTH/ FRANK. HE *is well dressed in an overcoat and muffler. It has been snowing out and* BOTH *are covered with melting flakes.*

JOY (*Waving her hand around the apartment, her voice mixed with embarrassment and an attempt at lightheartedness*): Well, this is it.

FRANK *watches her move about swiftly, doing a last bit of straightening up: sofa pillows plumped, a dress gathered up, the floor lamp turned on, the phony flame in the phony fireplace set revolving.*

JOY (*Continued*): I'm really sorry the apartment is in such a state. You'll have to excuse it. I wasn't expecting any visitors. (*Going over to him*) Let me take your coat. It's soaked through. (*Helping him off with his coat*) I hate it when it turns sleety that way. It soaks through everything. (*Holding his coat*) I'll hang it up in the bathroom. I'll be right back. Please make yourself at home.

JOY *exits through a beaded archway on the Stage Right side of the reenactment set, the archway presumably leading to her bedroom and bathroom.* FRANK *stares about the room, examining the bric-a-brac and the dust.*

FRANK (*Calling out as* HE *lights his pipe*): How long have you lived here, Joy?

JOY (*Offstage*): Three years. I used to have a much nicer apartment on 23rd Street, but my girlfriend got married and the rent was too much. (*Returning to the room. The dress* JOY *has been wearing under her coat is tight, cheap, and provocative. It matches her manner, now*) What would you like to drink, Frank?

FRANK: Nothing for me. I think I just about had my limit at the bar. I'm feeling kind of woozy.

JOY: Oh, come on, don't be a spoilsport. What'll it be? I've got scotch, wine, brandy . . . whatever you like.

FRANK: I really shouldn't. I've got to deliver a paper tomorrow at the Modern Language Association meeting, and I haven't finished working on it yet.

JOY (*Waving the bottle*): One little drinky?

FRANK: Okay. Just one and then I gotta get going. I really do.

JOY: Sure. Just one. (*Pouring out two drinks and handing one to him*) Well, here's to . . . whatever.

THEY *both take a swallow.* JOY *sits down on the couch and looks at* FRANK *provocatively.*

FRANK (*Uneasy*): I just wanted to make sure you got home safely, Joy. It's not much of a neighborhood out there.

JOY: Why don't you sit down beside me on the couch, Frank?

FRANK: All right.

JOY (*Moving over toward him on the couch*): This is much better, isn't it? (*Touching his face*) You have a nice face.

FRANK (*Grown visibly nervous*): I usually take my wife and kids into New York when I come, but our youngest came down with the flu, so I had to make the trip alone this time.

JOY (*Seductively continuing to touch him*): That's too bad.

FRANK: Yes.

JOY: Such warm-looking eyes. (*Running her fingers over his lips*) Sensitive mouth. (*Starting to unbutton his shirt*) All these buttons. So many buttons. I'm going to show you a very good time, Frank. I think we're going to have a very good time together.

FRANK: Joy, I think you misunderstood why I came up here. I really didn't intend . . .

JOY (*Placing her finger over his lips to silence him*): Do you like to dance, Frank?

FRANK: Sure.

JOY: Why don't you finish your drink, and I'll put on some music.

FRANK: I don't think I ought to drink anymore. I feel a little dizzy.

JOY: Oh, come on. One more little drink won't hurt anything. (*Lifting his glass to his mouth*) Bottoms up.

FRANK *finishes his drink.* JOY *walks over to the radio, a visible sway to her hips, and turns it on.* SHE *stands by the radio, arms out, fingers gesturing for him to join her. The music is slow, romantic, and her body moves provocatively to it. For some long moments* FRANK *watches the lewd grinding of her hips, and then* HE *gets to his feet.* HE *is slightly unsteady, apparently due to the influence of alcohol.* THEY *begin to dance, her arms around his neck.*

JOY (*Continued*): This is nice, isn't it?

FRANK: Yes.

JOY: You really should learn to relax. Your body is tense all over.

FRANK: I'm just not used to drinking. I feel so damn dizzy.

JOY (*Wetting her lips with her tongue*): Don't you like me?

FRANK: I can't do this. I can't. I've got a wife, kids . . .

JOY (*Overtly pressing her body into his groin as* THEY *dance*): But it feels so good, doesn't it?

FRANK: Yes.

JOY: You don't really want me to stop, do you, Frank? Should I stop?

SHE *continues to grind her pelvis against him.* FRANK's *breathing has become audible as the passion of the moment overcomes him.*

JOY (*Continued*): I'll stop if you want me to, Frank. (*Sliding her body up and down against him*) I'm going to make you feel good all over, Frank. I want to show you the best time you ever had. You want that, don't you, Frank? Every man wants a good time.

As FRANK *holds her around the waist,* JOY *leans slightly back and unbuttons the front of her dress, pulling it back to partially expose her breasts.* SHE *places her hands under her breasts, cupping and squeezing them.* FRANK *tries to draw her close to him, kiss her, but* SHE *starts to slightly resist, laughing.*

JOY (*Continued*): I want it too, Frank. I want it as much as you do, but we have to settle the money thing. We have to get the money thing out of the way so we don't have to think about it.

Suddenly from the darkness, BUCK *yells out.*

BUCK: Hold it! Hold it! (*Striding toward the reenactment set, waving his arms, shouting*) Gimme the lights! Just cut it! Cut everything!

The lights for the entire stage come on. The TWO ACTORS *playing the parts of* JOY *and* FRANK *stand motionless, perplexed, on the set.* CHARLIE *hastens toward* BUCK.

CHARLIE: What the hell's the matter now?

BUCK: What the hell isn't the matter now. It's wrong! It's bullshit, and it's all wrong!

CHARLIE: What's wrong?

BUCK (*Stepping onto the reenactment set*): The fucking yellow lamplight! What does she live in? An apartment in the East Village or a Chinese brothel? And that goddam dress! The woman spent the day working in a department store! You think she waited on customers in a department store looking like that?

CHARLIE: Who the hell cares? We're in the middle of a rehearsal here. I'm about to set up my shots. This goddam thing shoulda been in the can three days ago!

BUCK *angrily strides over to the worktable and grabs a copy of the script.*

CHARLIE (*Continued*): What are you doing?

BUCK: What I shoulda done the first time I saw this goddam script! (*Starts to tear up script*)

CHARLIE: You can't do that!

BUCK: Yeah? You just watch me! (*Tearing the script and tossing it into a wastepaper basket*) It's a total crock of shit! You're turning her into a goddam whore! That pipe-smoking son-of-a-bitch is coming out like St. Francis of Assisi, and she's coming out like a goddam whore!

At the mention of "pipe-smoking son-of-a-bitch," the ACTOR *playing the part of* FRANK *strides Off in a huff, almost as if* HE *personally had been insulted.*

CHARLIE: What difference does it make? Who the hell cares? You're not doing a remake of *War and Peace*! You're doing a lousy reenactment of some whore's murder for cable TV!

BUCK: Shut up, Charlie! Don't tell me what I'm doing!

CHARLIE: No, I'm not going to shut up! You're giving Milly and Nathan everything they want—action, violence, sex! That goddam script is right on the money, and you know it! So what the hell is coming down here?

BUCK: I want the truth up there, Charlie. The truth!

CHARLIE: I don't believe this. The truth? You want the truth? We're filming lousy cable TV one step up from the pornos we used to film for them in the Eighth Avenue bookstores, and you want the truth? You're talking fartsy-craftsy? You better get your head on straight before one of those bastards from upstairs comes down here and cuts your balls off!

BUCK: I want this rescheduled for next week. I'm reworking the script.

CHARLIE: I'm the scriptwriter.

BUCK: Not on this one.

CHARLIE: There's no time open next week.

BUCK: Then make some!

By this point some STAGEHANDS *have entered to listen to the fight.*

BUCK (*Continued; to* STAGEHANDS): What are you waiting for? The A train from 125th Street? I want this goddam set outta here! Let's move it! Let's move it! We're going in ten minutes with the wino murder!

CHARLIE: Okay. Okay! You want time next week, you got it! You just tell Milly.

CHARLIE *walks over to the* ACTRESS *playing* JOY, *and throwing up his hands, says something to her.* SHE *exits the stage. The* STAGEHANDS *have already begun their work.* THEY *will rotate the* JOY BONNARD *set around on its wheels and place it against the Upstage wall, the outside scrim walls of the apartment facing the audience. The "set" for the wino murder, when it is brought in, consists of nothing more than a couple of garbage cans spilling over, a fire hydrant and a single flat painted to look like a graffiti-covered brick wall. These items will be placed directly on the stage floor.*

BUCK (*Picking up the worktable phone*): I want an outside line. (*Dials a number*) Hello? Hello, Douglas, this is Buck. How you doing? (*Pause*) Good. Good. Listen, could I talk to Marion for a minute? I've got to make some changes about picking Kenny up. (*Pause, picking up the child's archery set* HE *bought and looking at it until Douglas comes back on the line*) I know she has a headache, Douglas, but she always has a headache when I call, doesn't she? (*Pause*) I'm not being sarcastic, Douglas. I'm being accurate. If I don't pick the kid up with machine regularity, she finds a reason why I can't have him. If I have to switch from a Saturday to a Sunday, it's a big problem. If I'm five minutes late, she's taken the kid someplace for the rest of the day because she thought I wasn't going to show up. Now that's the truth, isn't it?

CHARLIE, *busying himself with some paperwork at the other end of the table, just lowers his head, shaking it.*

BUCK (*Continued*): Why can't we behave like civilized human beings just once, Douglas . . . just once! All I want to do is switch pickup dates! I bought Kenny a little gift and . . . (*Pause*) Just let me talk to her! Let me explain! (*Pause, then totally losing control of himself*) I don't give a shit if she has a headache! That doesn't stop her from letting me change a date! Douglas? Douglas! (*Jiggling the phone button, but Douglas has hung up.* HE *puts the phone down*)

CHARLIE: Boy, you sure know how to get what you want. Why do you let that son-of-a-bitch stick it to you like that?

BUCK: Mind your own business, Charlie. Maybe I deserve it.

CHARLIE: Nobody deserves it.

BUCK *picks up the archery set and stares at it again.*

CHARLIE (*Continued*): What the hell's happening to you, man? Ever since we started on this Joy Bonnard thing. Everything else is in the can in two days. This thing's been going on a week. You're tearing up scripts, you're starting to cost them money. What the hell is coming down?

BUCK: I just want it to be right . . . one lousy thing right.

CHARLIE: It is right! It's just as right as any other reenactment we do. Listen to me, Buck. You came up with a big money winner for them. This murder reenactment idea of yours is the biggest idea to ever hit cable TV, and they appreciate it. All they wanted to do was launder their lousy money through cable, but you showed them how to make a profit. They're grateful. So let it go. Let it go before they dump us back down into the sewer!

BUCK: You should have put in something about her kid, Charlie. The girl at the perfume counter told me she told you Joy Bonnard had a kid.

CHARLIE: Yeah, so what? Who the hell cares what she had beside a pair of tits and an ass?

SHIRLEY, *the actress playing the part of* JOY BONNARD, *enters.* SHE *wears a coat and is on her way out.*

SHIRLEY: Mr. Halloran? Was I okay?

BUCK *goes over to her.*

BUCK: Yeah. You were fine, Shirley.

SHIRLEY: Mr. Corvanni said you didn't like the way it was going. Maybe if I had a few more lines I could do something better with it.

BUCK: It's not you, Shirley. I just gotta change some things around. You were just fine.

SHIRLEY: You really mean that, Mr. Halloran? I know I'm not much of an actress, but I really feel I understand the part and I want to do the best I can with it.

BUCK: You are, Shirley, and you're just right for it. You're doing a great job.

SHIRLEY: Thank you, Mr. Halloran. It means a lot to me to hear you say that.

CHARLIE: I got a feeling you'll probably get an Emmy nomination, sweetie.

SHIRLEY: I don't expect an Emmy nomination, Mr. Corvanni. I just want to give a good performance, that's all.

CHARLIE: You are, baby, you are. (*Holding up a tape cassette*) I'm gonna get it all down in here. Seven minutes of skin. You're gonna be a big hit in the living room.

SHIRLEY (*Ignoring* CHARLIE's *comment*): Mr. Halloran? I'd like to call some agents to see my work. Could you tell me when you think this is going to be shown?

BUCK: I'll let you know next week, Shirley. I really don't know right now.

SHIRLEY: Thank you. I enjoy working for you, Mr. Halloran. (*Starts to exit*)

CHARLIE: If I hear anything about an Emmy nomination, where's the best place to reach you?

SHIRLEY (*Turning and coldly staring at* CHARLIE): You can't reach me at all, Mr. Corvanni. (*Exits*)

CHARLIE: Ooooh!

BUCK has begun sticking tape marks on the stage to indicate to the STAGEHANDS where HE wants the elements of the wino murder reenactment set placed.

CHARLIE (*Continued; turning to* BUCK): You wanna guess where Mr. Milly sent me to find that piece of meat? In the back of a men's boutique in New Jersey! She was wriggling her ass under a pair of five-hundred–watt photo lamps while thirteen guys and a cocker spaniel were pretending to take pictures with a Brownie Instamatic. I shoulda left her there.

BUCK: See what's happening with Mr. Goglas and Mr. Berman.

CHARLIE: Bimbos like that really piss me off. You oughta get a load of her bio. She's been stripping since she was fifteen. Smokers in Columbus, lodge halls in Philly, Texas, Oklahoma. That's her chief reference. The high point of her life? Four pornos filmed for Mr. Milly in a bookstore in Philly. You like that? And then she's got the guts to come in here and ask for more lines.

BUCK: See what's happening with Mr. Goglas and Mr. Berman, Charlie. I wanna get going with the derelict murder.

CHARLIE is fiddling with his camera equipment, still too annoyed with SHIRLEY to sense BUCK's mounting anger.

CHARLIE: "If I had a few more lines, I could do something better with it." Jesus, can you believe that? You give a piece of meat like that a chance to wriggle her ass all over the metropolitan area instead of a bookstore porno machine and she's got the gall to ask for more lines.

BUCK (*Blowing up*): I told you to find out what's happening with Goglas and Berman, didn't I? So do it!

CHARLIE (*Replying in kind*): The goddam suit you want don't fit him! They're still working on it!

BUCK: You check it, Charlie! You check it!

CHARLIE starts to go.

BUCK (*Continued; as* CHARLIE *walks past him*): And the next time you talk to a performer on my stage like that, I'm gonna pick up that fucking camera of yours and bust it over your fucking head, you understand?

CHARLIE: I was just kidding around with her, that's all. You know me.

BUCK: They're on that stage, they're artists, you understand? I don't care where you dig them up from, they're on that stage they're entitled to respect!

CHARLIE: Yeah. Okay. Take it easy.

The brick wall flat has now been put in place for the wino murder. CHARLIE *stands by the wall and shouts Offstage Right.*

CHARLIE (*Continued*): What the hell's happening with the suit?

BUCK (*Still not finished with* CHARLIE): I'm still the producer around here, not you!

VOICE (*Offstage, answering* CHARLIE *in Spanish*): Tu quisiste ojales en los panta-lones, así que los estoy poniendo! Tu crees que puedes hacerlo más rápido, pues aquí tienes la máquina . . . y mientras la usas, puedes besarme el culo! [You asked me to put cuffs on the pants, so I'm putting cuffs on the pants! You think you can do it any faster, I'll give you the machine . . . and while you're at it, you can kiss my ass!]

CHARLIE: Then forget about the cuffs on the pants! Just get 'em out here! (*Walks over to the worktable and sits down. Reaching out for a jelly donut,* HE *takes a bite, is disappointed, and puts it down*) Just for once I'd like to get a blueberry one.

For some long moments there is silence between BUCK *and* CHARLIE, *neither look-ing at the other. When* BUCK *speaks all the anger seems drained away.*

BUCK: They got me back in the playground again, Charlie. The same cruddy playground across the street from the apartment I spent five years of my life in with Kenny . . . first rocking him in the carriage, then watching him walk, holding onto my fingers, then one day just going off by himself. And I can see the two of them standing on the terrace, staring down at me through those rotting ficus bushes he planted. And when the reconnais-sance is finished with, they move inside for the discussion: "Should we send the kid out, or risk another battle over visitation privileges?" You know how many times I've been to court with them in the last year-and-a-half since the divorce? Four times. Four times! And I always win because we always get the same judge—a sixty-year-old lesbian who knows injustice when she sees it. She issues order after order demanding that I be allowed to see my son. The only problem is it never does any good. My wife has a special dispensation from God which allows her to throw my court orders into the garbage can while I have to obey hers down to the letter of the law or suffer immediate death. "If you don't have him back in four hours, I'll get a court order!" And, by God, she will. She's got an East German refu-gee with stainless-steel eyeglasses who represents her as a special favor to Douglas's accounting firm. He specializes in court orders. You could call him when he's just starting to boil a soft-boiled egg, and by the time the egg is ready to eat he's got the court order and fifteen documents proving he spent all of World War II as a medic on the Russian front. He keeps dumping me back in the park again with the rest of the divorced leftovers. I sit there watching them waiting for their kids to come out with little gift boxes on their laps, and I'm scared, Charlie. I'm so scared. Scared that they're not going to bring him out to me, scared that if I can't keep up my support payments they'll keep him away from me for good, scared that no matter what I do I'm gonna lose him anyway.

CHARLIE: That's why you gotta keep doing what you're doing, Buck. That's why you gotta give 'em what they want. You start screwing around with them here, they'll get rid of you and they'll get rid of me, and they'll just find somebody else. You'll lose your job, you'll lose Kenny, and it won't change one fucking thing here.

BUCK: He used to circle around the block with his car, waiting for Marion to come out. The last three months of my marriage they didn't care what I knew, what I felt.

CHARLIE: Forget about them, Buck, and listen to me . . .

BUCK: I hated them so much, Charlie. All I wanted was to walk in on them somewhere . . . in my living room, my bedroom . . . somewhere. That's how I got the idea for my first reenactment, Charlie . . . seeing myself kill them. Did you know that?

CHARLIE: No, Buck, I didn't.

BUCK: Now all I want is just for it to be ordinary again between me and Kenny. But it's never gonna be ordinary again. Ever. The first few months I tried, pretending Saturday or Sunday or whatever the hell day it was they let me see him was just another day of the week . . . but after a while it sinks in. It's gone. The whole damn cord of life that used to hold the two of us together is pulling apart like a piece of wool from an old sweater. And even if I wanted to live with the pretense, I can't, because sure as hell he comes into the park one day and I can see in his eyes he's pretending, too. And he tells me this jerk, this accountant, this Mr. Perfect Mate Lovey-Dovey with three college degrees and a Jaguar, wants him to call him Dad. "Just call me Dad." Well, I told Kenny, "You just call him Douglas. You tell him your Dad told you to call him Douglas."

The elevator comes to life with its usual shrill whine and pulsing red light, and CHARLIE, *as usual, is sent into near panic.*

CHARLIE: Oh, shit!

CHARLIE *hastens over to his camera, adjusting it for height on the tripod, as the elevator comes to a stop and the door opens. There is a different reality now:* FRED MILLY *is dressed as handsomely as before, only the suit is different; the monstrous club foot has somehow metamorphosed into a simple built-up shoe that compensates for a slight deformation in one of* MILLY's *legs; the blinding white light that issued from the elevator in the first scene has muted into the ordinary.*

CHARLIE (*Continued*): How ya doin', Fred.

MILLY (*Coming forward*): Good afternoon, boys. How's it going?

CHARLIE: Right on schedule, Fred. We just finished shooting the death of the girl with the vibrator, and in about ten minutes we're gonna tape the wino murder in the East Village.

MILLY: That was yesterday, Charlie. The girl with the vibrator was yesterday.

CHARLIE: Yeah, that's right. Time sure flies by when you're having fun.

MILLY *is unamused.*

CHARLIE (*Continued*): Well, we're right on schedule with the wino. In fact we're thirty minutes ahead of schedule with that.

MILLY: What about the prostitute? The one that got killed by the college professor.

CHARLIE: Buck?

BUCK: We're a little bit behind on that one, Fred. I'll get it in the can by next week.

MILLY: You got a problem?

BUCK: No problem, Fred. We just got a little behind, that's all.

CHARLIE: Cup of coffee, Fred?

MILLY *just nods his head.*

CHARLIE (*Continued*): Just black, right?

MILLY: So what's the problem?

BUCK: There isn't any problem, Fred. Just some stuff in the schedule, that's all.

MILLY: The girl I suggested to Charlie working out okay?

CHARLIE: Hey, listen, Fred, she's terrific. You sure know how to pick 'em.

MILLY: I'm talking to Buck, Charlie.

CHARLIE: Yeah. Sure, Fred. Sorry.

BUCK: She's fine, Fred.

MILLY: So what's the problem?

BUCK: There isn't any problem, Fred. I just want to rethink some things.

MILLY: You want me to get rid of her, I'll get rid of her. No problem.

BUCK: She's okay, Fred. Everything's okay.

MILLY: Mr. Nathan likes this one about the whore. He thinks it'll make a good reenactment. He can't wait for it to be in the can.

BUCK: It'll be in the can by the middle of next week.

MILLY: Monday?

BUCK: Tuesday, Fred.

MILLY: Tuesday?

BUCK *nods.*

MILLY (*Continued*): All right, Tuesday. I'll tell Mr. Nathan he can expect to see it on Tuesday. (*Placing his attaché case on the table and opening it up as* HE *speaks*) Mr. Stein wanted me to tell you that he thinks you guys are doing a terrific job. He asked me personally to convey that to you.

CHARLIE: Thanks a lot, Fred. It means a lot to us having Mr. Stein say that.

MILLY: According to the figures on our latest survey, these reenactments have upped our percentage of the cable audience four point seven percent.

CHARLIE: Boy, that's really something, isn't it, Buck?

MILLY: The advertising boys translate this into additional revenues of almost a quarter mil, give or take twenty-five thou.

CHARLIE: That's great, Fred. Old Buck was really on the ball with his reenactments idea.

MILLY: The question now is—where do we go from here? Now that we've grabbed an additional four point seven percent of the market, what's the topper? (*Pausing for a moment as if expecting an answer*) The answer is five point two percent. As Mr. Jacobs put it to me this morning, "We've hooked the magic fish. We've asked him for four point seven percent and he's given it to us. Now we gotta come back and hit him for more." At five point two percent gross revenues punch up to . . . (*Punching in some numbers on his calculator, the calculator noisily printing out the answer*) Three-tenths of a mil.

CHARLIE: Wow!

BUCK: It ain't all numbers.

MILLY: What?

BUCK: I said, everything ain't all numbers, Fred.

MILLY: Sure it is. The height of the Eiffel Tower—nine hundred eighty-four feet. The speed of light—one hundred eighty-six thousand miles a second. The chance of croaking of a heart attack at age sixty-five—one in eight. Everything's numbers.

As MILLY *continues to speak, one of the actors in the next reenactment,* MILTON BERMAN, *enters.* HE *is in his 60s and is dressed as a* DERELICT.

MILLY (*Continued*): You don't pay attention to numbers you end up in Central Park with a pair of baggy pants and a lollipop. Mr. St. George says . . .

MILTON (*Suddenly calling out, interrupting* MILLY): I was promised something to drink!

BUCK: Take it easy, Mr. Berman. (*To* CHARLIE) Give Mr. Berman a cup of coffee.

MILTON: Not that shit! Something to drink!

CHARLIE: Whatta ya want me to give him, Buck? Your artiste don't want no coffee and donuts.

BUCK: As soon as we're finished with the taping, Mr. Berman, I got a fifth of Johnny Walker for you.

CHARLIE: You hear that, Milton? A fifth of Johnny Walker! You keep your mouth shut and do a decent day's work for us, you're gonna get it. You don't show some respect while Mr. Milly's talking, we're gonna kick your ass out on the street with the rest of the artistes! (*Turning to* MILLY) You were saying, Fred, Mr. St. George was saying?

MILLY: Problem: success breeds imitation. CBS, NBC, ABC are getting on their track shoes. They're beginning their own programs. They want to cash in on our breakthrough in the market. Solution? Mr. Stein says . . .

MILTON: I used to be an engineer!

CHARLIE: That's fantastic, Milton! An engineer! Only I'll tell you something, Milton, you don't look like an engineer to me. You look like a dried-up piece of horseshit! So why don't you keep your mouth shut while Mr. Milly is talking?

MILTON: You got no right talking to me that way! I was an engineer! I was what I said I was!

CHARLIE: So what's the story with you now, Milton? You in-between jobs? You just waiting around to latch onto one of those big engineering jobs? (*To* BUCK) That's a lesson for you and me, Buck. You ain't happy with what you got, you're just liable to end up a piece of horseshit, talking about yesterday. (*To* MILLY) You were saying, Fred, Mr. Stein was saying?

MILLY: Solution: advance to the next level. So far we've limited our reenactments to local murders. But the public's appetite has been whetted. They're ready to ask us for more, but they don't know yet what more is. Well, gentlemen, Mr. Jacobs says . . .

MILTON: I had a wife, three kids, and a damn good job as an engineer!

CHARLIE (*Angrily grabbing a newspaper off the worktable and approaching* MILTON): Well, then, you know what you need, Milton? A copy of the *New York Times*. It's easy as hell getting a great job. All you gotta do is look in the Help Wanted section.

CHARLIE *throws the newspaper at* MILTON. MILTON *throws the newspaper back.*

MILTON: I helped build the Verrazano Bridge! I put down the pilings for the Verrazano Bridge!

CHARLIE (*Throwing the newspaper at* MILTON *again*): Then you won't have any trouble getting another job, will ya, Milton?

MILTON *throws the newspaper back.* CHARLIE, *as crazily angered now as* MILTON, *whips open the paper.*

CHARLIE (*Continued*): I'll even get one for you!

MILTON: I sunk the pilings on the Verrazano Bridge!

CHARLIE: Oh, underwater! You work underwater! I'll get you one for underwater!

BUCK: Charlie!

CHARLIE (*Too lost in his own anger to pay any attention to* BUCK, *pretending to read an ad from the paper*): "Engineer needed for underwater. Long confinement with naked women testing the effects of Johnny Walker Black Label. Interested applicants contact our representative in the main bar of the New

York Hilton. Starting salary half a mil a year." You got a dime on ya, Milton? Ya got a dime, I'll make the call!

BUCK: That's enough, Charlie!

CHARLIE: No dime? Gee, what a pisser. Losing out on a swell job like that 'cause you don't have a dime to make a call!

BUCK (*Starting toward* CHARLIE): I said that's enough, Charlie!

CHARLIE (*Breaking off his attack against* MILTON, *having satisfied his need to publicly humiliate the* DERELICT *in front of* MILLY): You were saying, Fred, Mr. Jacobs was saying?

MILLY: Expand: the world is big, the world is more. (*Pulling 8 x 10 glossy photos out of his attache case and tossing them one by one on the table*) A school bus blows up in Haifa, children explode into pieces! A Malay strangles a tourist for a pocketful of change in Kuala Lumpur! The wife of a French diplomat is raped and torn apart by communist guerrillas in San Salvador! A South African farmer is gutted by his houseboy in Pretoria, "Freedom" scrawled in blood on the wall!

CHARLIE: Wow! These are great, Fred. Really great.

MILLY: It's our next level, Charlie. Mr. Nathan says . . .

MR. GOGLAS *enters to blaring Spanish music coming from the large portable radio* HE *carries on his shoulder.* GOGLAS *is in his 20s, thin and supple as a snake.*

GOGLAS: Hey, how you like this suit? This is some crazy suit. It don't fit for shit! (*Goes into his dance routine, obscenely thrusting his pelvis*)

CHARLIE: You like that, Buck? That's Mr. Goglas's entrance theme. I found Mr. Goglas dancing in front of a music store on West 50th Street.

GOGLAS (*Pointing to* MILTON): Oye! You better give this man a drink. Tu sabes? He don't look so good to me. He's behind in his drinking. (*Putting the radio down*) Hey, papi chulo! (*Walking over to* MILTON *and grabbing his arm*) Come on, let's dance. You look half dead, man.

MILTON (*Pulling his arm free*): Take your hands off me, you son-of-a-bitch!

GOGLAS (*Suddenly snapping open a switchblade*): Come on, man, come on. I'll cut you up!

BUCK (*Hastening over, shutting off the radio*): Put the knife away, Mr. Goglas.

GOGLAS: Sure. Sure. I'm just kidding. You think I'm serious? (*Raising both his arms in the air, a large smile on his face*) I don't cut him up till we get on the camera. (*Closing the knife and putting it away*)

CHARLIE: You were saying, Fred, Mr. Nathan was saying?

MILLY: Devour the world! Go international! Use everything! Everyone!

CHARLIE: God, what a fantastic idea! Look at these photos, Buck. Did you ever see anything as fantastic.

When BUCK *seems to offer no enthusiasm,* MILLY *walks over to him.*

MILLY: Mr. Nathan wants enthusiasm on this, Buck. Real enthusiasm. When he talks about tourists strangled in Kuala Lumpur, he wants to see the juices flow. Mr. St. George says . . .

GOGLAS struts over to MILLY and thrusts a torn-out page from a porno magazine under his nose. The picture shows a woman lying provocatively with her legs spread apart.

GOGLAS: What do you think of that? She gave it to me. This is my woman. We are getting married. Her father is Don Antonio de Vega Becquer, a rich man. I'm going to make her my queen. What do you think of my woman?

MILLY just stares at him. GOGLAS shoves the picture practically into MILLY's face, seems very angry.

GOGLAS (*Continued*): I ask you something! What do you think of my woman?

For a moment there is silence and it is difficult to say if GOGLAS is serious or not. Then HE laughs, picks up his radio and exits.

CHARLIE: You were saying, Fred, Mr. St. George was saying?
MILLY (*Still not fully recovered from his moment of fright with GOGLAS*): Mr. St. George thinks . . .

A STAGEHAND signals BUCK.

BUCK: I gotta do the lead-in, Fred. Charlie, I want you on camera.
MILLY: Mr. St. George is talking international, Buck.

The lights snap on over the reenactment set.

BUCK: I have to get on with the taping, Fred.
MILLY: Mr. St. George is talking tourists strangled in Kuala Lumpur, Buck!
BUCK: "A man died in this city. . . ." How's audio, Mickey?

BUCK gets an okay signal from one of the STAGEHANDS who now stands by the monitoring equipment, earphones on his head. BUCK holds a white sheet of paper up to the camera.

BUCK (*Continued*): Gimme a white balance.
MILLY: A South African farmer gutted by his houseboy!
CHARLIE (*Looking at the white paper through the camera*): Got it!
MILLY: The wife of the French ambassador torn apart in San Salvador!

BUCK: Roll tape!

MILLY: Children blown to pieces in Haifa!

BUCK *stands by the brick-wall flat some feet away from* MILTON *and speaks directly into the camera.* MILTON, *in his role as the* DERELICT, *sits on the ground, a bottle of cheap wine in his hand.*

BUCK: A man died in this city. A man without a definite name, a definite address. Witnesses to his death remember him only as a man who looked for handouts along the street, a man who cleaned the windshields of passing cars for a few coins to buy a bottle of cheap wine, a man content to sit on the ground and watch through a wine-soaked mind the endless bustle of a great city whirling about him. This man had no part in the life of the city he lived in. There is no record of him in the mission houses, or on the rolls of any city agency. Only now in his death are we, the living, made aware of this invisible man. Only now in his death is this city for the briefest instant of time made aware that it has lost an inhabitant. Only now in his death can we imagine we see him for the first time: the fine network of nerves beginning to form, the skeletal pattern of his bones laid out, the channels of his blood beginning to flow, the bands of fiber and muscle contracting. Only now in the humiliation and death of the invisible man is the measure of our loss made visible.

BUCK *steps away from the reenactment set as* GOGLAS, *playing the part of the murderer,* RAMON LUIS CARPIO DE LA BARCA, *enters, dancing to the music of the radio* HE *carries. The* DERELICT *watches him.*

RAMON (*To the* DERELICT): Hey! Hey, you! What are you looking at? (*Shutting the radio off and putting it down*) You hear me? I ask you what you're looking at?

The DERELICT *just tries to roll himself into a ball and go to sleep.*

RAMON (*Continued*): Hey? (*Walking over to the* DERELICT) Hey, you!

When there's no response RAMON *nudges the* DERELICT *with his foot.*

RAMON (*Continued*): I'm talking to you!

DERELICT: Leave me alone. I got nothing.

RAMON: What are you looking at me for? You never seen nobody dancing?

When there is no response RAMON *prods the* DERELICT *again with his foot.*

RAMON (*Continued*): What are you looking at?

DERELICT: I'm not doing anything to you. Leave me alone.

RAMON: You were looking at me. I don't like people to look at me. You think you can just look at me? (*Kicking the* DERELICT) Eh? Eh? You better answer me!

The DERELICT *tries to get to his feet, but is pushed down.*

RAMON (*Continued*): You don't look at me because I cannot be looked at! I am the King of the World! You hear what I say to you? Nobody looks at the King of the World unless he tells them to!

DERELICT (*Trying to crawl away*): Get the hell away from me!

RAMON (*Shoving the* DERELICT *down with his foot and strutting about*): You see this suit I'm wearing? This is some suit! I don't dress like you dress. This is the only suit like this in the world. I have it because I am King of the World! You understand what I say to you?

DERELICT: You rotten bastard! Get away from me or I'm going to call the police!

RAMON: Whatever I want, I can do! Nobody can stop me! I am the King! (*Squatting down in front of the* DERELICT *and pulling out a switchblade*) You see what I got?

DERELICT: Please leave me alone. I don't have anything. I'm nobody. I'm just sitting here.

RAMON (*Snapping the blade open*): You know who gave me this? (*Taking out his magazine photo*) She gave it to me. This is my woman. We are going to be married. Her father is a rich man—Don Antonio de Vega Becquer. I am going to make her my queen. What do you think of my woman? (*Shoving the picture in the* DERELICT's *face*) Eh? Eh?

DERELICT: What do you want from me? I haven't done anything. Please.

RAMON (*Standing up and straddling the* DERELICT, *holding out his knife*): I could kill you with this and you don't know nothing. You don't feel nothing. When I kill you, I dedicate you to her. I will prove myself worthy of her love by dedicating you to her. (*Raising the picture above his head, looking at it, speaking in Spanish*) Oh, bella reina, yo, Ramón Luis Carpio de la Barca, le dedico a ustéd este toro y mi vida en el nombre de la santa madre de Diós que siempre nos vigila.
[Oh, beautiful queen, I, Ramon Luis Carpio de la Barca, dedicate this bull and my life to you in the name of the sacred mother of God who watches over us.]

RAMON *squats down behind the* DERELICT *and thrusts the picture in front of his face.* CHARLIE, *camera off tripod, moves in.*

RAMON (*Continued*): Kiss her feet!

Placing the knifeblade against the DERELICT's *cheek,* RAMON *forces him into a kneeling position.*

RAMON (*Continued*): I tell you to kiss her feet!

For a moment the DERELICT *just stares at the picture, and then* HE *slowly begins to lean forward.*

RAMON (*Continued*): I am the King of the World and this is my woman whose feet you kiss.

As the DERELICT *kisses the photo,* RAMON *plunges the knife into his back. The* DERELICT *lets out a cry of pain.* RAMON *lets out a cry of exaltation.*

RAMON (*Continued*): Oh, beautiful queen, I, Ramon Luis Carpio de la Barca, dedicate this bull and my life to you, proving my worth in the name of the sacred mother of God who watches over all things. (*Placing his hand over the* DERELICT'*s face*) Oh, mother of God, let the blood of this sacrifice pour forth and strengthen our marriage that our life may be fruitful and blessed with many sons. I, Ramon Luis Carpio de la Barca, ask it of you!

RAMON *draws the blade of the knife across the* DERELICT'*s throat. The* DERELICT *raises his arms out in front of him as if making a silent plea for help. For a moment the* DERELICT *seems frozen into his position, and then* HE *pitches forward, collapsing to the ground as* CHARLIE *moves in for a closeup of his face.* RAMON *bends down, wipes off the blade of his knife on the* DERELICT'*s coat, closes it and puts it away.* CHARLIE *focuses now on* RAMON *as* HE *picks up his photo and radio. Turning on the radio, giving a final strut and smile to the camera,* RAMON *exits. Lights up on stage. For some seconds there is no motion, then* MILLY *gets to his feet and snaps shut his attache case.*

MILLY: Monday we go international. Monday a Malay strangles a tourist for a pocketful of change in Kuala Lumpur. (*Heads for elevator*)
CHARLIE (*As* MILLY *goes*): I don't think I can find a Malay by Monday, Mr. Milly.
MILLY: Sure you can, Charlie. Check out the Chinese restaurants. New York's full of Chinese restaurants. (*Pressing the elevator button, and then turning around to look at* BUCK *as the doors open*) Oh, by the way, Buck. You know the stuff you did at the beginning . . . the lead-in? (*Stepping into the elevator and turning around to continue looking at* BUCK) Mr. Nathan don't like it. Mr. Nathan says talking is a crock of shit.

MILLY *presses the button to shut the elevator door.* CHARLIE *and* BUCK *stare at one another. Sound of the elevator rising as the lights dim and out.*

END OF ACT ONE

ACT TWO

The studio, the following week. The movable platform used for the Joy Bonnard living room, has now been converted into a dining room to tape the reenactment of "The French Ambassador's Wife Gets Raped in El Salvador." A small table is elegantly laid out with two silver candlesticks, a bowl of fresh cut flowers, some covered silver serving dishes, and a single place setting. Upstage of the table is a large multipaned window, beyond which can be seen the tops of palm fronds.

Bright Caribbean music is heard as the lights come up. A servant (VIN-CENTE) enters the room with a covered silver dish. As HE enters HE gives a slight "out-of-character" nod to CHARLIE, who is filming the scene. VINCENTE is in his early 20s, and wears a white serving jacket over his black pants. HE places the dish down on the table, stands back to admire the perfectly set table just as a woman (MADAM) calls out, presumably from the next room. Music fades.

MADAM (*Offstage*): Jean-Paul? (*Pause*) Jean-Paul?

VINCENTE stands motionless by the table. In a moment MADAM, the French am-bassador's wife, enters. SHE is a handsome woman in an attractive yellow suit, gloves, and a wide-brimmed hat. The suit jacket is cut low enough to expose the top of her generous breasts.

MADAM (*Continued*): Oh, Enrique, is the ambassador at home?
VINCENTE: Excuse me, madam. I am Vincente. Enrique has left for his vacation.
MADAM (*Really looking at the servant for the first time*): Oh. I don't recall him say-ing anything about a vacation. How awkward. We are entertaining this evening.
VINCENTE: I'm sure I will be able to perform his duties to your satisfaction, madam. My family has produced a long line of dining-room servants. My great-grandfather worked for the German ambassador, my grandfather worked for the English ambassador, my father was employed by the Amer-ican ambassador, and, with your permission, it shall be my pleasure to serve you and the French ambassador.
MADAM: But where is the place setting for the ambassador? You have forgotten it.
VINCENTE: No, madam, I have not forgotten it. The ambassador has been called away. He will not be joining you for lunch.
MADAM: Where has he been called away to? He said nothing to me about hav-ing to leave.
VINCENTE: His departure was sudden, madam. May I take your hat and gloves?
MADAM (*As SHE removes her hat and gloves and gives them to VINCENTE*): I really don't understand what is happening today. First Enrique is not here who is always here, and then my husband is called away and leaves no message for me, and now all morning in the street the sound of gunfire.

VINCENTE: A few malcontents, madam. They come in from the hills, the slums, other provinces. The police will take care of it in a matter of a few hours. It is nothing to concern yourself about.

MADAM: I hope so. This sort of thing is very disturbing. I can't understand what it is your people want. General Rojas is such a perfectly civilized charming gentleman. His government has instituted land reform, social reform, economic reform, elections to take place within two years. What else is it they want?

Having deposited the hat and gloves on a chair, VINCENTE *now returns to* MADAM *in time to help her be seated at the table.*

VINCENTE: Some people are just never satisfied, madam. They are never content with what they have. It is in their nature. A condition caused by the constant oppressive heat of the tropics.

MADAM: But the buildings are all air-conditioned.

VINCENTE: Not all of them, madam.

MADAM: You think the answer to this constant unrest is air-conditioning?

VINCENTE: It is impossible to state with any degree of certainty, madam, but it wouldn't surprise me. It is my opinion that this fever in the blood of my people is not caused by social inequality, political fascism, or economic deprivation—but merely by a lack of decent air-conditioning.

Sound of gunfire in the distance.

MADAM: There! Some more of it! This is all intolerable! Absolutely intolerable!

VINCENTE: Shall I serve, madam?

MADAM: What is it the chef has made?

VINCENTE: The chef did not prepare this meal, madam. I did.

MADAM: You? But you are the dining-room waiter!

VINCENTE: In these times we must all play many roles, madam.

MADAM: But where is the chef?

VINCENTE: He has gone also on his vacation, madam.

MADAM: But this is grotesque. I am hosting a dinner party tonight for sixty people.

VINCENTE: The dinner party has been canceled, madam.

MADAM: Canceled? How can it be canceled? Who canceled it?

VINCENTE *lifts the lid to two of the dishes, neither of which appeals to* MADAM.

VINCENTE: Mushrooms jardinier, madam. Cold bean salad. (*Replacing the lids and lifting a third*) Pate?

MADAM *samples the pate as* VINCENTE *puts a little on her plate.*

MADAM: What kind of pate is this?

VINCENTE: Pate Ambassadorial, madam.

MADAM: It has an odd flavor. I can't quite place it. (*Taking another taste*) It isn't goose liver?

VINCENTE: No, madam, it isn't goose liver.

MADAM: Duck?

VINCENTE: No, madam.

MADAM: It has a slightly gritty texture.

VINCENTE: But not unpleasing?

MADAM: No, it is not unpleasing.

VINCENTE: I would not want to serve madam something that was not up to her usual refined gastronomical standards.

MADAM: Such an odd flavor. I can't quite place it. Is it lamb? Veal? Pig?

VINCENTE: Pig, madam? Does it taste to you like a pig?

MADAM: I don't know. It has a very strange taste. What is it?

VINCENTE: Pate Ambassadorial, madam.

MADAM: But what is in it? What is it made out of?

VINCENTE: The ambassador, of course.

MADAM (*Abruptly looking at* VINCENTE): What did you say?

VINCENTE: I said it was made out of the ambassador, madam.

MADAM (*Jumping to her feet*): Oh, my God! My God!

VINCENTE (*Pushing* MADAM *back down in the chair, grabbing her neck in his hands*): But you must finish it, madam. You must finish it all. We are a poor country. We cannot afford to waste any of our food. Your husband and his wonderful French culture, and the wonderful American culture, and the wonderful English and German cultures, have fed off my country for so long they must be very appetizing. They must be pleasing to the palate! Gastronomical delights!

As VINCENTE *speaks* HE *takes the fork, fills it with pate and begins pushing it into* MADAM's *mouth.* MADAM, *screaming, tries to spit it out, tries to escape.* CHARLIE, *the camera handheld now, moves in for his closeups.*

VINCENTE (*Continued*): Eat him, madam! Eat him the way he has helped General Rojas devour my people! Eat him the way he has sent in guns and bombs for General Rojas to kill my people! Eat him, madam, the way he has helped stuff our prisons with the innocent! Destroyed lives! Murdered children! (*Shoving the pate in with his fingers*) Tortured countless victims while you had your dinner parties, fed yourself to the gills, and stopped your ears to the screams of the suffering!

VINCENTE *thrusts* MADAM's *head down so her forehead bangs on the table.* MADAM *gets to her feet, staggering around the room, screaming for help.*

VINCENTE (*Continued*): Scream, madam bitch! Scream! Add your screams to the screams of my people! No one will hear you!

VINCENTE *slaps* MADAM *so hard* SHE *falls against the table, sending everything scattering to the floor.* VINCENTE, *spreading her legs, crawls on top of her on the table, ripping open her jacket as* HE *begins trying to rape her.*

VINCENTE (*Continued*): No one will save you! You who were deaf to the massacre of thousands of my people, pleading, begging your wonderful culture for help, will find no help from the dead! You are now the dead, madam! The raped, maimed, mangled, mutilated dead! And there will be no mercy or forgiveness because you have shown none! Pitiless whore from a pitiless world!

VINCENTE *raises one hand to the sky in a final grandiloquent gesture.* CHARLIE *keeps filming for some moments until* BUCK *calls out.*

BUCK: Okay, that's a take, Charlie. That's a take.

CHARLIE *stops filming and walks over toward* BUCK. *For a moment neither man seems to notice that* VINCENTE *has not stopped his assault on* MADAM. *In fact the assault seems to have grown more real, more violent, the* YOUNG ACTOR *tearing at* MADAM's *jacket, raising the* ACTRESS' *legs, thrusting his groin into her. The* ACTRESS *slaps out hard at him.*

ACTRESS (*Screaming*): Get your hands off me, you son-of-a-bitch!

The ACTRESS *tries to get up, but the* YOUNG ACTOR *holds her down on the table, continuing his assault.*

BUCK (*Running over*): I said that's a take! What the hell are you doing?
YOUNG ACTOR: Nothing.

The ACTRESS *finally manages to push the* YOUNG ACTOR *away and sit up.*

ACTRESS: You ever grab me like that again, I'll claw your face into shreds! I'll tear your eyes out, you ignorant bastard!
BUCK: What the hell is going on here?
ACTRESS: He was hurting me! He was purposely trying to hurt me and it had nothing to do with what we were acting! Look what he did to my breast! (*Showing* BUCK *a large scratch on her breast*)
YOUNG ACTOR: You're crazy, lady! I wasn't doing anything to you.

The ACTRESS *suddenly jumps off the table and starts attacking the* YOUNG ACTOR *with her fingernails.*

ACTRESS: You lousy Puerto Rican pimp!

BUCK *and* CHARLIE *have to separate them.*

BUCK: All right! Come on! Knock it off! Scene's over! You were terrific! You were both terrific! Take her backstage, Charlie! Get her to cool off!

CHARLIE *has to literally lift the* ACTRESS *off the floor to carry her out.* SHE *is still screaming.*

ACTRESS: I'll cut your heart out, you lousy pimp! You hear me? You ever lay a hand on me again, I'll cut your heart out!

CHARLIE *and the* ACTRESS *exit. We can still hear her screaming Offstage.*

ACTRESS (*Continued; Offstage*): Look what he did to my breast! He dug his lousy dirty fingernails into it! (*A final scream back at the* YOUNG ACTOR) You lousy dirty Puerto Rican pimp!

BUCK (*To the* YOUNG ACTOR): What the hell were you doing to her?

YOUNG ACTOR (*With great hostility*): Nothing! That lousy Park Avenue bitch should be pulled into an alley somewhere! I know people like her all my life! They don't give a shit about anybody! They think they're better than anybody! They come walking down the street with their fur coats and their two-inch–big poodles with diamond collars around their necks and they see somebody like me they cross over to the other side of the street because we're just shit on the street to them! She thinks she can do that to me or my people, I'll pull her into an alley somewhere and show her what she can do! (*Grabbing his genitals with his hand and shaking them*)

BUCK: What the hell is the matter with you? She was only playing the part that was written for her!

The YOUNG ACTOR *continues his tirade, not really listening to* BUCK. *A number of* STAGEHANDS *have come out to watch the action.*

YOUNG ACTOR: I'll give her a mouthful of this! That's what she needs, her and all the rest of those Park Avenue whores who think the rest of the world exists to take their hat and gloves!

The YOUNG ACTOR *throws* MADAM'*s hat and gloves in the direction of* BUCK. *The* YOUNG ACTOR *seems genuinely confused and flustered over his own behavior as* HE *stares wildly about him at* BUCK *and the* STAGEHANDS.

YOUNG ACTOR (*Continued*): Oh, man!

Picking up the white jacket HE had taken off during his assault on MADAM, the YOUNG ACTOR flees the stage, almost crashing into CHARLIE.

CHARLIE (*Returning from Offstage*): What the hell was that all about?
BUCK (*Truly perplexed*): I don't know.
CHARLIE: She's got a scratch mark from the top of her tit all the way down to her nipple.
BUCK (*To the STAGEHANDS*): Let's go! Let's go! I want the Joy Bonnard reenactment set up and ready to rehearse in fifteen minutes. Let's see if we can get out of here before midnight for once!

The STAGEHANDS turn the reenactment set around and, rolling it Upstage to the back wall, begin converting it into the Joy Bonnard living room. The triptych of panels that had been the ambassador's dining room will be removed, revealing behind them the already-in-place scrim walls of Joy Bonnard's apartment. As the STAGEHANDS begin their work, BUCK returns to the worktable and CHARLIE wheels his camera out of the way Upstage Left past the elevator steps.

CHARLIE: You know what I think? Some of these jerkos can't tell the difference between what they're acting and what's real. The son-of-a-bitch probably thinks we hired the French ambassador's wife for him to rape!

Finishing with his camera, CHARLIE wanders Midstage. For some moments HE watches the STAGEHANDS busy with their work, and BUCK, seated at the worktable, busy with his paperwork.

CHARLIE (*Continued; suddenly blurting out what's on his mind*): Hey, listen, by the way, I gave her the suit.

BUCK doesn't answer.

CHARLIE (*Continued*): Is that okay?
BUCK: What?
CHARLIE: I gave her the suit. Is that okay?
BUCK: Yeah.
CHARLIE: It's all torn up, but she thinks she can fix it.
BUCK (*Trying to concentrate on the expense figures in front of him*): Fine.
CHARLIE: I figured it was worth it, just to shut her up. (*Pause*) You heard the way she was screaming, and then she started asking about the suit, so I figured what the hell better give her the suit, shut her up.

Pause. No response from BUCK.

CHARLIE (*Continued*): The way I figure it if Milly or one of those other bastards from upstairs starts asking about what happened to the prop suit, we can always tell 'em the woman was going to sue us and we managed to quiet her down with the suit. Right?

BUCK (*Closing his eyes and rubbing his temples with his fingers*): Right.

CHARLIE: That's the way I figured it too, Buck. (*Pause*) Of course you never know with those sons-of-bitches. You think they'd be grateful we saved them from a lawsuit, but you never know with them. (*Pause*) You don't think that's gonna cause any problems, do you?

BUCK (*Still rubbing his temples as if trying to erase a terrible headache that is getting worse and worse*): What is?

CHARLIE: The suit.

BUCK: Why should the suit cause any problems?

CHARLIE: You ain't listening to me, Buck. I told her she could take the suit.

BUCK (*Finally exploding*): So she took it! She took the lousy fucking suit! Whatta ya want me to do about it, Charlie? You want me to follow her out on the street and tear it off her back?

CHARLIE: No.

BUCK: Because if that's what you want me to do, Charlie, I'll do it! I'll get up right now and do it! (*Standing up and throwing the stack of cost figures in his hand back down on the table*) And fix up your lousy cost figures. There's a four-dollar error in here.

CHARLIE (*Hastening over to the worktable*): On what?

BUCK: I don't know on what! You tell me. If you're going to nickel and dime 'em on the props, you oughta at least learn how to add! (*Walking over to the* STAGEHANDS *and speaking to them*) And make sure there's a white light in that lamp. That apartment gets lit up like a whorehouse again, you're gonna be picking tungsten wire outta your teeth.

The phone on the worktable begins to ring. CHARLIE *just looks at it for a moment as if it might be a rattlesnake shaking its tail, and then picks it up.*

CHARLIE: Reenactments. Charlie Corvanni. (*Listens for a moment and then covers the mouthpiece; to* BUCK) Your attorney's on the phone. You wanna speak to him?

BUCK *just throws up his hands.*

CHARLIE (*Continued; into the phone*): Hold on a minute. (*Presses the hold button and puts the phone down*)

BUCK: Ask Milly to come down. I want him to see the rewrites I made in the Joy Bonnard reenactment.

CHARLIE: The hell with it. Let's just tape it.

BUCK: I'll tape it after he sees what I've done. Just get him down here.

CHARLIE (*Walking Midstage to* BUCK): You're making a mistake. As big a mistake as all that revolutionary crap talk you added to my last reenactment. You already got the word what they think about your crap talk. Whatta ya think Milly's gonna do when he hears that South American banana-eater of yours spouting left-wing bullshit when all he's supposed to do is pull her bloomers off and stick it to her?

BUCK: The man was a revolutionist, Charlie! If all he wanted to do was stick it to her, then he just would have stuck it to her! He wouldn't have spent the morning grinding her husband into a pate!

CHARLIE *starts to exit Stage Left.*

BUCK (*Continued*): Why don't you ask yourself what was the meaning of the pate, Charlie?

CHARLIE *throws up his hands as* HE *exits.*

BUCK (*Continued; raising his hand to the sky and shouting after* CHARLIE): The pate! (*For a moment* HE *just stands there, then walks over to the worktable and picks up the phone*) Hello, Phil. How are you?

As BUCK *begins his conversation the* STAGEHANDS *wheel the Joy Bonnard set into place Downstage and exit. The apartment is different now than when we first saw it: the beaded curtain is down, replaced by a plain cloth one; a number of cheap reproductions of paintings by Degas and Monet hang on the wall; on the mantle there is a collection of photographs; a small imitation Christmas tree complete with tinsel stands on the floor near the phony fireplace. All the changes reflect* BUCK's *concept.*

BUCK (*Continued*): Yeah. Yeah, that's right. I was over Marion's apartment on Sunday. What about it? (*Listens*) No. No. There wasn't any banging on the door, Phil. I just knocked with my knuckle. One knuckle. (*Starts to wander about as* HE *talks*) Oh, that's beautiful. She's got four witnesses willing to testify I was pounding on the door. That's really beautiful, Phil, considering the fact that there's only one other apartment on the floor and I know those people. They wouldn't open their door if the Virgin Mary was being raped by a Nazi panzer division! So what the hell is she trying to pull now? (*Listens*) What kind of court order?

As BUCK *listens to his lawyer,* SHIRLEY *enters onto the reenactment set through the scrim door.* SHE *wears a pink terrycloth bathrobe and slippers.* SHE *holds some pillows in her hand, which* SHE *places on the couch.* SHE'*d like to talk to* BUCK, *but doesn't want to interrupt his phone conversation.*

BUCK (*Continued*): How in the name of God can she get a court order keeping me outta that apartment house when I'm the one still making the mortgage payments on that fucking co-op the two of them are living in? (*Listens*) No! No! I don't give a damn about her court orders! As far as I'm concerned they oughta take that motto they got chiseled in stone over the courthouse that says "Equal Justice Under the Law," and change it to "Abandon Hope All Ye Who Enter Here!" (*Listens*) If she had brought the kid out to me in the playground the way she was supposed to I never would have gone near that apartment. You know how long I waited in that fucking freezing playground with a bow and arrow on my lap, waiting for her to send Kenny out? Two hours! (*Picking an arrow out of the toy archery set* HE *has just been talking about, and walking around with it and the phone in his hand*) No! There was no confusion. She knew I had to exchange a Saturday for a Sunday because I was working. For God's sake, Phil, doesn't she ever ask herself what would happen to my child-support payments if I lost my job down here because I didn't make myself available when they needed me?

SHIRLEY, *without having ever been seen by* BUCK, *exits the reenactment set through the same door* SHE *entered.* SHE *waits, out of sight, behind the set for* BUCK *to finish his call.*

BUCK (*Continued*): She's got to be flexible! She can't use that as a weapon to keep me from seeing my son! (*Listens*) I want to see him, Phil! Can you understand that? I love him! He's my son and I love him and they won't let me see him! He's growing up and I'm not part of his life anymore! (*Almost broken down in tears,* HE *listens to his attorney. When* HE *finally speaks there is a deadly serious tone in his voice, a frighteningly obvious truth to what* HE *says*) That's right, Phil. You call their attorney and you fix it so I can see my son, because if you don't, I'm gonna go over there and kill the both of them.

BUCK *hangs the phone up and sits down where his wanderings have brought him—the edge of the reenactment set. As* HE *stares off into space,* HE *keeps jabbing the suction-tip arrow into the reenactment-set floor, over and over again.* SHIRLEY *watches him for some moments through the scrim door, and then opens the door and pokes her head in.*

SHIRLEY: Mr. Halloran?

After a slight pause, BUCK *looks up.*

SHIRLEY (*Continued*): Can I talk to you for a minute? (*Pause*) It's about the robe.
BUCK: What about it?

SHIRLEY (*Entering onto the set*): I'm not quite sure how I'm supposed to wear it when I come out of the bedroom. When I asked Mr. Corvanni, he told me to ask you because it was your reenactment.

BUCK *just looks at her.*

SHIRLEY (*Continued*): Should I open the robe a little at the neck so you can see the top of my breasts, or should I open it all the way so you can . . . you know?

BUCK: Just leave it closed. (*Lowering his eyes, staring downward still lost in his own thoughts*)

SHIRLEY (*Starts to exit and then turns back*): I spoke to an agent last Friday. Fred Milly set it up for me. He said he represented a lot of people who are real stars now. At first I thought he was just coming on to me . . . you know what I mean, the way they look at you sometimes . . . but I think he was really interested in my career. We're going to have dinner together next week and talk over how he could get started on a publicity program for me. You know, get me dates with important people, things like that, and then, maybe, have a couple of lines written up in one of the On The Town columns.

BUCK: That sounds terrific, Shirley.

SHIRLEY: I think this agent represents Johnny Carson. At least he had a picture of him on the wall.

For a moment BUCK *and* SHIRLEY *just look at each other.* SHIRLEY *turns to exit, and then finally getting up the courage to say what's on her mind, turns again to* BUCK.

SHIRLEY (*Continued*): Mr. Halloran, could I ask you something?

BUCK *turns around to fully face her, resting his back against the scrim wall.* SHIRLEY *sits down on the couch.*

SHIRLEY (*Continued*): Do you think I could be an actress? I mean if I went to one of those acting classes and had lessons and really worked at it? Or do you think I'm just fooling myself? You see I've put aside a little money over the years and I wouldn't mind spending it if I thought I had a chance of really becoming a good actress. But if I was just fooling myself . . . it wouldn't be just losing the money . . . you know what I mean? When you stopped the rehearsal last week and I thought it was because of me . . . wow! I just said to myself, "Wow . . . well, shit, Shirley, what did you expect?" And my heart almost stopped.

BUCK: Then you oughta take the chance, Shirley. I think you could be a fine actress.

SHIRLEY (*Sliding down off the couch to a position in front of it*): Because that's what I really want, you know? I've been thinking about it for a long time, ever since I was stripping down in Dallas . . . . I guess Fred Milly told ya about that . . . I mean the stripping part.

BUCK: I don't remember what he told me, Shirley.

SHIRLEY: Yeah . . . well, what it was was that I was always trying to put some words in my act . . . nothing set, or anything like that . . . just what came into my mind. I'd come out and say . . . (*Getting to her knees, snapping her fingers, and in an instant creating her character: a shimmying, breast-jiggling stripper*) "Hi. My name is Francine. What's yours? (*Stopping her motion and turning to* BUCK) That's the name I was using down in Texas. I changed it to Babette in Oklahoma because it sounded more French. And they'd say, "Frank," or "John," or whatever. And then I'd say . . . (*Getting up on her knees again and going through the same routine*) "I need a bodyguard. Would you like to be my bodyguard?" (*Sitting back down again*) You see my full stage name was Francine the Body, so there was a double meaning for the words. I also had a routine I did with a rose. That was when I was supposed to be the Rose of Sharon. You see I had a lot of parts I made up for myself: Babette the French maid . . . the Devil's Angel . . . (*Placing a finger on her hip and making a sound suggestive of heat*) tsss! Very hot! Marie Antoinette . . . (*Drawing her finger across her throat*) Sinderella. Sinderella, with an S. . . . When I was Sinderella I showed the whole transformation using little hand puppets like mice to take off my clothes . . . (*Getting to her knees again, making little "eek, eek" sounds as* SHE *pretends her fingers are little mice pulling at her clothing. Finishing,* SHE *sits down again*) But my favorite was the Rose of Sharon. When I was the Rose of Sharon all the decorations on the stage were like petals, and I pinned a rose to the front of my G-string, and then I would lift my skirt and ask if anyone would like to pluck my rose. And someone would always say he would, and try to reach out and grab the rose, but I would never let him. I did it all by myself. (*Lying down on the stage and simulating the action* SHE *describes*) I laid down on the stage and I plucked all the petals of my rose and blew them away. (*Sitting up again*) The manager thought it was a good idea because the boys like to say things to you while you're working, and it works out great if you can give them little bits of prop to keep or say things back. Most of the girls just made noises . . . little kissy sounds or things like that . . . but I was the first one there to actually use words, or tell a story.

BUCK: Sounds like you had a really nice act there, Shirley.

SHIRLEY: It was okay. I was doing what I had to do.

There is a silence between them as THEY *look at each other.*

SHIRLEY (*Continued*): Fred Milly tell you why he picked me for this job?

BUCK: I really don't talk much to Fred Milly.

SHIRLEY: I got this job because I was sleeping with him. I told him if he wanted to sleep with me, I wanted to get a job out of it.

BUCK: I hope it was worth the effort.

SHIRLEY: It was.

BUCK (*Standing up*): Listen, Shirley, if you don't mind, why don't we just drop this. I really don't want to hear about Fred Milly's sexual prowess, and I've got some work I've got to finish.

SHIRLEY: He doesn't have any sexual prowess. He stinks. He tries to make love, but all he does is screw. Fred Milly never went to bed with anyone but himself.

BUCK (*Crouching down near her*): Why are you telling me all this, Shirley?

SHIRLEY: You think sleeping with pigs wears it out, Mr. Halloran? You think every time a woman is forced to open her legs to a pig, it wears out what she is? She's something less for it? Because I don't. Not if I was screwed by a hundred different pigs in a hundred different ways would it ever make me feel any less clean or decent inside. They got what they wanted from me, and I got what I wanted from them, and I never gave them anything inside of me that mattered. You're a nice guy, Mr. Halloran. I don't care what the pigs around here think of me, but I do care what you think.

CHARLIE *enters in a semi-run as if the devil might be in pursuit.*

CHARLIE (*Shouting at* BUCK): You had to give Milly a copy of the new script! We shoulda taped the damn thing as it was last week!

SHIRLEY (*Seeing that her conversation with* BUCK *is about to end, starts to exit*): Maybe we could have dinner together sometime, Mr. Halloran. I'd like that. (*Exits backstage through the scrim door of the set*)

CHARLIE: What the hell did that cuckoo bird want now?

BUCK: Nothing. (*For some long moments* HE *just stares after the departed* SHIRLEY. *Then* HE *turns around and heads over to the worktable*) Just something about the robe.

CHARLIE: Yeah? What the hell's the matter with the robe? (*Spraying his mouth with a portable mouthwash,* HE *begins rooting around in the papers on the table*) Goddam broad thinks she's Marilyn Monroe! (*Sticking his face close to* BUCK) Smell my breath. You can't smell any booze on it, can you?

BUCK: No.

BUCK *watches* CHARLIE *pick up the cost figures and start rapidly turning the pages.*

BUCK (*Continued*): What's the matter with you?

CHARLIE: You gave a copy of the script to Milly.

BUCK: Yeah, so what?

CHARLIE: I'll tell you what so what. Nathan saw a copy of it sticking out of Milly's pocket as he passed him in the hall and he pulled it out and read it. And now he's on his way down here with Milly.

BUCK: Nathan never reads anything.

CHARLIE: That's what you think. He had Milly up against the wall and he was grinding the end of his cane into Milly's toes. He was really pissed off. He was grinning from ear to ear.

BUCK: Maybe he was happy about something. People grin when they're happy, too, Charlie.

CHARLIE: Not Mr. Nathan. The last time Mr. Nathan grinned three guys from the fourth floor turned up in New Jersey as part of the foundation for the Meadowlands Raceway. (*Throwing the papers down and picking up another set*) Oh, shit! Oh, shit!

BUCK: Take it easy.

CHARLIE: Don't tell me to take it easy! You couldn't leave well enough alone, could you? We had everything in the world going our way, and you had to fuck it up! You just had to fuck it up like everything else in our lives!

BUCK: What the hell are you looking for?

CHARLIE: The cost figures! Where the hell are they?

BUCK picks them up and hands them to CHARLIE, who immediately flips through them until HE locates what HE's looking for.

CHARLIE (*Continued*): Well, this is wrong. Who the hell said the prop couch cost three seventy-nine? It's only three nineteen. (*Furiously erasing the figure, and shouting as if for the benefit of some unseen presence who might be listening to him*) I catch whoever fucked up these cost figures, he's finished here! He's through! I don't give a shit who he is. I'm not going to take responsibility for somebody else's mistakes!

BUCK: You did the cost figures, Charlie.

CHARLIE: Don't say that! I didn't do these cost figures! I never touched them!

The elevator comes to life with its shrill whine and its pulsing red light above the door. CHARLIE is thrown into an instant panic as HE struggles to right all the wrongs in his cost figures. HE keeps glancing at the elevator as HE works.

CHARLIE (*Continued*): Oh, shit! Oh, shit! Not now! Gimme a second!

CHARLIE is still talking to himself and trying to fix up the figures when the elevator door snaps open. MILLY and MR. NATHAN have arrived. NATHAN is a short man in his 60s, spiffy in neither dress nor grooming. The suit HE wears is a generation out of fashion, and the sweater beneath it with its row of buttons looks ratty. For a second the two of them stand inside the elevator as if THEY were posed statues—MILLY staring straight ahead, NATHAN with his cane in front of him, both hands resting on it. Then NATHAN smiles and speaks.

NATHAN: Good evening, my children, good evening. May God be on your side and not grudge you the profits of your labors.

BUCK: Good evening, Mr. Nathan.

CHARLIE: How ya feelin' tonight, Mr. Nathan?

NATHAN *and* MILLY *come forward, descending the stairs simultaneously, step for step.*

NATHAN: Strong, Charlie. Always strong . . . like a pack of Canadian wolves that have brought down a moose, tearing its hamstrings so it cannot run, sinking their teeth into its soft organs, ripping them, eating . . .

MILLY: Mr. Nathan says he feels good tonight, Charlie.

NATHAN *gives a little wave of his cane.*

MILLY (*Continued*): Mr. Nathan says sit down, boys, sit down, relax.

BUCK *and* CHARLIE *sit down, about as relaxed as a man with a scorpion crawling up his back.*

NATHAN (*Sticking his hand in his pocket and taking out some nuts and raisins*): Currants, raisins, seeds?

BUCK: No thanks, Mr. Nathan.

NATHAN: You should eat, Buck. Always eat to keep up your strength for your work.

BUCK: I had a chicken salad sandwich a couple of hours ago, Mr. Nathan.

CHARLIE (*As eager as ever to make points*): I'll have some, Mr. Nathan.

NATHAN *pours the nuts and raisins into* CHARLIE's *outstretched palm. For a moment* CHARLIE *just stares down at his palm.*

NATHAN: What are you looking at, Charlie?

CHARLIE: Nothing, Mr. Nathan. Just some pieces of lint in here. (*Popping the nuts and raisins into his mouth and chewing*) Boy, these are good. You should try some of it, Buck. Where did you buy this stuff, Mr. Nathan? The health food store around the corner?

NATHAN: No, Charlie. It came with the suit.

MILLY: Mr. Nathan bought the suit secondhand in a bazaar in Damascus in 1967, Charlie, and when he put his hand in the pockets there it was. Isn't that right, Mr. Nathan?

CHARLIE *has stopped chewing, his facial expression turned sour, his teeth seemingly stuck together.*

NATHAN: Eat up, Charlie. You waste my time, you waste my life.

CHARLIE, *almost gagging, swallows the food down.*

MILLY: Mr. Nathan says his time is limited, boys. He has to fly to Istanbul tonight to discuss international distribution rights for our programming with
a Japanese consortium.

NATHAN: I am looking forward to meeting with the Japanese again. (*Walking directly Downstage as* HE *speaks*) Kagoshima, Kitakyushu, Nagasaki, Kyoto,
Yokosuka, Yokohama, Hamamatsu, Yamaguichi, Wakayama . . .

MILLY: Mr. Nathan has had extensive experience in dealing with the Japanese,
Buck. He met them during the war.

NATHAN (*Turning to* BUCK *and pointing his outstretched cane at him*): I incinerated
twelve cities! (*Lowering his cane, continuing to speak as* HE *walks behind the
worktable*) I blew up dams and drowned the livestock. I razed their shrines
and destroyed their gods. I leveled their railroads and their homes, the
places where they lived and the places where they prayed. I gave them rack
and ruin!

CHARLIE: Boy, I can sure see why you're looking forward to this meeting, Mr.
Nathan. Nothing like talking over old times, eh, Buck?

CHARLIE *nervously watches as* NATHAN *begins rooting around in his papers.*

MILLY: It's because Mr. Nathan has this sentimental attachment to the Japanese, Charlie, that Mr. St. George has given him carte blanche to pursue
these negotiations to a successful conclusion.

NATHAN *finds the paper* HE's *looking for, the one* CHARLIE *has been erasing.* HE
holds it up to the light, smiles at CHARLIE, *and then sticks it under his arm as* HE
turns his attention to BUCK.

NATHAN: You're a good boy, Buck. (*Leaning close to* BUCK) Out of the eater came
forth meat; out the strong came forth sweetness.

Lifting BUCK *up by the arm,* NATHAN *walks* BUCK *away from the worktable to a
Midstage position in front of the reenactment set.*

BUCK (*As* THEY *walk*): What does that mean, Fred?
MILLY: It means Mr. Nathan likes you, Buck.
BUCK: Thank you very much, Mr. Nathan. I appreciate . . .
MILLY: I'm not finished with the analysis of Mr. Nathan's remark, Buck.
BUCK: Sorry.
MILLY: Mr. Nathan likes you, Buck, but he's very disturbed that you didn't seek

his advice before your marriage went down the tubes. He feels he may have to question the corporate judgment of a man who is too proud to seek help when he needs it.

As NATHAN *begins to walk back behind the worktable,* MILLY *takes over his spot, standing a few feet away from* BUCK, *staring at him, almost as if riveting* BUCK *to his place.*

BUCK: I wish you wouldn't look at it that way, Mr. Nathan. I know I should have come to you, it's just that . . .

MILLY: Mr. Nathan's not finished, Buck.

CHARLIE: Mr. Nathan sure says a lot in a few words, Buck.

MILLY: Mr. Nathan says a man who feeds his wife with vinegar will suck no honey from her lips.

CHARLIE: Boy, that's really a great thought, isn't it, Buck? Advice like that could really save a marriage.

CHARLIE, *increasingly frightened by* NATHAN'*s presence at the worktable, tries to light a cigarette, but everything shakes: his hands, the cigarette, the match.*

MILLY: Mr. Nathan hopes you will remember these words of advice as you go forth to seek a new life and a new woman to shack up with.

BUCK: Thank you very much, Mr. Nathan. I certainly . . .

NATHAN *crashes his cane down on the table.*

MILLY: Mr. Nathan doesn't have time for idle chitchat, Buck. Mr. Nathan says you are almost ready to move up in the food chain. You do want to move up in the food chain, don't you, Buck?

NATHAN (*Before* BUCK *has a chance to answer*): Oh, Charlie, Charlie. What am I going to do with you? Man that is born of woman has but a short time to live and is full of misery.

CHARLIE: What is he saying, Fred?

MILLY: He's not saying anything, Charlie.

NATHAN: I knew his father when he was running numbers on 125th Street. An honest man from the day he was born to the day he died from ulcers and a liver condition. And now comes the progeny with a couch marked up from three hundred nineteen dollars and ninety-eight cents to three hundred seventy-nine dollars and ninety-eight cents, not including tax! (*Crushing the paper* HE *had taken from* CHARLIE *into a little ball and throwing it away,* HE *squeezes* CHARLIE'*s face in his hands*) Oh, Absalom, Absalom, my son, why hast thou risen against me?

CHARLIE: What's he saying, Fred? For the love of God tell me what he's saying!

MILLY: It's nothing to worry about, Charlie. Absolutely nothing.

NATHAN: Why does he tear my heart out like this? What have I done to deserve this injustice? (*Thrusting* CHARLIE's *face away from him in disgust*)

CHARLIE: He's saying something, Fred. He's definitely saying something!

NATHAN (*With mounting ferocity as* HE *raises his hands to the heavens*): Lord, gird up my strength unto the battle! Give me the strength to crush into the earth those that rise up against me! Burn the bones of my enemies into lime! Stone them with stones that betray me! Deliver up their children to the famine! Pour out their blood with the point of a sword!

CHARLIE: It sure sounds like something, Fred. What is it? Some kind of prayer?

MILLY: I don't know what it is, Charlie.

CHARLIE: Buck? Buck?

NATHAN (*Rocking back and forth as* HE *chants*): The heart of the sons of men is full of evil, and madness is in their heart while they live, and after that they go to the dead! (*Hiding his face in his suit jacket*) For to him that is joined to the living there is hope, for the living know that they shall die, but the dead know not anything . . .

CHARLIE: Oh, my God, my God, it's a prayer for the dead, isn't it? He's reciting a prayer for the dead over me! Fred! Fred! Oh, God! Oh, God!

NATHAN: Better a living dog than a dead lion. Better a living cockroach than a dead dog. For the dead rot in the ground and the memory of them is forgotten.

CHARLIE (*Grabbing* NATHAN's *hands, pulling the lapels of the jacket away from his face*): I'll never do it again, Mr. Nathan! I swear to God Almighty I'll never do it again! Just give me another chance! Please, Mr. Nathan, please! I didn't know what I was doing! I didn't! Please! Please!

NATHAN *pats* CHARLIE *on the cheek and then starts to walk away, back to his position near* BUCK. CHARLIE *tries to follow, to continue his pleading, but* MILLY *steps in front of him, forcing* CHARLIE *to sit down again.*

MILLY: Mr. Nathan thinks you don't look well, Charlie. He's arranged to have you driven home in his own private limousine. All you have to do is walk out the door and tell the three men waiting for you in the limousine where you live.

CHARLIE *suddenly throws his head back, his hand clutching his chest, his mouth gaping open in what looks like a heart attack. Great gasps of pain come from his throat.* BUCK, *instinctively, starts to move toward* CHARLIE. NATHAN *blocks his way with his cane.*

MILLY (*Continued*): You live out by the Meadowlands, don't you, Charlie?

At the mention of "Meadowlands," CHARLIE's *agony becomes unbearable. His mouth moves, but only a gasping sound comes out.*

NATHAN: What's he saying?

MILLY: What's he saying, Buck?

BUCK: He says he lives on West 55th Street.

MILLY: He says he lives on West 55th Street, Mr. Nathan.

NATHAN: In that case he doesn't need the limousine.

MILLY (*To* CHARLIE): Mr. Nathan says if you live on West 55th Street, you can just walk home. You won't need the limousine . . . this time.

> CHARLIE, *reprieved, struggles to recover from the death sentence. But reprieved or not,* CHARLIE *has been totally destroyed. His arms hang limply at his side, his eyes are glazed.*

MILLY (*Continued*): Mr. Nathan is ready to see the rehearsal of the Joy Bonnard murder, Charlie.

> CHARLIE *slowly gets up from the table and starts to head backstage.* HE *walks like a dead man.*

MILLY (*Continued*): There's no rush, Charlie. All Mr. Nathan wants you to remember is that you waste his time, you waste his life.

> CHARLIE *picks up his pace. Now* HE *stumbles Off like a dead man in a hurry.* NATHAN *walks over to the worktable and sits down in the Upstage chair,* CHARLIE's *chair. Lifting both of his legs onto the table,* NATHAN *heaves out an audible sound of having achieved great comfort.* MILLY *follows* NATHAN *to the table, sits down in the middle chair, and crashes both of his feet down on the table.* THEY *both stare at* BUCK.

BUCK: What you're going to see, Mr. Nathan, is the second scene in the Joy Bonnard murder reenactment. The scene in which she gets killed.

MILLY: Mr. Nathan has varicose veins, Buck. The only way he can get any relief is to lift his legs on top of something. Isn't that right, Mr. Nathan?

NATHAN: This is a great relief.

MILLY: Why don't you put your feet on the table, too, Buck?

> BUCK *walks over to the worktable and, sitting in the remaining chair next to* MILLY, *lifts his legs on the table.* MILLY *has spread his feet so wide there is hardly room for* BUCK's *feet to fit.*

MILLY (*Continued*): Best way to avoid varicose veins, isn't it, Mr. Nathan?

NATHAN: It's a great relief.

BUCK: As I was saying, Mr. Nathan, what you're going to see is the second scene in the Joy Bonnard murder reenactment. The first scene takes place in the bedroom and we're going to be taping that . . .

BUCK *momentarily loses his train of thought as a strange battle begins between* NATHAN *and* MILLY. NATHAN *has just placed his left foot on top of* MILLY's *foot. It rests there unchallenged for a moment.*

BUCK (*Continued*): . . . first thing tomorrow morning. It's going to follow our usual format. Charlie's going to be able to gets lots of . . .

MILLY *challenges* NATHAN's *foot by lifting his left foot on top of* NATHAN's *foot. There is a big smile on* MILLY's *face as* HE *places his foot down.*

BUCK (*Continued*): . . . skin because both the girl and the man are going to be naked in the bed, and we're going to be able to get lots of good . . .

NATHAN *drops his remaining foot on top of* MILLY's. *The feet are now stacked up four high.*

NATHAN: Muff!
BUCK: I beg your pardon, Mr. Nathan?
NATHAN: Muff!
MILLY: Mr. Nathan wants to know how many good shots of her muff you're gonna get out in this scene.
BUCK: Well, that's the thing, you see, Mr. Nathan. In this scene we're not really going to be concentrating on her muff. We're going to concentrate on her muff in the first scene, but in this scene, the one you're going to see . . .

MILLY *begins trying to extricate his left foot from the pile. Although* NATHAN *and* MILLY *are smiling at each other, the battle is joined and great pressure is being applied.*

BUCK (*Continued*): I want to pull back the camera, in a sense. I want to show the viewing audience that there was more to this girl than her . . .
NATHAN: Muff!
MILLY (*By dint of great effort, finally managing to wrench free his left foot*): Excuse me a minute, Mr. Nathan. (*Turning to* BUCK) It sounds to me like you're not rowing with both oars on this, Buck. You can't tell Mr. Nathan you ain't shooting . . .
NATHAN: Muff!
MILLY: Without good muff shots we lose seventeen percent of the viewing audience.
BUCK: I understand that, Fred.
MILLY: Ass eleven percent, tits fourteen percent, muff seventeen percent. It's all in the computer, boy! (*Dropping his left foot on top of* BUCK's *right*)
BUCK: If you'll listen to me for a minute, Fred, I'll try and . . .
MILLY: Because it sure sounds to me like your elevator ain't got no top floor, Buck. Your refrigerator door's open, but the light ain't comin' on!

BUCK *begins struggling to extricate his foot as* HE *argues with* MILLY, *but* MILLY *is tenacious.*

BUCK: All I'm trying to say is that we gotta start putting these pieces of people together so that some kind of whole human being comes out. You can't keep breaking people down into tits and muffs and say that's all there is to them!

BUCK *continues to violently try to pull his foot out from under* MILLY'*s foot, but* MILLY *holds on.*

MILLY: The hell we can't, boy! The twenty-one percent share of the cable market we've grabbed sure as hell says we can!

BUCK: I'm not talking about market shares, Fred! (*Giving up trying to extricate his right foot,* BUCK *drops his left foot on top of* MILLY'*s foot*) I'm talking about meaning! I'm talking about the meaning of human life!

MILLY *looks from one of his legs to the other, suddenly realizing* HE *is spread-eagled on the table—his right leg held down by* NATHAN, *his left caught in a scissors grip by* BUCK'*s feet.* HE *tries to pull his feet free, but* NATHAN *and* BUCK *hold on.*

BUCK (*Continued*): How long can you keep filming people cut up into butchered parts, Fred? How long can you pretend human life is nothing better than dead organ meat?

NATHAN *slips his cane under* BUCK'*s and* MILLY'*s legs and begins pulling them closer to him.*

BUCK (*Continued*): If we see people die and then we take away everything that gave their life meaning, what is there going to be left for any of us, Fred? What is there going to be left when the world has pulled itself down into a sewer, Fred?

As all the feet are brought together, a tremendous melee of thrashing legs breaks out in a battle for dominance. The battle continues for some seconds, reaches its frantic pitch, and then suddenly stops: BUCK'*s feet on the bottom,* MILLY'*s feet in the middle,* NATHAN'*s feet on top.* NATHAN, *in triumph, pokes his cane into the air, screaming out as if in answer to* BUCK'*s question.*

NATHAN: Muff! Muff! Muff!

Lights dim on the worktable and come up full on the reenactment set.

JOY (*Offstage*): You make me feel like dirt! You make me feel like a whore!

Entering the room through the archway, JOY *is in a highly agitated state.* SHE *moves about the room for some moments, making spastic little motions with her hands, shaking her head, before* SHE *finally comes to a stop by the phony fireplace.* SHE *has obviously been crying.* SHE *wipes her eyes.* FRANK *enters barefooted and wearing only his briefs.*

FRANK: What the hell is happening here? It's one in the morning. Let's get back into bed. I'm not finished yet. (*Waits a moment for an answer, and when there isn't any, comes forward*) I don't know what the hell you're trying to pull, but I don't have time for this. I gotta get outta here in a couple of hours. I got a paper to deliver at the MLA convention in the morning. I told you that. So come on, let's go. I'm ready to go again. (*Grabbing at her arm when* SHE *doesn't answer*) Did you hear what I said?

JOY (*Pulling her arm free*): Keep your hands off me!

FRANK: I told you I'm ready to go again, so let's do it!

JOY: No!

FRANK: Don't tell me no! Two lousy fucks and that's supposed to be it? Well, let me tell you something. Two lousy fucks isn't worth the cab fare it cost me taking you home! (*Pulling her*) Now come on!

JOY (*Wrenching her arm free again and moving away*): Get out of here! Why don't you just get your clothes on and get out of here! I'm not your whore! I'm not any man's whore! So just leave me alone!

FRANK: Sure, I'll leave you alone . . . when I'm finished.

JOY: You're finished now! I'm not getting back into that bed with you!

FRANK (*Grabbing both her arms, his anger suddenly boiling up to terrifying proportions*): Don't you tell me what you're gonna do! Don't you ever tell me what you're gonna do! (*Thrusting her violently down on the couch*)

JOY: I thought we could be good for each other! I thought because you had an education you would be capable of some sensitivity! I could get the smallest touch of understanding from you!

FRANK: Who the hell do you usually pick up in that bar? Leonard Bernstein? The Sultan of Morocco? Rimski Korsakov? Why don't you get off your high horse and take a good look at yourself? You're nothing! Nobody! A hole walking around on two legs, too stupid to even realize that the only reason any man ever comes up here is just to stick it to you!

JOY: That's not true! The only men that ever came here were men that I wanted here . . .

FRANK (*Beginning a litany that continues throughout her reply*): Stick it to you! Stick it to you! Stick it to you!

JOY: Men I invited up here because I thought a relationship might develop, something worthwhile, something . . . . Stop it!

FRANK: I'll tell you the kind of men you brought here. The scum of the earth, stinking of liquor and sweat. Tired old men with bloated bellies and suspenders . . .

JOY: Why are you doing this?

FRANK: Teenage jocks from the garage with car grease dripping from their fingers, and their tongues lolling outta their mouths like the bovine numbskulls they are.

JOY: Why are you turning what we could have felt for each other into a sewer?

FRANK: And you took them home with you, and you let them stick their fingers into every crevice of your body. And you took them to bed with you and you lay there next to them and under them, laughing at their moronic jokes.

JOY: They were decent men!

FRANK (*Kneeling down on the couch beside her, pressing his face close*): But that's what every whore tells herself, isn't it? Lying there in the dark while those sweaty stinking bodies pound down on her. "I am the Snow Queen and Prince Charming has come to slide his bloated tongue into my mouth!"

JOY (*Standing up and moving a few feet off to get away from him*): And what did you do with your tongue? And what hole in my body didn't you shove your fingers into? What am I guilty of, Frank? Thinking you would turn out to be different than the rest of them? Believing there was a chance I could meet someone capable of giving love for love? Was that my crime, Frank? Not believing that love is shit and people are scum?

FRANK *covers his face with his hands, rubbing his eyes, his temples, as if trying to soothe a terrible headache.*

JOY (*Continued*): All the way home in the cab I thought how good tomorrow was going to be with you: waking up, going to the hotel, listening to you deliver your paper. I was going to be there for you, to listen to you. I wanted that because you made me feel in the bar that you were someone I could open my heart to. That everything was possible. What was that all about, Frank? Just to turn it into a screw job in a fourth-floor walkup, without any gentleness, without any meaning—like an animal? Well, how dare you do that to me? How dare you do that to any human being? I have love inside of me, and poetry inside of me, and . . .

FRANK: The hole that walks on two legs has poetry inside of her? (*Standing up and walking over to her*) What kind of poetry? Hallmark cards? "Trees"?

JOY: If you wanted a whore, Frank, why didn't you just pick up a whore? Why did you come looking for someone like me?

FRANK (*Ignoring her remark, or pretending to*):
"I think that I shall never see
A poem lovely as a tree,
A tree that may in summer wear
A nest of robins in her hair . . ."

FRANK *runs his fingers through his hair to show what it would be like having robins walking around in your hair.* JOY *sits down on the couch, turning away from him.*

FRANK (*Continued*): Now that we've exhausted everything you know about poetry, maybe you'd like to talk about philosophy? Maybe you'd like to enlighten me with your perceptions on Schopenhauer, Nietzsche, the will to live and the will to be Superman. I could use it in my lecture tomorrow. No? How about a thousand words on Kafka and Camus, Jean-Paul Sartre and the failure of existentialism to solve anything? Yes? No? What do you want to talk about? Polly wanna cracker? Talk. Talk. Squawk. Squawk. You tell me what the salesgirl behind the department-store perfume counter thinks anybody would be interested in hearing her talk about? (*Silence*) That's right! Zippo! Nada! Nothing! (*Opening the liquor cabinet and pouring himself a drink*) God, this whole stinking society makes me sick! Always whining. Always bellyaching.

FRANK *swallows down the drink. For some moments there is nothing but silence between them as* FRANK *stands there, facing away from* JOY.

JOY: You're as lonely as I am, aren't you, Frank?

For some moments more FRANK *stands there rigidly staring forward. But the question has been heard and has had a visible effect upon him.* HE *suddenly turns toward* JOY.

FRANK: Come on. Let's get back into bed. It's colder than hell out here. (*Squatting down in front of her*) Didn't I show you as nice a time as you showed me? (*Opening the bottom of her robe*) Wasn't that a nice couple of sweet screws we had? (*Stroking her legs, kissing them*) Such beautiful legs . . . such sweet beautiful legs . . . I just wanna bury myself in them.

As JOY *watches* FRANK *burying his face between her legs, a slight smile comes to her face; but it is not a pleasant smile, and her eyes are filled with ice and hate.*

JOY: Do I excite you, Frank? Does it excite you being here with someone like me?
FRANK (*Too lost in his passion to really pay attention to what* JOY's *saying, or sense the change that has occurred in her*): Yes.
JOY: So much nicer than having to stay in that stuffy hotel room, or that stuffy little university town where you teach, isn't it, Frank?
FRANK: Yes.
JOY: Having to pretend all sorts of things to all sorts of people all the time, when you can come down here and get off on the crumpled sheets of an unmade bed.

FRANK *tries to climb up on the couch beside her, but* JOY *places her foot against his chest and pushes him down to the floor.*

JOY (*Continued*): But you gotta stay down on the floor, Frank. If you wanna get a good look at everything I am, you gotta stay down on the floor.

JOY straddles FRANK, *sitting on him.*

FRANK: I like it when you tease me. When you pretend you don't want it and you make me work for it.

JOY: I can do anything you want, Frank. I know lots of tricks.

FRANK (*Squeezing her breasts*): Oh, God, this feels so good. Your boobs feel so good in my hand.

JOY (*Grabbing his wrists and forcing his hands away*): I want it too, Frank. I want it as much as you do, but we have to settle the money thing. We have to get the money thing out of the way so we don't have to think about it.

FRANK: I just want to squeeze them . . . kiss them . . . suck them in my mouth . . . no thought . . . no thought anymore . . . oh God, just kiss, just . . .

Lowering her head as if to kiss him, JOY *spits in his face. Before* FRANK *has a chance to react,* SHE *moves away, sitting down on the couch.*

FRANK (*Continued*): You whore! You lousy whore! (*Getting to his feet, and wiping the spit off his face*) You're like all the rest of them! Every face I have to face in the lecture hall!

FRANK *goes over to* JOY *and rubs the spit from his hand into her face.* JOY *jumps to her feet, trying now to get out of the room, get away from* FRANK *as* HE *stalks after her.*

FRANK (*Continued*): A universe of dull, boring, whining, stupid mediocrities! And I watch them filing in every day . . .

FRANK *pushes the couch so* JOY *is blocked against the fireplace wall.*

FRANK (*Continued*): And I'm like a god to them . . .

JOY *tries to climb over the couch and run past* FRANK, *but* HE *grabs her, pulling her down to the floor, choking her.*

FRANK (*Continued*): And I let them feed from the trough of my intelligence: the loudmouth and the bully, the coward and the cunning, the pathetic, the false, the debased, the insignificant!

JOY, *desperately trying to save herself, reaches out for one of the knitting needles stuck through the half-finished sweater lying near the arm of the couch.* FRANK *grabs her wrist before* SHE *has a chance to strike out at him, and turning the needle around in her hand, begins driving it down into her chest.*

FRANK (*Continued*): Dismal gray eaters of another man's intelligence! And before them I spread out the feast of my skull, my consciousness, my being . . . and year after year I watch them dine on all the dainties . . . munching me, tearing me, sucking out of the marrow of my existence! And when the year is over they leave, and a new horde of useless, brainless . . .

As the needle drives into JOY's *heart,* SHE *screams—and for a long moment her scream rends the air.*

FRANK (*Continued*): They're eating me alive! They want me to have answers and I don't have any answers! They want me to be God and all there is to me is a sack of testicles between my legs!

FRANK, *almost in tears, lies down against the still body of* JOY BONNARD. *For some seconds there is only silence. Nothing moves. Then the stage lights abruptly come up.* MILLY, NATHAN *and* BUCK, *their feet on the floor now, are still seated at the worktable. For some moments more the silence continues as* NATHAN *stares at the reenactment set and the drama that has been played out for him.* BUCK *looks over at* NATHAN, *trying to read some reaction.*

BUCK: As I said, Mr. Nathan, this is only part of it. I'm going to have the introduction, and then there's the scene between the two of them in bed. I just wanted to show you this particular scene because I think it helps us understand something of what Joy Bonnard was really like as well as some of the motivations of the . . .

NATHAN *scrapes his chair back as* HE *gets to his feet, the sound cutting* BUCK *off in mid-sentence.* NATHAN *looks at* BUCK *for a moment and then walks over to the reenactment set,* BUCK *trailing, pleading his case.*

BUCK (*Continued*): She was a decent human being, Mr. Nathan. She went into that bar, she drank, she took men home with her, but it wasn't because she wanted money from them. It was just something to push away the loneliness that was in her life.

Under NATHAN's *withering glance, the* ACTOR *playing the part of* FRANK *quits the stage.* BUCK *seems even more desperate now.*

BUCK (*Continued*): She was suffocating, Mr. Nathan, and she couldn't find anyone to listen to her! She listened to all those men, but which one of them ever listened to her? Which one of them . . .

NATHAN *abruptly turns and heads for the elevator.* BUCK *stares at* SHIRLEY *left alone on the stage, and then* SHE *lowers her head and exits.*

BUCK (*Continued*): You can't walk away from it, Mr. Nathan! You can't pretend the agony of the world doesn't matter!

NATHAN *enters the elevator, followed by* MILLY. THEY *turn around to look at* BUCK.

BUCK (*Continued*): You do that you're gonna wake up in the middle of the night, crying out for the sound of a human voice, and all that's gonna come back to you are the screams of baboons rubbing their asses on the ground!

MILLY (*Continuing to look at* BUCK *for a moment longer*): Mr. Nathan says . . . throw the garbage out and shoot what you had last week.

MILLY *presses the elevator button. The door shuts and the elevator begins its shrill ascent.* BUCK *takes the toy arrow* HE's *been carrying around in his hand and throws it at the elevator. It harmlessly bounces off the shut door.* CHARLIE, *seeing the coast is clear, enters.* HE *thrusts out his hands, still trembling.*

CHARLIE: Boy, look at that! They're shaking like a leaf.

BUCK *sweeps his arm across the worktable, sending a pile of papers flying.*

CHARLIE (*Continued*): When he started reciting that prayer for the dead over me, I thought for sure I'd bought it. I thought for sure I was going to be part of the Meadowlands. He wasn't kidding, was he, Buck?

BUCK: No.

CHARLIE: Wow! I'll tell you something—this was worse than what happened to me last week. I woke up in the middle of the night, grabbing my guts. I couldn't believe it. I thought my insides were coming out. I didn't know what the hell it was. I ended up crawling on the bed on my knees, bent over like some goddam Moslem bowing to a prayer wheel. I was going around like that for two hours: in the bed, in the tub, walking around. The pain was terrible. First it was in the kidneys, then it was in the side, then it was about three inches over the groin. I thought something blew up in there. I was scared, I don't mind telling ya. I thought I really had it. I thought I was going to the hospital, the whole works! And then you know what it turned out to be? Gas! Would you believe it? Gas! I sat down on the toilet and let out a fart that almost blew the door off the wall. I was never so happy in my life. That's the way I feel now, Buck. This is the happiest moment of my life!

BUCK: Go on home, Charlie.

CHARLIE: Yeah. Sure. What the hell time is it anyway? (*Looking at his watch*) Christ, it's after midnight, already.

CHARLIE *hunts around the elevator steps for his rubbers as* BUCK *walks over to the reenactment set.*

CHARLIE (*Continued*): What the hell did I do with my rubbers? The radio said it was going to snow like a son-of-a-bitch tonight. (*Finding his rubbers under the steps,* HE *sits down and puts them on*) So whadda ya gonna do now?

BUCK *bends down and picks up the knitting needle.* HE *holds it in his hand, staring at it.*

CHARLIE (*Continued*): You want me to clear some time to shoot the Joy Bonnard thing on Friday?

BUCK: Yeah. Sure. Friday's fine, Charlie. (*Wanders for a few moments about the set*)

CHARLIE (*Putting on his leather jacket and winding a muffler around his neck*): We can shove it in right after the tourist gets strangled for a pocketful of change in Kuala Lumpur. Or is it the school bus that gets blown up in Haifa on Friday? I can't keep the fucking things straight anymore.

BUCK (*Coming to rest on the arm of the couch*): It's the school bus on Friday, Charlie.

CHARLIE: Yeah, that's right. I keep thinking about this piece of meat I've got coming in to play the part of the tourist. She's gotta go two hundred pounds, but when she sits there in the tub with her balloons floating on top of the water, the shot I'm gonna get looking down is gonna be unbelievable. When she gets strangled and goes under, the fadeout's two nipples comin' up to the surface. You got any idea what half those clown directors they got in Hollywood would give to come up with a shot like that? Their left nut! But they didn't do it. Charlie Corvanni did it! Charlie Corvanni working for Shit Enterprises did it! (*Clapping his hands as if trying to work up some exuberance in* BUCK) Okay! So Friday it is! (*Walking over to* BUCK *and touching him*) Listen to me, old Buckeroo. It just don't matter. By the time we do a reenactment of it they're all dead anyway. You're dead you don't have to give a shit about anything. (*Turns and starts to exit*)

BUCK: It's going to be pretty out there tonight, Charlie, with all that new snow coming down.

CHARLIE: Sure. And by tomorrow morning when they get done sanding it and a million bums get done pissing into it, it's gonna end up like it always ends up—a pile of sopping shit!

BUCK: That's right, Charlie. That's just what happens to it.

CHARLIE *exits.*

BUCK (*Continued*): The wonder of it is is that it ever bothers coming down at all.

Lights fade and out.

END OF PLAY

Mercenaries
James Yoshimura

About James Yoshimura

James Yoshimura was born and raised in Chicago and attended Catholic schools in the city. After graduating from Mundelein College, he attended Yale School of Drama on John Golden and Shubert fellowships, and was awarded the CBS Foundation Prize in Playwriting for best thesis play (*Stunts*). Yoshimura is also the author of *Lion Dancers* and two teleplays, *Reelroom* and *My Elvis*. He was a writer-in-residence for the Illinois Arts Council for five years and received a project completion grant from them. In 1982 he was selected as a national member of New Dramatists. His play *Ohio Tip-Off* was presented at the O'Neill Theater Center's 1983 National Playwrights Conference.

Production History

Mercenaries was nominated for TCG's *Plays in Process* script circulation series by Colette Brooks, dramaturg of the Interart Theatre in New York City. It was presented there from June 9 through August 1, 1982.

Margot Lewitin directed. The set was designed by Kate Edmunds, lighting by Ann Wrightson and costumes by Kate Edmunds and Tom McAlister. The cast was as follows:

Spike	Andrew Davis
Jimbo	Kenneth Ryan
Yogi	William Winkler
Wells	Reg E. Cathey
Mockis	Roger Brown
Doctor	Anna Deavere Smith
Guard	L.B. Williams
Attendant	Jeffrey Joseph

Prior to the Interart production, *Mercenaries* was given readings at the Goodman Theatre in Chicago and at Interart.

Characters

SPIKE, real name Michael Robert Whaley, white, a cold intellectual, over six feet, just under 200 pounds, big-boned, all lean muscle, in his early 30s.

JIMBO, real name Gerald O. Ryan, white, a boisterous spirit, initiates action to satisfy his need to displace all his hyperkinetic energy. An even six feet, under 170 pounds, in his early 30s.

YOGI, real name James Mark Milliken, white, quiet, jovial, with the physical presence of a mountain. Over six feet, five inches, 225 pounds of massive strength, in his middle 20s.

WELLS, black, the island representative, a high-fashion dresser, with elegant understatement in selection of clothes and manners. In his early 40s, no older.

MOCKIS, white, the American representative, a neat, clean dresser with midwestern tastes in clothes and manners. Nothing flashy or garish, just simple, long-wearing clothes. Late 50s, early 60s. A man with a voracious appetite for food and drink, enjoys the small quirks of his personality, and is a genuine, jovial soul. The simple midwestern American.

DOCTOR, black, Wells' associate, a beautiful light-toned woman. An efficient clinician. In her early 30s, dresses with her professional standing always in mind.

GUARDS, ATTENDANTS and WORKMEN, black, some young, some middle-aged. The GUARDS should be big, physical individuals. There is only one scene (Act Two, Scene 2) in which a GUARD has a sustained section of dialogue; this GUARD should be in his early 30s. Ideally at least six actors should play and double in these roles, but it is possible for as few as two actors to suffice.

Time

The present.

Place

The resort area of a Caribbean island.

The Play

Mercenaries

ACT ONE

Scene 1

An airplane hangar. It contains no airplanes, but there are boxes and crates of airplane parts: engine bolts and blocks, parts of propellers, disassembled gears, sections of a fuselage.

Reggae music is on pre-set, a heavy steel-drum beat dominating the music.

WORKMEN are finishing the construction of three steel plates that have been bolted to the floor. There is an individual set of neck, wrist and ankle irons attached to each steel plate by a thick chain that runs through a soldered steel loop in the center of each plate.

The reggae music segues into deafening thunder from a passing overhead jet. The sound of the jet diminishes, segues back into the music. The WORKMEN exit.

Lights down. Music down. Lights up.

WELLS and the woman DOCTOR come Onstage in a rush, WELLS following on the heels of the DOCTOR. The DOCTOR is dressed in a gray surgeon's gown over a floral print dress, and is carrying a stethoscope and a medical black bag. WELLS is dressed in an expensive pair of gray slacks, a light blue silk bathrobe and a pair of handmade Italian designer shoes. HE is sockless. DOCTOR begins checking the neck irons and the chain. WELLS stalks the stage, wringing his hands, occasionally untying and adjusting his bathrobe's sash.

WELLS: No! No, this can't be possible! Not now. (HE *kicks the chain from one of the plates*) Why does this happen now? They lied to me!

DOCTOR: Yessir.

WELLS' ATTENDANT *enters, carrying three suitcases and a briefcase.*

WELLS: The arrogance of them. Who the hell are they? To order me around. (HE *grabs a chain from a steel plate*) Three months of waiting, and now they decide what has to be done. We make the concessions? They decide, we jump. In the middle of the night. Damn this country. Damn this world. I take it from everyone. (HE *kicks a chain at the* DOCTOR) These things mean nothing to me! Pay attention to me, not these things!

DOCTOR (*Opening her medical bag*): Can I give you anything?

WELLS: Give me? (*Giggles nervously*)

DOCTOR: Would you like something then?

WELLS: Why? Should I be relaxed? Who am I to complain? I've been selected for this honor. It's a privilege, isn't it? No one else wanted it!

DOCTOR: You're not responsible for what's happened. No one thinks that.

WELLS: I don't want to hear that. I shouldn't have to listen to any of it! You should know better. (*Beat*) These damn butchers! They can come here and do whatever they please. They're from America. That makes them special. What the hell is our country, a playground for them?

ATTENDANT (*Struggling under the weight of the bags*): Sir? May I put the suitcases down for you?

WELLS: Stand and have some pride for once! (*Beat*) Why do they move everything to this place? This is a resort area. We have tourists here! It's our vacation season. (*Beat*) It's always on their time, forever on their terms. (*Beat*) I don't want to hear about my responsibilities! (*Sounds of* PEOPLE *entering the airplane hangar*) Oh, we'll see now. We'll see about this damn American representative and his schedule for us, at this hour! (*To* DOCTOR) Am I presentable?

DOCTOR: Of course. Yessir.

WELLS: You're a damn liar, of course.

The three MERCENARIES *are led in by a detail of* GUARDS. SPIKE, JIMBO *and* YOGI *are dressed in filthy military greens.* THEY *are shackled wrist to ankle by a chain that loops through a metal body brace.* THEY *are layered with grime and sweat, their hair matted and tuffed with grime.* YOGI *and* SPIKE *are wearing wornout dress shoes that are without heels or shoelaces.* JIMBO *is barefoot. The* GUARDS *stand the three* MERCS *to attention. Silence.*

WELLS (*Continued*): What the hell is this! Where is the American representative! Who did this! (*Hissing*) I want an answer.

DOCTOR: I don't know, sir. It was scheduled.

WELLS: When? Whose damn schedule! I am not up in the middle of the night for this! (HE *comes up to the three* MERCS) You are the three mercenaries? (*To* DOCTOR) These are the survivors? (*Chuckles*) There has to be a mistake somewhere. (*Beat*) Lovely to make their acquaintance.

YOGI *spits.*

WELLS (*Continued; wheels to* YOGI): Where are the rest of your friends? What was it, twenty-one or was it twenty-three others that came with you? Each and everyone of you a fine human being. (*Beat*) That's right, I almost forgot. They're all dead. (*To* DOCTOR) These three? These are what remains? They were going to take over our country? They don't look capable. They don't even know how to dress up for an occasion! (*Beat*) They have two hands, two arms, a nose, eyes. Something is missing. Has to be. What would it be. (*To the* MERCS) You look so damn average. (*Laughs*)

JIMBO (*Singing*): When you wish upon a star, makes no difference what color you are. . . .

WELLS: What was that? Did you address me, young man?

JIMBO (*To* SPIKE): He's the head nigger?

SPIKE (*To* WELLS): One moment, please. We gotta sort out who's who with all you colored folks.

YOGI (*Gestures to the* DOCTOR): She's in charge.

SPIKE: Naw, she don't look official. (*To* DOCTOR) You don't look hungry enough.

JIMBO (*Gestures to* ATTENDANT): He's the top boy. He's the only one who looks like he owns something around here.

SPIKE: Good point. (*Smiles*)

WELLS: I am the head "nigger."

JIMBO (*To* SPIKE): He can talk, can't he?

SPIKE: But can the boy dance? That's the test.

The MERCS *laugh.* GUARDS *bring them to attention.*

WELLS: Oh, you can celebrate now. You can whoop it up. You have the news. America sends someone for you. It's the good news! It travels quickly. (*Beat*) It had to happen. I made it happen. (*Pause*) The rumors, all the conjectures, it's over now. Finally. We will have a trial. You, your scavenger, and us. We have something firm. Now we can give the world the little show it wants. (*Smiles*) Let your representative stand up to me. Me! It won't matter how well he makes a case for you. (*Beat*) Your country always makes a case for anyone and anything. (*Beat*) It's all been fixed ahead of time, this time, by me!

The MERCS *laugh.*

WELLS (*Continued; whirling to* JIMBO): Where are your shoes? (*To* DOCTOR) Where are his shoes? He was issued them, wasn't he? I want him in shoes!

DOCTOR: If that is what you want, yessir.

WELLS: Do I need to repeat myself? (*To* JIMBO) I can't shoot you if you're barefoot. It would be too emotional a scene for me.

YOGI *surges towards* WELLS. GUARDS *restrain him.* WELLS *jumps away, almost tripping over his own feet. Pause.* JIMBO *laughs.*

DOCTOR (*Rushes to* WELLS' *side*): Are you okay, sir?

WELLS: What? What are you saying? (*Smiles, fakes a yawn*) I need a new bathrobe. I keep tripping over this one.

JIMBO: If that ain't fucking lame.

SPIKE *laughs.*

WELLS (*To* DOCTOR): What are those things on them? Bugs? (*Brushes off his sleeves*)

DOCTOR: Sir?

WELLS: I say they have bugs!

DOCTOR: Yessir, they have bugs.

WELLS: I want them cleaned off. You have that as a direct order, is that clear!

DOCTOR: Yessir.

WELLS (*To the* MERCS): Your country finally acknowledges you? That took courage? How could we put you on trial if you didn't exist? To your own country. How silly that would have been to the world. (*Beat*) America sends a show to us? The world needs a show from us? We have a responsibility now. (*Smiles*) Be big, be wonderful. It will be damn light entertainment! (*To* DOCTOR) I want a good appearance from all of them tomorrow! From all of us! (*To the* MERCS) Don't disappoint me, please. (HE *motions to his* ATTENDANT, *begins to exit*)

SPIKE: We'll give you a show. You choose the day, boy. Guaranteed laughs with you.

WELLS (*Whirls to* SPIKE): I'll have your ass!

JIMBO: I didn't know you were that way. (*To* SPIKE) Is there anything sadder than a black sissy?

SPIKE *laughs.* WELLS *lunges for* JIMBO. GUARDS *restrain the commotion.*

DOCTOR: Sir?

WELLS *pauses, looks to* DOCTOR, *then to* GUARDS, *exits.* ATTENDANT *follows, struggling with the suitcases.* HE *stumbles.*

DOCTOR (*Continued; to* ATTENDANT): Find the American representative and get him on schedule!

ATTENDANT *nods, exits.*

JIMBO (*Watching the* ATTENDANT): And there goes the little train that could. . . .
DOCTOR (*To the* GUARDS): Gentlemen.
GUARD 1: Assume the position, boys.
JIMBO: Why? There's no reason now that our representative . . .
DOCTOR: Do it!

GUARDS *shove the* MERCS *into lockdown position over the plates.*

YOGI: These goddam steel plates.
SPIKE: We can do it this one last time. (*Smiles*) I'm going to miss all the attention.

GUARDS *finish locking the* MERCS *down.* DOCTOR *takes her stethoscope and begins checking* SPIKE.

JIMBO (*To* DOCTOR): Your head boy, he's an excitable nigger, ain't he? He wants to make a big fuss now? Over what? You're all too goddam late. (*Laughs*)
SPIKE: That's life, just a bad comedy. We're going home, goddammit!
YOGI: Home!

The MERCS *laugh.*
Lights down. Reggae steel-drum music to bridge into the next scene.

Scene 2

An outdoor, screen-enclosed veranda. Potted flowers, tropical plants and trees abound. In the center of the room is a small breakfast table covered with a linen tablecloth. There are bowls of fresh fruit and the appropriate settings of silver, china, and crystal glassware.
Music fades to silence.
MOCKIS is paging through a newspaper distractedly, occasionally glancing at his watch. ATTENDANT is standing by a wheeled serving cart that holds a silver, heated coffee urn. HE is holding a silver serving pot for the coffee.

MOCKIS: This must be some place, not to believe in time. Mystical. Tell me, it's true, yes, that everything is always late in this country? Country? (*Smiles, bows his head to the* ATTENDANT) I suppose you're immune to all the bad jokes about your country. You have pride now, don't you? A new pride, yes, or some excuse for making me sit and wait. (HE *leans back and fiddles around with one of the Churchill cigars that have been set out*)

ATTENDANT *moves in with a lighter.* MOCKIS *waves him back.*

MOCKIS (*Continued*): No, no. Don't indulge me. I might come down with a case of humility. I could use some humor. Strange how tobacco leaves could convince a man that he has a certain, elevated position in the world. (*Smiles*) I don't smoke. (*Beat*) Pride, yes. Some real stature. (*Beat*) Do you smoke? No? Huh? (HE *stands*) No, you wouldn't have any idea what I'm saying, would you? You have a real way of life down here. An honest, nose-to-the-ground acceptance of things. A genuine feel for the earth. (*Beat*) I find that so precious. Isn't it damn precious? (HE *fingers his coffee cup*)

ATTENDANT *steps to refill the cup.* MOCKIS *waves him off.* MOCKIS *spreads his arms over the table.*

MOCKIS (*Continued*): This is impressive, yes? You do know how to impress, but, ah, when it comes to protocol, you people, (*Sighs*) the bad jokes just come up about you, yes? (*Beat*) Why should it be otherwise. (HE *fiddles with the cigar*)

ATTENDANT *steps forward with the lighter again.*

MOCKIS (*Continued*): You're damn intent, yes? Fine.

ATTENDANT *holds a flame to the end of* MOCKIS' *cigar.* MOCKIS *cannot get the cigar lit.*

MOCKIS (*Continued; puffing*): What am I supposed to do? (HE *finally gets the end of the cigar lit*) Good tobacco. Good country you have here. Right? Damn good country, yes? (*Beat*) What, boy, are you a handicap or something? (*Beat*) Right. Damn good country. Except for your man, or "mon"? Where the hell might he be? (*Beat*) Right.

ATTENDANT *steps away to his station.* MOCKIS *stretches, walks to the window.*

MOCKIS (*Continued*): All this quiet. Salt water. All around. All this salt in the air. (*Beat*) I once read that the blood in the human being contains the same percent of salt as the ocean. (*Beat*) What does that mean? What, I have no damn idea. What, that you have life in the air, yes? (*Beat*) The book never said. Damn useless information. (HE *flicks an ash from the end of his cigar*)

ATTENDANT *steps over and holds an ashtray for* MOCKIS.

MOCKIS (*Continued*): Have you ever seen snow? Yes or no? Come on, son, now answer me. I'm waiting on you. (*Beat*) Make some damn sound, will you?

ATTENDANT *returns to his station and begins shining the serving pot.*

MOCKIS (*Continued*): There's no damn mystery to snow. It's in this world to make your bones wet and ache, yes? It makes you aware of where you are and for how damn long. (*Beat*) How anyone could live in all this beautiful weather, day in and day out, it makes sense, not to be able to keep things on schedule. (*Smiles*) Ignorant of me to talk about snow. What would you know? (*Glances at his watch*) I'm standing here in all this beautiful weather, and I don't feel a bit mystical. I can't beat time, yes? (*Laughs*) Ah, but there are those times when there aren't any answers, yes? (*Beat*) All those cultures, all of them surrounded by salt water. The Greeks, the Japanese, Hawaii. Those Cubans. You people. (*Beat*) Those damn Cubans, they have their ways. There has to be something common among all of you, yes? I get fascinated. You all look so different. That's for sure. But common? It makes me wonder, it sure does.

WELLS *enters, briefcase in hand.*

MOCKIS (*Continued*): If there is anything to understand, why would anyone have to find it in a book? Why would anyone put it in a book? It's all out in the open, yes? (HE *turns and sees* WELLS) There must be something basic, yes? Why there are differences between salt and freshwater people? I'm sure there is a reason.
WELLS: Coffee.

ATTENDANT *bows, takes briefcase from* WELLS' *outstretched hand.*

MOCKIS: Some morning, yes?
WELLS: I hope a pleasant one. For you.
MOCKIS (*Glances at his watch, looks at* WELLS): The weather, yes? Real cooperation, from nature, do you think.
WELLS: We've had good days. We'll have better ones.
MOCKIS (*Chuckles*): Then I must be in heaven. (HE *walks to the table, begins to seat himself, stands quickly, and then holds out a hand to an empty chair*) Please, join me.
WELLS: After you.
MOCKIS: Please, I insist. Insist? (*Beat*) That's not like me, yes? (*Smiles*)
WELLS: I said, after you. Sir.
MOCKIS (*Still smiling*): I've had such an easy morning.
WELLS: We are all well aware how easy it has been.
MOCKIS (*Laughs*): I could have overslept then, yes? (*To* ATTENDANT) Hurry with

that coffee, will you? (*To* WELLS) As they would say around my house, have a seat, take a load off yourself.

WELLS: You are our guest.

MOCKIS: Is that right? Is that what I am? (*Puffs on cigar*) So I am. I'm confused. I am a guest. The guest. (*Beat*) The salt air.

WELLS: Excuse me?

MOCKIS *eases into a chair. Pause.*

WELLS (*Continued*): I have had the opportunity to go over your preliminary petitions. I would like . . .

MOCKIS: . . . some coffee. Hurry with that coffee for my host here, would you? (*Beat*) Never says a word, that guy. Is there something I should know? Nothing tragic with him, I hope.

WELLS: On the basis of your preliminary petitions . . .

MOCKIS (*To* ATTENDANT): Make that two fresh cups, come to think of it. (*To* WELLS) Do you take anything in your coffee? Please, take a seat. A guest should never worry about the comfort of his host, yes?

WELLS: You ignore all the legal precedents which . . .

MOCKIS: I am sitting. Do you see me doing that? I could stand, but then you wouldn't be able to lecture down at me, would you?

WELLS: You misunderstand, I think.

MOCKIS: Do I now? (*Smiles*) Haven't I forgotten it all. (*Beat*) You can join me, or I can stand and join you, but I'll be goddamned if you talk down to me. That's schoolboy crap, young man. (*Beat*) Put a little extra cream in that cup of mine, will you, ol' Silent Sam?

ATTENDANT *hesitates, returns to the serving station.*

MOCKIS (*Continued; to* WELLS): You ever see snow?

WELLS *looks confusedly to the* ATTENDANT. ATTENDANT *serves the coffee.*

WELLS (*To* ATTENDANT): Fetch my briefcase.

MOCKIS: "Fetch"? How charming. (*Chuckles to himself*)

WELLS: Pardon me?

ATTENDANT *holds the briefcase out to* WELLS.

WELLS (*Continued*): On the table.

MOCKIS (*To* ATTENDANT): Please, on the table.

WELLS (*Pauses, smiles*): Yes, "please."

ATTENDANT *places the briefcase on the table, returns to his serving station.*

WELLS (*Continued*): Perhaps we could begin with an examination of the evidence we have assembled.

MOCKIS (*To* ATTENDANT): The coffee is perfect. Nice job, ol' Silent Sam.

WELLS (*Opens his briefcase, takes out some photo folders*): You should have the opportunity to taste our coffee when we really want to make it. Someday, you might. (*Beat*) Pictures speak, how is it put, a thousand words.

MOCKIS: A thousand, you say? I've never counted. I wouldn't want to guess on the accuracy of that.

WELLS (*Holds out folders to* MOCKIS): These were taken by the mercenaries themselves. I give you the chance to be eloquent.

MOCKIS: You "give" me? (*Snorts, sips his coffee*)

WELLS: They are quite striking. It's only my opinion, but I do think they were trying to capture a holiday mood. As if they were holding up some prizes from a fishing trip. Perhaps you'll find them as amusing as I did?

MOCKIS: Your coffee is getting cold, did you forget?

WELLS: Look at these pictures! Then tell me what you have forgotten.

MOCKIS: I'm more partial, more inclined to books. Those thousands and thousands of words. Pictures never impressed me much.

WELLS: You're not going to examine these pictures?

MOCKIS: I can't be surprised anymore, by anything. I'm too old for that. Surprising to say that, yes? (*Sighs*) It's taken me a long time to get used to that idea. (*Beat*) Wisdom instead of facts, that's what counts. There's truth here, there, everywhere. (HE *stands, and steps from his chair*)

WELLS: I'd like an opinion of these. (*Gestures with the folders*)

MOCKIS: The humidity is rising, isn't it? This weather isn't all that perfect, yes? It must have been something you just said.

WELLS *dumps the folders on* MOCKIS' *place setting.* MOCKIS *pauses, removes his suitcoat.*

MOCKIS (*Continued*): You won't sit, and now you throw things. (HE *tosses his suitcoat to the* ATTENDANT) Could I have that pressed? I'd be most appreciative. (*Beat*) I should get out today and do some shopping. (HE *walks towards the windows, airing his underarms*) A couple of shirts, yes? Some natural fibers. A little of your traditional handstitching. That human touch. (*Beat*) Where are we today? Things have been made more convenient, more manageable, easier to take care of. Things get carried away by progress. Sometimes that's not what's best. (*Beat*) Small things come up all the time, and things go to hell so quickly, yes? It messes up everything. (*Beat*) Those small things, so important.

WELLS (*Holds out the photos*): Your opinion.

MOCKIS (*Wipes his eyes*): I trust that they've had their effect on you. That's good enough for me. Hell, I can't trust your opinion?

WELLS: I'm not the one who needs any convincing, mister.

MOCKIS: I see you own a watch. Get any use out of it?

WELLS (*Throws open the folders on the table*): Look at them, damn you! They did this to my people, and I would like to know why!

MOCKIS: It discourages me to see you reduce all of this to a personal problem of yours. (*Glances at his watch*) After all this time, yes? (*Beat*) Tell me that you got caught in traffic. Your traffic jams are notorious here, yes? Isn't that so frustrating, sitting and waiting, when things are so out-of-hand already. (*Beat*) It was the traffic, wasn't it?

WELLS (*Laughs, pauses, eases into a chair*): This is the best that America can do? This is the best they could send? What do they have in mind?

MOCKIS (*Sips his coffee*): If you could rate this country of yours, all its highlights, I think I have a second or two to get it all.

WELLS (*Removing his coat while remaining seated*): It is getting humid, isn't it?

MOCKIS: Another move on my host's part, yes? Am I supposed to take notice of it? (*Unbuttoning his shirt cuffs* HE *rolls them up*)

WELLS (*Points to* MOCKIS' *cup*): Cream in your coffee? Only women put cream in their coffee. (*Beat*) I prefer mine black.

MOCKIS: I prefer milk. Not for its taste. (*Beat*) What's lost in the taste is made up by, how should I phrase it, by a certain aesthetic color.

WELLS: And wouldn't your mother be the only source for your milk? (*Smiles*) That obsession for mother, it's everywhere in your culture. To imagine a major power so tied down.

MOCKIS: Then there are places that make a religion out of sticking pins into little dolls. Just some of your native charm, yes?

WELLS (*Bolting up*): You go to hell.

MOCKIS: That would be unfortunate. After making it here, to heaven? (*Beat*) You're a goddam nuisance. If that, yes?

MOCKIS *and* WELLS *square off.* ATTENDANT *fumbles with his coffee server, spilling coffee over* WELLS' *suitcoat.*

ATTENDANT: I'm so sorry, sir!

WELLS: Dammit! Pick it up! Pick all of it up! Get my coat up from that mess!

A knock on the door. A GUARD *steps in, comes to attention.*

WELLS (*Continued*): Goddammit! Now what!

GUARD: Sir, you had wanted to be informed when . . . (*Pauses, looks at* MOCKIS; *to* WELLS) Sir, if we could have a private word.

MOCKIS: Another surprise for me? Or is it "on" me?

GUARD (*To* WELLS): Sir, I was to inform you when a certain situation presented itself.

WELLS: What? (*Suddenly brightening*) Yes. Yes! (*Pauses, eases to a calm*) Thank you. (HE *gestures the* GUARD *out*)

GUARD *salutes, begins to exit.*

WELLS (*Continued; to* GUARD): Get a crease in those pants of yours, mister.

GUARD: Yessir. (HE *salutes, exits*)

MOCKIS: Snappy salutes you have here. Haven't seen one quite like it. You should have kept him here to help ol' Silent Sam here. (*To* ATTENDANT) Geezus, to think you were a handicap. Not too snappy of me, yes?

WELLS (*Standing Upstage, at a window*): Join me, won't you? There is something you'd appreciate.

MOCKIS: I could, yes? Of some concern to me? (*Beat*) A group of your best musicians? No, that couldn't be it. You people don't have any music to speak of, here. (*Beat*) Children waiting to serenade me with some local songs? No, that would be too easy for you, yes?

WELLS *laughs.*

MOCKIS (*Continued*): You would have the nerve, though, wouldn't you?

WELLS (*Looking out*): They sit so nicely. Smiling. One of them is laughing. (*Beat*) I could mistake them for tourists. No, you, you would make that mistake.

MOCKIS (*Comes back to the table, and eases into his chair; looks at* ATTENDANT): What would be your bossman's purpose? To embarrass me? (*Beat*) Yes, yes. Me up here, the three young men down there. Isn't it so provocative a moment? (*Smiles*) Ah, the stations in life we all serve, and for what reason anymore?

WELLS (*Calmly*): They talk so quietly. Who will share their secrets with them? (*Beat*) Set a cup up here for our guest. A fresh cup.

MOCKIS (*Rises, steps to grab his suitcoat and newspaper; looking over his suitcoat*): Nothing spilled on me? Another small blessing from heaven, yes? (*Beat; to* ATTENDANT) What's the time?

WELLS: A little past one. (*Holds out his watch to* MOCKIS, *smiles*)

MOCKIS: What would a "little" be? In minutes if it's not too difficult.

WELLS: We did anticipate a Jew to be sent.

MOCKIS: I'll bet you did.

WELLS: Those three bastards, I understand now why real talent wouldn't be wasted on them.

MOCKIS: If you can't tell time, you can't anticipate a goddam thing. (*Beat*) A Jew? Honest? (*Chuckles*)

WELLS: We're going to conduct an international war crimes trial.

MOCKIS: Is that right?

WELLS: Crimes against human nature.

MOCKIS: Whew. Something smells. Mothballs? Human, what? Where did you find that one?

WELLS (*Smiles*): Your country waits three months to respond, to acknowledge what has happened, and then, then, they send a comedian.

MOCKIS: Yes, real talent.

WELLS (*Turns to* MOCKIS, *walking to the table*): Mister, what is it, Mockis?

MOCKIS: Right.

WELLS: I think this has been a perfectly functional meeting.

MOCKIS (*Snorts*): On my good days, I'd have 'em rolling in the aisles.

WELLS *picks up his briefcase and begins to exit.*

MOCKIS (*Continued*): I would like a meeting to be arranged for me and the three young men. No real rush to it, tomorrow, the day after, sometime appropriate.

WELLS (*Turns back*): It's been set for this evening.

MOCKIS: Tomorrow evening, that would be ideal for me.

WELLS: It's been arranged. This evening. (*Steps to* MOCKIS) The preliminary hearing for the trial is scheduled for tomorrow morning.

MOCKIS (*Laughs*): Couldn't I have just guessed that? You arrange everything for me, yes? (*Beat*) Now there's a rush. (*Pause*) Neither of us wants to be here. Neither of us should be. I'm just as embarrassed as you that all of this happened, what, some three months ago, so you say it was? Hunh, that's quite a long time ago, yes?

WELLS (*Looks about in bewilderment*): I'm embarrassed? (*Laughs*)

MOCKIS: Where can I get some of those T-shirts? The ones with your country's name across the front? No one ever believes you've been somewhere unless you wear a T-shirt that says so. (*Beat*) One day it's books, the next, T-shirts. What can anyone believe anymore? (*Beat*) Clean the young men up before I meet them. It would save all of us some embarrassment.

WELLS: I have every intention of having the bastards shot!

MOCKIS: Son, you're going to have to learn to think. Simply think, that's the first step. Then you're going to have to work on getting it quick, yes?

WELLS *offers a hand to* MOCKIS.

MOCKIS (*Continued*): Yeah? A friendly shake? Hell, why not? (HE *smiles, shakes hands with* WELLS)

WELLS (*Gripping* MOCKIS' *hand tightly*): I had thought we could have had some discussion on whether you personally thought the three sons of bitches are worth the effort.

MOCKIS (*Pulls his hand away*): "Personally"? Uh-hunh.

WELLS: They are wrong, aren't they? Between me and you?

MOCKIS: Who am I to say? You'll find that out for me, yes? (*Beat*) I can't get over all this quiet. All the salt in this air. It's something, yes? So relaxing.

MOCKIS *pats* WELLS *on the shoulder, exits.* WELLS *stands by the door, walks slowly to the window and looks out.*

WELLS: That's all? It's this easy? (HE *loosens his tie*)

ATTENDANT *begins stripping down the table.*
Lights down. Reggae music bridge into the next scene.

Scene 3

An open courtyard, set away from the veranda setting of Scene 2.

A glaring, whitehot sun crushes and twists the air, distorting the features of the setting and the characters with waves of heat, as if the scene were set in an open sauna.

JIMBO, SPIKE and YOGI are seated on a long bench, facing the audience. THEY are shackled at the ankles. A long chain binds them together, very loosely, at their waists. A GUARD stands apart, at ease, sipping from a can of Pepsi. A SECOND GUARD is mixing a thin, soapy solution in a big plastic pail, sloshing the water around with a large sponge.

JIMBO: It's no one's business but ours, goddammit.

YOGI: He'll want to know. What if he asks?

JIMBO: He wouldn't have the balls. (*Looking up and out*) How much longer, goddammit! He's had his look by now. What's the delay? (*Beat*) This goddam sun.

YOGI (*Pausing*): Maybe we should have done something different. We didn't figure it right.

JIMBO: I don't want to hear it! That shit is old news, it's over with!

YOGI: Maybe if we had started off on a different day, huh? If we had done something, maybe the stars, the moon, something, huh?

JIMBO (*Sighs*): This heat. (*Calling up and out*) You've come to get me, boy. Here I am, dammit.

SPIKE: Patience.

YOGI: It should have been planned different, you understand. Maybe we didn't figure everything into it.

SPIKE: Enough of what didn't happen! We're the focus of the world right now. (*Beat*) All of this shit, it serves us. It's a matter of honor.

JIMBO: Honor? (*Spits*) No such animal.

SPIKE: They have to care about what happened, not us! They suck it from us! (*Laughs*) Ain't that some bullshit, hey. (*Beat*) They're goddam mental cripples, all of them. Let them play their games. We've got some fun coming, too. (HE *opens his hand flat, slowly makes a tight fist*) It'll be one fine day then. All of it, for us.

JIMBO (*Snorts*): I've had months of your "one fine days."

SPIKE (*Rising off the bench*): And you'll make it through a few more!

JIMBO: Then get some real action for me! Out of this goddam sun, for openers, boy!

SPIKE: Who the fuck is your "boy"?

JIMBO rises off the bench. GUARD 1 bangs his baton against the ground. SPIKE and JIMBO ease back.

SPIKE (*Continued*): I'm saying to you: patience. So they play. Let 'em tinker and tool around. What else can they do? We're on top of this goddam heap. They've moved this to us, they had to.

JIMBO: The shitpile moves to Mohammed, huh? (*Grunts*) When this is over with, there be some things to settle up. (*Beat*) They sit up there and discuss things about me? (*Up and out*) We'll see who's what and the good American! They didn't have the decency for three months. And now? (*Snorts*) I'll find out that, in particular.

SPIKE: Agreed. (*Nods*) First we come back and do this place again. We finish this one up.

JIMBO: Fuck that shit. I say we start it up in America. Get our own things clean first. If that hasn't been the one thought all this time, goddammit!

YOGI (*Lurches forward*): On my back! Someone get that thing!

SPIKE: We finish this place first, dammit!

YOGI: One of you, get it!

SPIKE (*To* JIMBO): We got more than enough back home. We scope that first!

YOGI: Damn youse!

JIMBO (*To* SPIKE): Get that thing for him.

SPIKE (*To* YOGI): Ignore it. It'll give you something to push you for the days to come!

YOGI: I want the goddam bug off now!

SPIKE: You can take it for now!

YOGI: Please. Please!

JIMBO: Geezus to hell. (HE *takes aim, smacks* YOGI's *back*)

YOGI: Ahhhh. (*Sighs, smiles, wiggles his back about*)

SPIKE (*To* JIMBO): You shouldn't have done that. You've gotten weak. It shows on you real clear.

JIMBO (*Grabbing length of chain between himself and* SPIKE): How about I show you your feet off the ground? How high you want me to hang your ass!

SPIKE (*Smiles*): That's another thing we can settle up, later.

JIMBO (*Snatches* SPIKE's *ankle chains and jerks them high*): Let's go, now! Now!

GUARD 1 *shoves* JIMBO *and* SPIKE *apart, then bangs the baton on the bench between them.*

JIMBO (*Continued; to* SPIKE): Patience, right? (*Laughs*)

GUARD 2 *comes over, peels back* YOGI's *shirt, begins rinsing him down.*

YOGI: Ah, this is so good. So nice. Yeah, oh.

JIMBO *reaches for the bucket of water.* GUARD *shoves him away.*

JIMBO (*Licking his lips*): You can give me some water!

GUARD 2 *continues to rinse* YOGI *down.*

SPIKE: You'll have all the water you want, soon. When we get back home.

GUARD 2 *soaks* YOGI's *face with the sponge.* YOGI *closes his eyes and catches some of the water with his tongue.*

YOGI: Ah, that's so wet, huh? (*Smiles in relief*)

JIMBO (*To* YOGI): Do you have to talk about it, too? (*Shoves* YOGI) Keep it to yourself! (*Softly*) Nothing can be that good. I'm so thirsty.

SPIKE (*Licking his lips*): We don't need anything from any of these morons.

JIMBO (*Chuckles*): Moron? (*Beat*) Up there, the good American, our best boy, he's having himself a nice, cold drink. A tall, cold ice tea. (*Licks his lips*) A tall glass, filled with ice, and a slice a lemon. The glass sweating from all that ice. (*Beat*) He's sitting in front of a fan. (*Beat*) Laying up in front of an air conditioner. Turned all the way up to frost. (*To* SPIKE) Who's the moron? Some fucking honor this is, you bet.

SPIKE: They're centered on us. That's the only thing that counts right now.

JIMBO: Yeah, and their nigger boy . . .

GUARD *steps to* JIMBO, JIMBO *pauses.*

JIMBO (*Continued; to* GUARD): . . . your top man, right. The hot-fudge-sundae-son-of-a-bitch, he's centered, huh? He's up there arguing to get some shoes on me. They're both having themselves a fashion show up there. (*Up and out*) Kinky about shoes, huh? That figures, they are that way! They all are. (*Beat;* "*falsetto*") Where'd you get yours? Oh, dearie, is that so? I should mail away for a pair of those. Give me the address. No, better yet, write it down. You say, who the fuck is out in this heat? Oh, they should get out of the sun. Don't they have better sense? ("*Basso*") And these shoes were such a bargain. They would just make for a new blue suit. (*Up and out; regular voice*) Talk about your blue suits, talk about your shoes. Then I'll talk, cuties, with a goddam can opener in my hand. Peel you, sons of bitches.

GUARD 2 *moves the bucket of water to* SPIKE. JIMBO *grabs the* GUARD.

JIMBO (*Continued*): I'm next! He said he can wait.

SPIKE: I can, damn you.

JIMBO: And you will, babe.

GUARD 2 *peels back* JIMBO's *shirt, begins rinsing him down.*

JIMBO (*Continued*): Oh, damn, whoooweeeeeee. . . . (HE *laughs, then dips his hands into the bucket and slurps some water*)

YOGI (*Giggles*): It's good, isn't it? (*To* SPIKE) It is, you know.

GUARD 2 *soaks the top of* JIMBO's *head.*

JIMBO (*Purring contentedly*): I'm new, once more. I've never been better.

SPIKE: I'll remind you of this one day. In front of these, these, you're worse than them.

JIMBO: You bear up to it, huh? Keep it going. Grace under pressure. (*Snorts*) No such animal.

SPIKE: Give these niggers the satisfaction.

GUARDS *laugh.*

JIMBO: The only nigger is our boy up there. (*Slurps more water from the bucket*)

GUARDS *laugh again.*

YOGI: He's a shine? Yeah? (*Looking at* GUARDS) Maybe?

SPIKE: What? Send a nigger for us?

JIMBO *laughs.*

SPIKE (*Continued*): Never!

JIMBO: Wouldn't that just "center" us? Wouldn't that be something to take back home? A spade comes to save us from his fellow spades? Some honor, huh?

SPIKE: Colored people can be intelligent. At certain times.

YOGI: Maybe we got one of the smart ones.

JIMBO: A cotton picker is going to save my ass. Wouldn't that be a "thank you"?

SPIKE: If that's what it has to be, it has to be. For now.

GUARD 2 *moves to* SPIKE, *begins rinsing him down.*

YOGI (*To* SPIKE): Feels good, huh?

JIMBO: Don't ask him petty questions. He's gotta figure how to oil himself up for our boy Willie.

SPIKE *glares at* JIMBO.

YOGI (*To* SPIKE): You know it feels good.

Pause. SPIKE *glares at* YOGI, *slowly smiles, nods, eases back.*

SPIKE (*To* GUARD 2): If you ever need a real job, fella, you come look me up in the States.

JIMBO *and* YOGI *join* SPIKE *in slurping water with cupped hands.*

JIMBO (*To* GUARD 2): So, Mr. Bojangles, what's with our boy? He wouldn't be a relation to all you tree-jumpers, huh?

GUARD 2 *pauses, then resumes rinsing* SPIKE.

JIMBO (*Continued*): Naw, he can't be. Bojangles, you'd be dancing around with your head up your ass if our boy was a soul brother of yours.

YOGI (*Bolting upright*): Maybe they sent a woman for us.

SPIKE: What? No!

YOGI: Women are something. They got some charms to 'em, don't they?

SPIKE: No woman! Never! Not for this! That's final!

JIMBO: Could you picture that right up there under bright lights, up there in the skies, across the whole wide world: "TITS SENT TO SAVE DICKS." Are you stupid?

YOGI: I only said, maybe. Or, wait to figure . . . uh . . . (*Beat*) could be our boy is one of them in-betweeners. Something between us and these shines here.

JIMBO: What, you find yourself at the end of the rainbow? I'll take a nigger before a Chink, Jap, or any other colored bullshit. This ain't a high tea ceremony for some goddam Buddah-head or one of them taco-sucking Cha-chas. (*Up and out*) And you're not a woman either! (*To* YOGI) You don't send tit to bail out dick, simple as that.

YOGI: A Jew-boy? Yeah, maybe.

JIMBO: 'The fuck is wrong with you!

SPIKE: The Jews had their days. It's over with.

JIMBO: What's a Jew-boy going to do, walk us home across the water?

YOGI: They can do that?

JIMBO: He's here, and that's it! (*Gestures up and out*) The son of a bitch is white, male, and Christian. That's the way it has to look, goddammit!

SPIKE: Whoever it is, we get him. When we start up again, we get whoever that boy is, first. You want something right, you gotta start right. From the end to the front.

JIMBO: Let him be a Jew then. (*Beat*) Three-quarters of them Jews think they're white anyway.

SPIKE: They wish.

A GUARD *laughs.* SPIKE *smiles.*

SPIKE (*Continued*): Even you boys don't like them Jews, huh? (*Beat*) Us and the Jews. Gotta get that one on the agenda. Gotta give that one some serious satisfaction, soon.

JIMBO: We ain't alone on that.

SPIKE (*Smiling*): No, we ain't. Never been. (*Beat*) Who says there's no God? We'll show them Jews who's God.

JIMBO: All them Jews and the rest of their liberal friends, huh? I live to see that shit up against a wall.

SPIKE: The job would never end. We'd be killing 'em for years.

JIMBO: All the big liberals, huh? All their ideas on how to operate everything for me. (*Spits*) Them first. All the top boys, huh?

SPIKE: The rest fall in line. Always have.

JIMBO: If we lined up every punk in America alone, we'd be lining up everybody. Damn discouraging, ain't it? Where'd we get enough shooters, huh?

The MERCS *laugh.* DOCTOR *enters, still wearing her gray surgeon's gown.* TWO GUARDS *follow her On, rolling a portable delousing tank on a wheeled handcart.*

DOCTOR: Stand up. Everyone, up.

SPIKE (*Grabs the bottom of the* DOCTOR'S *gown*): You're too much, honey. How about a preview?

DOCTOR (*Smacks* SPIKE'S *hand away*): Get on your feet!

GUARDS *draw their batons.* YOGI *and* SPIKE *stumble to their feet.*

SPIKE: I gotta little peek of things to come for you. (*To* JIMBO) Haul your butt up here, Jimbo.

JIMBO (*Lost in reverie*): There really wouldn't be enough shooters. We'd have to import some foreigners to help us do the job. That wouldn't be right, huh?

DOCTOR *signals* GUARD 3. GUARD 3 *turns on the tank and fogs the* MERCS. *The* MERCS *cover up, coughing.*

DOCTOR: Cover your eyes.

Obscenities from the MERCS *as* THEY *cover their eyes and mouths.* DOCTOR *runs her hands through their hair.*

YOGI: Get your nigger hands off of me!

YOGI *grabs hold of the* DOCTOR. GUARD *swats* YOGI *across the hips with his baton.* YOGI *locks a chokehold on the* GUARD.

YOGI (*Continued*): God, help me kill him! Kill this nigger for me!

A brief melee erupts. DOCTOR *turns the fog into the* MERCS' *faces, stopping the fight.* GUARDS *pin the* MERCS *to the ground with their batons.*

DOCTOR: This is so unnecessary! (SHE *quickly checks through the* MERCS' *hair and clothes*) We only want you to be presentable now, don't we? (SHE *quickly exits*)

GUARD 1 (*Points to* JIMBO): Him. Stand this one up. (*To* JIMBO) You with all the ideas.

A GUARD *chokes* JIMBO *into a standing position.* GUARD 1 *takes his baton and whips it across* JIMBO's *shins.* JIMBO *drops to the ground, covering up.*

GUARD 1 (*Continued*): Assume the positions, boys.
ANOTHER GUARD: Right to hell now!

SPIKE *and* YOGI *assume the lockdown position. A* GUARD *jerks* JIMBO *around into the lockdown position.*

JIMBO: One of these days, I'll have my day.
SPIKE: Believe it, fella. Keep it. We will have our run on things. Soon.
JIMBO (*Mimicking Martin Luther King's voice*): I have a dream, yes, I have a dream.

YOGI *and* SPIKE *pick up the melody of "We Shall Overcome."*

JIMBO (*Continued*): I have been to the mountaintop, and I have seen the promised land. (*Beat; normal voice*) And the fuck if the white boys own the mortgage to it. (HE *begins singing the KKK version of "White Christmas"*)

SPIKE *counterpoints the song with "I have a dream, I have been to the promised land."*
Lights down. Reggae music bridge into next scene.

Scene 4

The veranda of Scene 2. The room has been stripped of the flowers and the potted plants. A long conference table, one with folding legs, replaces the breakfast table. An aluminum pitcher of ice water and a stack of paper cups are set on a serving tray at one end of the table. Five metal folding chairs are set around the table.

Soft-focused lighting defuses the intensity of the sunset. The sun and the moon, opposite each other on the horizon, can be seen through the screen windows. The ceiling of the room is washed in purples and reds from the sunset. The moon throws iridescent blues and greens across the walls and along the borders of the floors.

MOCKIS *is airing his underarms at the windows.* WELLS *is paging through a stack of legal briefs. A* GUARD *is standing at the table, sifting through packs of cigarettes, rolls of mints, and packs of gum from* MOCKIS' *briefcase.*

WELLS: You do nothing but restate the facts. Do you understand the significance of that?

MOCKIS: Have you ever seen such a sky? It's beyond words.

WELLS: Where are your arguments against the charges? Don't you realize what you've done? You argue nothing!

MOCKIS: Everything to its appropriate time and place. (*Beat*) What incredible beauty you have here. Nature has a helluva imagination. (*Beat*) Those waterfalls there. Something I will always remember. The name of those waterfalls. (*Turns to* WELLS) Everything beautiful in nature gets named after someone, yes? The name becomes famous, to eternity. (*Beat*) Things in nature shouldn't have names. Let them be what they are, yes?

WELLS: We expect a full, written response to the evidence. When will that be coming? (*Beat*) How do you propose we go about tomorrow's opening proceedings?

MOCKIS (*Turns back to view the sunset*): These twilight hours? Is that what they really are? What made us call them that?

WELLS: If you have any requests, make them now. It's some sort of cooperation that we can extend to each other before tomorrow.

MOCKIS: They had themselves a party today at the U.N., yes? You have so many new friends. So I hear. Cuba, Iran, France. The French, they have to have it both ways, yes? (*Beat*) Albania, good God, Albania. How they discovered the Caribbean, after all these years, yes? (*Turns away from the sunset, walks into the center of the room*) What does nature matter to any of us anymore?

WELLS (*To* GUARD): Open the cigarettes. Open the damn gum!

MOCKIS: Yes, would you now? For all the oppressed of the world. Open it all up. Cheer them all on. (*To* GUARD) The one on the left there, the first pack, that will be the first cheer. (*Beat*) No, no, the first pack.

GUARD *looks to* WELLS *in confusion.*

MOCKIS (*Continued*): The Marlboros? No, no, not those. The red and white box, yes? (*Beat*) The first one. (*Giggling*) Counting to one, picking out the simple colors, how they remain mysteries to you? The third world, yes? Is this how it is going to be? Is it any wonder why your new friends have to make speeches for you?

WELLS: And then there's America? Such a good country once, wasn't it?

MOCKIS: How could we let it get away from us, yes? (*Beat*) What was it that might have gotten away?

WELLS: What did you ever have?

MOCKIS: Take the advice of your new French friends. Yes, soon America will be parking its cars on this island. America, the parking lot builder. How they heat up all their leftovers. (*Beat*) Those old cliches, they do comfort me.

WELLS: Cut the cigarettes open! Shred the damn things!

GUARD *begins shredding the filter and paper from the tobacco.*

MOCKIS: It's from your heart, I know. Open everything up. Cigarettes, candy, thoughts, feelings. (*Taps his forehead*) It's another memorable cliche, the heart. Hearts and minds. Right from those golden years. That was a time, yes? (*Shakes his head, smiling*) Without cliches, we'd have some very direct, very personal conversations, yes? Without interference from your friends?

WELLS: It would make the world too simple for you. Much too serious.

The door flies open, banging and rebounding against the wall. SPIKE, JIMBO *and* YOGI *are led in by* GUARDS. THEY *are cuffed and linked together at the waist.* THEY *are clean-shaven, freshly showered, their hair slicked back, still wet from shampooing.* THEY *are dressed in native tropical shirts of a floral pattern and dark brown or black slacks that are shiny from wear. The slacks have been let out at the cuffs, but are still too short, barely reaching the tops of their ankles.* THEY *are sockless and are wearing torn, scruffed dress shoes without heels or shoelaces.* JIMBO *is limping, supporting himself by holding onto the back of* SPIKE's *shoulders.* GUARDS *stand the* MERCS *to face* WELLS. GUARD 1 *moves to turn up the lights.*

WELLS (*Continued; to* GUARD 1): You lower those lights back down to where they were, damn you!

GUARD 1 *jerks the lights back to dim.* WELLS *moves to the light switch.*

WELLS (*Continued; to* GUARD 1): Stand away!

WELLS *pauses, then slowly raises the lights to a full bright.* HE *slowly spreads his hands in an elegant gesture to* MOCKIS.

WELLS (*Continued*): As ordered by you. (*Stalks the* MERCS) How are you tonight? (*To* MOCKIS) How are all of us tonight? (*Beat*) All dressed up for the occasion, I see. What is it that we should be celebrating?

The MERCS *shift about, glancing to* MOCKIS, *then to the floor.*

WELLS (*Continued*): They're all cleaned up. As requested. No dirt, no bodylice.

SPIKE (*To* MOCKIS): You our boy?

WELLS: "Boy"? Oh, that's good! (*To* MOCKIS) Boy. I like that.

MOCKIS (*Pausing, to* SPIKE): I am here for you, yes.

YOGI *moves forward, hand extended. A* GUARD *shoves* YOGI *back in line.* MOCKIS *gestures "hello" with a wave of his hand. The* MERCS *nod in acknowledgment.*

WELLS: What a moment! Aren't we so choked with emotion? Are there tears of joy and relief? (*To* GUARDS) Why are the guests of honor standing?

GUARDS *move the* MERCS *into seats.*

WELLS (*Continued*): One, two, three, three little boys who got lost and ended up here. Of all places. (*Beat*) Wouldn't that make a good defense? All of them found, safe and sound, that's such a story.

MOCKIS: Then there wasn't any reason to worry, yes? For any of us. As it always should be.

YOGI *laughs.*

WELLS (*Leans into* YOGI's *face*): How your boy stands us on our head with his wit? Isn't he amazing? Isn't that a relief for you! (*Whirls to* MOCKIS) Are you clever, sir? Be a magician. Make all of this go away!

MOCKIS: You pressure me to perform? A host should never have to promote his guest in anything, most of all this moment, yes?

YOGI *laughs.* MOCKIS *smiles at* WELLS. *The* MERCS *break up, laughing and nodding.*

WELLS (*Pauses to survey the* MERCS, *then slowly, deliberately sweeps everything from the table in three fluid motions*): Not from anyone! Not God, not this world, not America or this damn island. This is just among us here right now. A private one, among friends.

A GUARD *begins to gather up the cigarettes and gum.*

JIMBO (*Points to the pitcher of water and the cups*): When you clear a table, clear it correctly. Where is your training, boy?

SPIKE: It's his lack of proper upbringing.

YOGI: Yeah, maybe, huh?

SPIKE: Definite on that. His mama didn't whip his ass enough when he was a baby. Huh, boy?

The MERCS *laugh.* MOCKIS *gestures to silence them.*

WELLS (*To* MOCKIS): "Boy"? I am a "boy"? You are their "boy"? (*Grins*) We take that from this garbage? From these gentlemen? My, how everything comes together for them now! (*Snatches the water pitcher, pauses, drops it down on the tray; to the* GUARD) What are you doing?

GUARD *pauses, holding loose cigarettes and sticks of gum.*

WELLS (*Continued*): Leave it on the floor! I put it there, it stays! (HE *jerks* GUARD *to standing position*) Get up! Get away from that! Pick up after them? Stupid! (*Beat*) Get out. Get away from me!

GUARD *hesitates one beat, quickly exits, dropping the articles.*

MOCKIS: It will all go away, yes? Which of us is the magician?

WELLS (*Whirls to* MOCKIS): This pleases you? This is light amusement for all of you? (*Beat*) God damn this world of manners and respect! (*To the* MERCS) I will kill you with all due courtesy!

SPIKE: With a pretty please, if you would.

WELLS (*To* GUARDS): Does this amuse you, too? Who gives you the right to stand here and be amused? I do! Who do you think you are to watch this! (*To* MOCKIS) I'll damn you to be witty, mister! (*To* GUARDS) I'm sick of you and this country of yours!

WELLS *moves angrily toward the* GUARDS. GUARDS *exit.* WELLS *grabs* MOCKIS *by the lapels.*

WELLS (*Continued*): It's on my time! It's always been on my personal time! You and I, we have to waste our words. We have to spit out a few lines about right and wrong. (HE *releases* MOCKIS) Justice? (*Smiles*) Do I frame it properly? Let's not be naive. (HE *turns to exit, pauses, steps toward* SPIKE; *to* SPIKE) "Boy"? (*Exiting*) On your damn time, gentlemen. Your time is mine. (HE *slams the door shut after his exit*)

Pause.

MOCKIS: What energy. What a demonstrative young man, yes? (HE *gestures to the floor*) I had brought some things for you.

YOGI: They're still good. (*Reaching for a loose cigarette*) What's a little dirt?

MOCKIS: Leave it there.

YOGI: I don't mind.

MOCKIS: Leave it.

YOGI: They still gotta be okay.

MOCKIS (*Holds out a fresh pack from his pocket to* YOGI): Take these.

YOGI: Naw. Those are yours.

MOCKIS: I'd like you to have them.

YOGI: I can't, sir.

MOCKIS: You'll take them, dammit! Please.

YOGI *pauses, takes the pack, looks long at it, holds it out to show* JIMBO *and* SPIKE, *smiles up at* MOCKIS *with tears, nods repeatedly.* MOCKIS *smiles.*

MOCKIS (*Continued*): Quite a display just now, yes? Caught me, all of us off guard for a moment. One of those unavoidable messes. Necessary, yes? (*Beat*) A resolute young man, someone to be respected. (*Beat*) But at another time, yes? (HE *takes out a folded sheet of paper*) Gerald Ryan? Gerald O.?

JIMBO: Yo, yessir.

MOCKIS: Michael "Wall-lee"?

SPIKE: "Way-lee." It's a long "a." (HE *shoves an outstretched hand at* MOCKIS)

MOCKIS (*Unaware of* SPIKE's *gesture*): Long "a." (*Taps his forehead*) I'll remember that.

SPIKE's *hand nudges* MOCKIS.

MOCKIS (*Continued*): Oh? Yes, of course. (*Shakes hands with* SPIKE) Yes, sure.

JIMBO (*Stands, stiffens, shakes hands with* MOCKIS): It's been a long time. Good to finally have you, sir.

SPIKE: Damn good.

JIMBO: It's an honor.

YOGI (*Stands*): I'm Milliken. James M. "M" for Mark.

MOCKIS (*Glances at his paper*): Yes, correct. Milliken.

YOGI *grabs* MOCKIS' *hand, shakes it vigorously.*

MOCKIS (*Continued*): Your name, here on paper. Yogi, is it?

YOGI: Yessir.

MOCKIS: You go by that, yes?

YOGI: Yes, I do. Yogi, it is.

MOCKIS: Is that from the baseball player?

YOGI (*Still pumping* MOCKIS' *hand*): I don't know. Maybe. I got it, that's all.

MOCKIS: Some New York team, aways back, yes?

YOGI: It could be from baseball, huh?

MOCKIS (*Gently frees his hand from* YOGI's *grip*): I would think so, yes. Only a guess, though. (*Taps his forehead*) All of you with nicknames. (*Glances at the sheet of paper*) Jimbo, Spike . . .

SPIKE: . . . Yessir.

MOCKIS: . . . Yogi here. Unusual. (*Beat*) A sign of affection from others, yes. How nicknames come about, from someone else's affection.

JIMBO: Something the matter? You're staring.

MOCKIS: Oh. It's nothing. (*Smiles*) Excuse me. (*Beat*) I had always imagined you all as being bigger. Somehow much taller.

SPIKE (*Gestures to his clothes*): You see how these coloreds slaughtered us in these clothes. You can't tell these niggers anything, can you?

The MERCS *laugh.*

MOCKIS: I am Anthony Mockis.

JIMBO: Mockis? What is that, Jewish?

SPIKE: Easy, Jimbo.

MOCKIS: You would spite me that way, yes?

Pause; the MERCS *shift about in their seats.* MOCKIS *smiles.*

MOCKIS (*Continued*): My God, if I was, yes?

ALL *relax.*

YOGI (*Holding the pack of cigarettes up to* MOCKIS): Thank you, sir. (*Chokes back tears*) I wish I could find some words to tell you how much . . .
MOCKIS: . . . Don't. It's okay. (*Beat*) Thank you.
SPIKE: How's home, sir? What the hell is America up to?
JIMBO: Where the hell has America been?
MOCKIS (*Pausing*): America does what it does. (*Shrugs*) It's doing well.
SPIKE: Our families?
MOCKIS: Families? Your families, yes? (*Beat*) As well as they would be, I would assume.
JIMBO: The other guys, our buddies? They get home? They get some sort of ceremony? They deserve that much for what they gave.
MOCKIS: I don't have any recall on how it was handled. (*Beat*) Arrangements were left to their families, I would suppose. (*Beat*) It was never an official concern. (*Beat*) What you all were thinking about doing here, yes?
JIMBO: That's none of your goddam business! (*Beat*) Twenty-three damn fine citizens, all of them. They never asked for a thing from anyone. Why don't things turn out the way they're suppose to?
SPIKE (*To* MOCKIS): When does this all end? How much of a fuss?
JIMBO: It's been a damn headache for us.
MOCKIS: It will be resolved soon. Hopefully very soon, yes?

Relieved smiles from the MERCS.

SPIKE: Gotta love our America, don't you? (*Making a fist*) How she always pulls it off, always in the clutch! And she doesn't have to be shy about it either, that's what kicks it all, huh! (*Laughs*)
MOCKIS: It's been difficult for us, all the same, yes? (*Pauses, points to* MERCS' *wrist irons*) Is there something we can do about these things? What are they, handcuffs of some sort, yes? They're horrible.
YOGI (*Smiling*): Hell, I don't even notice them anymore.
SPIKE: They're second skin to us.
MOCKIS: It's embarrassing, yes. (*Beat*) We should do something.

The MERCS *hesitate, lower their hands beneath the table.*

MOCKIS (*Continued*): Ah, much better now, don't you think?
SPIKE: What's the official word? What's the order of business now?
MOCKIS: There will be no trial for you.

SPIKE: How soon on our release then?

MOCKIS: There will never be a trial. That has been waived. Are we clear on that point, young men?

JIMBO: 'The fuck, what, what motions are we going to run then? We can run any goddam routine you want from us. "Are we sorry," that kind of crap? (*Beat*) I've danced that one in my sleep. (*Laughs*)

SPIKE: But are you *real* sorry? (*Laughs*)

JIMBO: Am I?

MOCKIS: Are you?

SPIKE: What's this? We got a man of conscience? (*To* MOCKIS) Don't be one of those. (*Beat*) To these niggers, hell.

YOGI (*Stands, points a finger at* MOCKIS): I'm going to build a hospital for the shines here. We're going home, yeah, but me, I'm coming back, reloaded, and they're going to need a hospital. A big one, you understand.

MOCKIS: I should appreciate that, yes?

YOGI: I'm gonna build a hospital for the poor shines. I want you to know that.

MOCKIS: I should applaud that, yes? How much applause would be sufficient, son? Why are you standing? Sit down! I don't need this from you!

SPIKE: Tony, Tony.

MOCKIS: Not "Tony," never "Tony." It is Mister, Mister Mockis.

YOGI *slowly sits down.*

MOCKIS (*Continued*): Is this what I have to listen to, yes? This damn nonsense? (*Beat*) There's no choice on my part.

JIMBO: He meant it in fun.

MOCKIS: Where was the humor? What was funny?

JIMBO: It was just silly, huh? Just some goofs.

MOCKIS: All too subtle for me then, yes? It must have been.

YOGI: Did I say you had to laugh?

MOCKIS: Do you see me laughing?

YOGI (*Bolts up*): Who asked you to, goddammit!

JIMBO (*Stands, wedging himself between* MOCKIS *and* YOGI): Let him go on this, Yogi.

YOGI: I want to hear his jokes. (*To* MOCKIS) You tell me something funny then, huh?

MOCKIS: You can have some self-respect for what you say and how it's said.

YOGI: Damn right, self-respect! That's a good one! Damn right, that's a joke! You understand, mister?

MOCKIS: Do I, yes?

YOGI (*Shoves* JIMBO *aside*): Don't you, huh? Sure, you do. (*Pausing*) I've been locked down here for three months, you understand? Three months. That's funny, huh? I've been kicked and hit on. These niggers, they hit on me. They kicked on me. They spit on me. Spit, you understand? That's real funny. Laugh if you want! (*Beat*) You understand, I don't stink from my own shit right now. I'm clean. That's a joke, you understand. I'm clean, but (*Bangs his fists on the table*) I'm still locked down. Anyone ever spit on you, mister? Especially a nigger, you understand? You ever been pissed on, you understand? I've been pissed on. How's that for jokes? I've been shit on for laughs. (*Bangs his hands again*) They shit on me. Got the joke.

JIMBO (*Shoves* YOGI): That's personal business for later, you clown!

YOGI: Dressed for it, ain't I? Ain't we all? Self-respect? (*Points to* MOCKIS) He's ignorant, not me! (*To* JIMBO) And you are, too. (*Pauses to hold back tears*) I was feeling so good. (*Clutches cigarettes to his eyes*) I started getting human again. So good, you understand, for a couple of seconds. (*To* MOCKIS) Tell me you got understanding for me. I got understanding for you, you understand. I got three months here to understand, and all you can do is come here and tell me what to think, how to talk? I need a few things of my own, you understand. I can't be anything, not a goddam thing, until I can get something definite back again, you understand. (*Beat*) Respect that! Respect me! I'm an American, too! You understand? I don't have to be anything else. Is that funny enough for you?

JIMBO: I'm ashamed of this, goddammit!

YOGI: I ain't! You can all see me like this! I've been worse. I didn't have any shame, you understand. There wasn't anything left. They shit on me, and they still could, you understand? (*To* MOCKIS) But right now, right now they can't because you're here, and I love you for that. Not a big thing, I understand, but I still love you for that, you understand? (*Beat*) You understand me? (*Breaks into stifled sobs*) That's a joke. You don't step on my dick that way, you understand. That ain't respect, you understand?

SPIKE: Slow down, Yogi.

YOGI: What could I do? He stepped on my dick! (*Sits back down, wiping his eyes, sniffling*)

Pause.

MOCKIS (*Holds out a handkerchief to* YOGI): You'll catch a cold. (*Beat*) Take it. This dry air isn't good for you. (*Beat*) Take it, dammit.

YOGI *grabs the handkerchief, turns away to wipe his face.*

JIMBO: A family fight, huh? Out of love, huh? For love, yeah.

MOCKIS (*Hands* YOGI *a paper cup of water*): A good cry cleans things up, yes? Drink it slowly.

YOGI *grabs the cup, gulps it down.*

SPIKE: So. So. What's the timetable?

MOCKIS (*To* YOGI): Another cup of water? (*Pouring a refill*) This air really dries up the sinuses, yes?

YOGI *looks away.*

SPIKE: What is the plan, Mister Mockis?

MOCKIS (*To* YOGI): You needed that, yes? Let it all out.

YOGI *nods, smiles.*

SPIKE: What's the plan?

MOCKIS: I'm at my damndest, trying to expedite the situation.

SPIKE: What's your guess on time?

MOCKIS: Everything would be best resolved here.

SPIKE: The time, goddammit! What's the timetable for us?

MOCKIS: There is no timetable. There never was a timetable, gentlemen.

SPIKE: When the fuck are we out of here!

MOCKIS: You're not. (*To* YOGI) Drink your water, son.

SPIKE (*Forces a laugh*): Something you just said, what didn't I get?

MOCKIS: You are to be executed here. All of you. Here and (*Beat*) hopefully soon.

JIMBO: Do what!

MOCKIS *pours himself a cup of water.*

JIMBO (*Continued; smiling*): You're pulling my ass, ain't you? (*Beat*) I get it, you're just fucking with me. Yeah, I get it.

MOCKIS *sips some water.*

SPIKE: When are we going home? We're suppose to go home! We have to go home!

MOCKIS (*Gingerly places his cup on the table, sits down on a chair*): Damn good water. (*To* YOGI) No fluoride taste is there?

SPIKE: You said, resolved!

MOCKIS: Not much of a counsel, am I? Just a damn errand boy, yes? (*Beat*) Damn fine boys, all of you. Much bigger than I could have ever imagined. I see that now.

YOGI: Why?

MOCKIS (*Sighing*): Who knows anything anymore? Don't we all wish we could, yes? (*Beat*) What terrible beauty there is sometimes, in everything, yes?

SPIKE: I want to hear a plan! You think of something!

MOCKIS *rubs his eyes, looks away.*

SPIKE (*Continued*): You're lying, ain't you? You're a lying son of a bitch!

MOCKIS (*Stands and walks to the window*): Everyone has suffered enough, yes? Long, damn enough. We've shared that with you, yes?

JIMBO: Three months of this, for this?

MOCKIS: The delay, it was intentional. It was a simple courtesy to you! Why couldn't you see that?

JIMBO: That was some big favor to us? To me, huh?

MOCKIS: You and those other twenty-some young men, this was your own personal affair, yes? Some smart, little something on your own, for your own, and for whose benefit? (*Beat*) Under what obligations from us? From anyone? Whose say-so? What flag? (*Smirks*) Just a little private enterprise on your own, yes? (*Beat*) Simple courtesy was the most you could have expected!

SPIKE: Fuck the formal talk. I give a hell about what flag. That's not the point, boy.

MOCKIS: It's the only point! (*Beat*) Why didn't they shoot you the first day? This would have all been behind us. (*Beat*) What were we free to do? What were you expecting? Understanding? Forgiveness. You have that, now. (*Beat*) A free pass on this? Oh, that was never possible. (*Beat*) Haven't you humiliated us long enough?

JIMBO: You're not pulling any numbers on me! No one tells me what the hell I have to do! I've carried the load for America across the whole goddam world. It was always for our best interests. You can pick up my sticks this one time.

MOCKIS: We've had to get up every morning and go to our jobs, for three months. Did you ever consider us? How we had to feel? (*Beat*) Why didn't you kill yourselves? That would have been decent.

JIMBO: What? I was to what?

SPIKE: I ain't dying here. (*Crumples the sheet of paper with their names on it, tosses it to the floor*) We don't need a list from you or from America. Fuck that shit. We ain't anybody's goddam laundry list. (*Beat*) Now, you will get the situation readjusted.

MOCKIS: You give me orders, yes?

YOGI: Maybe if we apologize. If we did, now, something could change. If it was a real apology, maybe it could.

MOCKIS: It's past that point, son.

JIMBO: Then offer them money, dammit! Money always spells the difference!

MOCKIS *sips some water.*

JIMBO (*Continued*): That's what they want, isn't it? Money. Okay, money and an apology. Right? It would give us something, more time to come up with something! Right?

MOCKIS *stares straight at* JIMBO. *Silence.*

JIMBO (*Continued*): Oh, God, what?

YOGI *opens the pack of cigarettes, offers one to* SPIKE.

SPIKE: From him?

YOGI *pushes the cigarettes back into the pack, closes it, glances at* SPIKE, *who is still glaring at him, then slides the cigarettes across the table to* MOCKIS.

MOCKIS: You don't have to do that, son.
YOGI: Sure I do.
SPIKE: I should be grateful, what the hell. It took the spades here to show me who the fuck the real niggers are. I'm truly thankful for that small favor. (*Laughs*)
MOCKIS: Be bigger than that, yes?
JIMBO: I could kill you, boy.
MOCKIS (*Leans across the table*): Son, you don't have the courage to do anything. You couldn't do a damn thing for three months, yes?
SPIKE: Bless America. Don't you take it all, huh? Thank you for your poor, your tired, and your sick. Here he is. From you to me, with sincerity written all over his ass. (*Beat*) We should get down on our knees and thank America for this moment.
MOCKIS: That would be desirable, yes, but not essential.

Lights fade as MOCKIS *pockets the pack of cigarettes from* YOGI.

END OF ACT ONE

ACT TWO

Scene 1

The airplane hangar. It is being converted to house an electric chair. Stacks of pipe, coils of steel banding and electrical cables. Boxes and odd-sized crates of plugs, connectors and conductors, cans of paint, various power tools litter the area. The steel plates from the first scene have been uprooted and set against a side wall.

Reggae music on pre-set; it segues into the din and dissonance from the power tools being operated by the WORKMEN. *The music and the noise from the power tools counterpoint each other and then marry into a cacophonous symphony. The din will diminish into muted background noise from the power tools as the scene begins.*

WORKMEN are hastily constructing the electric chair and the panel of conducting switches and the master throw switch on the wall. The activity and conversation of the WORKMEN *is atmospheric and unobtrusive. This work activity goes on for 15 seconds.*

Lights down. Lights up.

JIMBO *is being tape-measured and examined by the woman* DOCTOR. JIMBO *is wearing a T-shirt and briefs.* HE *is slouching and moving about, making the measurements impossible. A* GUARD *is positioned next to him.* JIMBO *is in leg irons and his wrists are chained to the leather body brace around his waist.*

DOCTOR (*Stepping back from* JIMBO): Stand still. You're being childish. Arms out now. Hold them straight out!

GUARD *taps* JIMBO *on the back with his baton.*

JIMBO: You put me up against a wall and shoot me! You ain't getting me into that chair!
DOCTOR: Straight out. Come on now, you can lock your elbows.
JIMBO: You're making a goddam mistake! You know that!

GUARD *grabs* JIMBO's *arm and straightens it out.* DOCTOR *quickly runs the tape measure down* JIMBO's *arm, then jots the measurement down on an index card.*

DOCTOR: That was painless, wasn't it? (SHE *runs the tape measure across the back of* JIMBO's *shoulders, jots the measurement down*)
JIMBO: Measure me. Do that. You'll get measured by someone one day yourself.

SPIKE *is swept Onstage from a side room by a* GUARD. SPIKE *is shackled as in the first scene.* HE *is wearing a starched military uniform and spitpolished black combat boots. An American flag patch has been sewn onto his upper left sleeve.*

SPIKE (*To his* GUARD): You dumb son of a bitch! (*To* DOCTOR) I ain't wearing these pants! Give me pants that fit! You call this a shirt? Look at these goddam lapels!

DOCTOR (*Loops the tape measure around* JIMBO's *waist*): I want you to take a deep breath now.

SPIKE: America ain't going to let this go by. They'll make a move.

JIMBO: Right, some big moves. (*Spits*)

DOCTOR: Come on now, inhale, young man. As deep as you can. You're a big boy. You've been a big boy for a long time.

SPIKE (*To* DOCTOR): I want some decent pants! I'm a military man!

DOCTOR: You'll wear those or nothing! It's up to you. (*To* JIMBO) Deep breath, one time, please. You don't want to be the only one not to. You can do it, I know you can.

JIMBO: You know you can't kill me this way!

DOCTOR: No one is killing anyone. We just want these measurements. (*Beat*) Tuck your waist in, please. Just one big breath. I want to see those good, strong muscles of yours.

JIMBO: There'll be a full accounting of you niggers. You want to be responsible?

DOCTOR: We want your waist size, don't we now?

SPIKE: It'll come back at them, Jimbo.

DOCTOR: Just one last deep breath. Inhale, right through your nose.

DOCTOR *steps aside, pauses, then jabs* JIMBO *in the stomach, lightly.* JIMBO *stiffens,* DOCTOR *measures* JIMBO's *waist.*

DOCTOR (*Continued*): There we are. Very nice. Thank you so much.

JIMBO: You tricked me, damn you. You know what you did? (*To* SPIKE) She tricked me!

DOCTOR: It's routine. Nothing personal. (*To* JIMBO'S GUARD) He's yours now. I want him on plenty of fluids. Lots of sugars and juices. Don't force him. (*Steps to* JIMBO *as an afterthought, rubs his forearm with her finger*) Get him into the sun. His skin tone is terrible.

JIMBO (*Knocks* DOCTOR's *hand away*): To hell with my skin tone!

DOCTOR: I think it would be a good idea for all of them to have some sun. (*Beat*) I don't want them sunburnt. (*To* GUARDS) Have I made myself clear on that? No sunburn.

GUARDS *nod.*

JIMBO: Fuck your suntans!

DOCTOR: I am responsible for your well-being now, not you.

JIMBO: What kind of shit is that? Be decent!

DOCTOR *moves away to check* SPIKE's *uniform.*

SPIKE: Take the tan, Jimbo. She's playing with us. If this was for real, they'd be a lot more efficient.

JIMBO: I don't need your crap either! You take the goddam tan, boy!

SPIKE: This is just a hype, huh? We're getting out of this! They want to scare something out of us, out of America. When they get it . . .

JIMBO: . . . Bullshit from all directions now, oh, God.

SPIKE: That ain't an electric chair. I've seen them before. Believe me.

> YOGI *is brought On by two* GUARDS *as* JIMBO *is being led Off to the side room by his* GUARD. YOGI *is wrestling with his* GUARDS. HE *is shackled as in the first scene and is prepped in a military uniform and boots.* GUARDS *struggle to lockdown* YOGI *to one of the uprooted steel plates.*

YOGI: Spikey, what are they doing to me? What do they want from me?

SPIKE: They're teasing us!

YOGI: I'm scared!

SPIKE: Shut the hell up! Be a professional, act with honor. Never give that up!

YOGI: They're getting us all fixed up for what, Spikey boy?

SPIKE: Don't be a virgin, Yogi! They're pimping us!

DOCTOR (*To* SPIKE): Okay, mister professional. (*Checks* SPIKE's *eyes*) Not so good. I want him on vitamins with his fluids. Plenty of vitamin C. Give him fresh fruit. (*Looks over* SPIKE's *hands*) Clean his fingernails. I want them clipped. (*Beat*) Get his hair trimmed. Around his backside here, get it off his shirt collar. Just a touch. (*Beat*) Some off his sides here, but nothing too short. Nothing severe. We don't want him looking too young. (*Checking the American flag patch*) This is sloppy. We can do a better job of stitching, can't we?

> SPIKE's GUARD *nods.*

SPIKE: Genuflect when you touch my flag, bitch! Where's your respect!

DOCTOR (*To* SPIKE's GUARD): Shine his shoes again.

> JIMBO *is swept back Onstage from the side room by his* GUARD. HE *has been dressed in a starched military uniform.* HE *is shackled as in the first scene.* DOCTOR *moves to* JIMBO.

DOCTOR (*Continued*): That's fine. Very good. (*Checks the American flag patch*) This is better, what I'm looking for. (*To* WORKMEN) Okay, gentlemen, allow me some room here.

> WORKMEN *back away from the chair quickly.*

DOCTOR (*Continued; to* SPIKE): Young man, I don't want you to get excited. We have to check something now, that's all.

SHE *signals* SPIKE's GUARD *to bring* SPIKE *to the chair.*

SPIKE: What the hell is going on?

DOCTOR (*Stepping to the chair alongside of* SPIKE): Just relax now, for a few moments.

DOCTOR *motions* WORKMEN *and* SPIKE's GUARD *to ease* SPIKE *into the chair.*

SPIKE: Hey, now. (*Forces a short laugh*) Guys, you guys, don't fool around.

DOCTOR: Slide him in. (*Beat*) This is for you, the last thing you have to do.

SPIKE (*Twisting in the grasp of the* GUARD): You guys, you've made your point, okay? Fine! Don't, it ain't necessary. Get your goddam hands off of me!

DOCTOR: No one's going to hurt you now. Just sit and we can finish up quicker. Then you can take it easy. How's that? (*To* WORKMEN) Hold him down! On the chair, damn you!

SPIKE: Let me up! For God's sake, no! Let me go!

WORKMEN *lift* SPIKE *into the chair, force him down on the seat.*

JIMBO: Let me out of here! Get me out! I don't have to watch this, you fucking bastards!

JIMBO's GUARD *braces* JIMBO *backward with his baton.*

SPIKE: Get 'em off of me! Did I ever do anything to you?

DOCTOR *moves* SPIKE's *arm over to an electrode.*

SPIKE (*Continued*): Leave my arm alone. Let it go!

DOCTOR *magic-markers* SPIKE's *wrist and forearm.*

SPIKE (*Continued*): What the hell are you doing? What are you touching me with?

DOCTOR: Stop fussing, damn you! We just have to see something! (SHE *markers* SPIKE's *other forearm and wrist, then quickly folds back* SPIKE's *pants cuff*)

SPIKE: Leave my pants alone! They're fine! I'll wear the pants, I'll wear the goddam things just the way they are! (HE *struggles, kicking his legs out*)

GUARD *pins* SPIKE's *legs.*

SPIKE (*Continued*): I'll kick you in the teeth, bitch! Don't touch me, don't take my legs, please!

DOCTOR: We didn't hurt your arms. We're not going to hurt your legs.

SPIKE: You're going to do something. Yes, you did. You did hurt my arms! (*Moans, fighting terror in his voice*) You're hurting me!

DOCTOR *clamps down on* SPIKE's *ankle.*

SPIKE (*Continued*): She's taking my legs! Jimbo, Yogi!

JIMBO *collapses against a stack of pipes.* YOGI *begins to moan a low, barely audible whine.* DOCTOR *quickly markers* SPIKE's *shins.*

DOCTOR: Bravo, young man. There we are. That wasn't bad, was it? You are a big boy. I knew it all along. (*To* SPIKE's GUARD) He's all set for tomorrow.

WORKMEN *and* GUARD *haul* SPIKE *to his feet.*

DOCTOR (*Continued*): Go easy on him. Hold him up until he gets his legs back. (*To* SPIKE) You'll be fine in a few moments.
SPIKE: No good, rotten sons of bitches. You have no right! (*Giggles*) Didn't you fool me? You did. You wanted to upset me. I knew what was going on. (*Beat*) All the time, I knew. I was just giving you a show. What you wanted. I know you can't go through with this shit! You just proved it to me! (HE *laughs, a muted, nervous giggling*)

DOCTOR *motions to* YOGI's GUARDS. GUARDS *move to* YOGI.

YOGI: Hands off of me!
SPIKE: It's nothing, Yogi! Didn't I show you? I showed them, too! It's a, a damn looneytune! They're dreaming!
YOGI (*Lunges towards* SPIKE): Help me then, you understand!

WORKMEN *rush over and restrain* YOGI *from* SPIKE.

JIMBO (*To* DOCTOR): We have to talk. We have to work this out. What kind of deal, huh? Whatever you want, I know I can make a deal with you.
DOCTOR: There's no need for that.
JIMBO: You can hear me out!
DOCTOR: No deals. (SHE *begins checking* YOGI's *eyes*)

YOGI *struggles to keep his face away from the* DOCTOR's *hands.*

YOGI: There's no choice, you understand? It's God's fault, not mine. He loves me.

DOCTOR *eases* YOGI *into the chair, with the* WORKMEN *and* GUARDS *assisting.*

DOCTOR (*While moving* YOGI): Yes, God loves you. He loves everyone.

YOGI (*Straining to stay off the seat of the chair*): No, no, God doesn't love you. Just me. He doesn't love you niggers. That's why he put me here.

DOCTOR: Relax, and we'll have you feeling better in a little bit. Just as soon as we do a couple of things here. (*Beat*) Think about something else for awhile.

YOGI: Why? Why did I get fucked into this world? It could have been some other time, a different day!

DOCTOR (*Struggling to put* YOGI's *wrist to the electrode*): Hold him! Dammit, he's strong! (*To* GUARD) Get him on sugars, plenty of them! We can't have him like this!

DOCTOR *markers* YOGI's *wrist and forearm, then moves quickly to roll his pants cuffs up.* YOGI *gurgles a sound as if* HE *is being burned. We hear the singular sound of the magic marker against* YOGI's *shins.*

DOCTOR (*Continued; to* WORKMEN): We'll need to elevate the chair, just for him. Will the change be difficult?

A WORKMAN *pats the* DOCTOR's *arm reassuringly.*

DOCTOR (*Continued*): Good. Fine.

WELLS *bursts into the room.* MOCKIS *follows, right on* WELLS' *heels.*

MOCKIS: You won't do this!

WELLS (*Whirls and sticks a finger in* MOCKIS' *face*): I'll do what I choose to! Go back to your country! You tell them, there was no trial! You don't give me that much, to hell with you!

MOCKIS: I want them shot!

WELLS: These sons of bitches? They're common criminals. Isn't that how it's done by you! (*To* DOCTOR) Are they ready!

JIMBO (*Straining to get hold of* MOCKIS): You make a fucking deal with these niggers!

MOCKIS: What are you doing in uniform? (*Looks*) All of you! What the hell is this!

WELLS: If there was any other way, but there isn't, is there? (*To* JIMBO) You'll have your way, you'll get your last dinner. Isn't that how it's done? Rules of decorum for every damn situation.

MOCKIS (*Sees the patch on* SPIKE's *sleeve*): This is the flag! What are you doing with that? (*Steps to* WELLS) You take my flag off of them!

WELLS (*To* MOCKIS): They took pictures? I want some, too! For the whole world to have! (*To* WORKMEN) I want it tested and in working order. Now! What are you standing around for? Don't waste my time!

WORKMEN *begin working on the chair again.*

JIMBO: Give him what he wants! Give him the goddam trial!

MOCKIS (*To* WELLS): You kill them the way you want, but you take the American flag off of them! I'll be damned before they wear the flag! You won't do this. You have better sense than that. (*Beat*) You line them up against a wall without the flag!

WELLS: Without the flag? Then they're not official? You don't represent them? (*Beat*) Then I'll decide what they wear and how they wear it.

Sudden sparks and dimming of lights. YOGI *is jolted and thrown out of the chair by an accidental surge of electricity.* HE *lies motionless.* DOCTOR *jerks* YOGI's *mouth open, begins CPR on him.*

WELLS (*Continued; running to the* DOCTOR): What are you doing? What did you do? (*Beat*) He's all right, isn't he? He is. He has to be. He can't die yet!

DOCTOR (*To* WORKMEN *and* YOGI's GUARDS): Get him up! Let's go!

WORKMEN *and* GUARDS *haul* YOGI *up, rush him Off, the* DOCTOR *running alongside, continuing CPR.*

WELLS (*Calling after* DOCTOR): You get him alive! That's an order! (*To* MOCKIS) She did this! You saw her. You, see what you caused to happen? All of you! (*Spotting* JIMBO *and* SPIKE) Get them out of here! What's wrong with you!

GUARDS *begin to haul* JIMBO *and* SPIKE *out of the hangar.*

JIMBO (*To* MOCKIS): Give him something!

WELLS (*To* JIMBO's GUARD): Pray that he lives. You're responsible for what's happened! I have to have three bodies tomorrow. I will have three if you have to take his place.

GUARDS *exit with* JIMBO *and* SPIKE. *Silence, as the smoke clears from the room.*

WELLS (*Continued*): It was an accident. You saw that.

MOCKIS (*Pausing*): What you will have to answer for, yes?

WELLS: How can you prevent an accident? (*Beat*) They're responsible, not me! He has to be okay. He will be fine. (*Beat*) I can't do it. I can't go through with this.

MOCKIS (*Pausing*): They are responsible, yes.

WELLS: You could have done something for them! Why couldn't you have given me another way! (*Wipes his face quickly*) What do I have to prove? Why do I have to prove anything! (HE *is suddenly seized by dry heaving*)

MOCKIS: Mother of God, look what they've done to you.

WELLS: I can't do it. We have to stop this somehow.

MOCKIS: You don't deserve this. (*Pausing*) See what they're doing to you? To us, yes? Could they care? (*Beat*) What do you owe them? The world has seen what they've done to you, to your people.

WELLS (*Pausing*): They murdered people. Butchered them! (*Beat*) We did nothing to provoke them to come here!

MOCKIS: You deserve that, yes? (*Beat*) They don't give a hell about you.

WELLS: They aren't human. They're nothing! They've provoked everything from us! (*Beat*) I, you and I, we owe them nothing then. (*Beat*) It's finished then. They've forced this on themselves, all of it! (*Pause*) There has to be some other way.

MOCKIS (*Pausing*): They did take pictures, yes? Of their fun? I can't imagine how sick those pictures are. (*Beat*) What kind of mind operates that way? They took pictures of all those unfortunate people. Your people, yes?

WELLS: What can I do? (*Beat*) He'll be fine, that boy. I know it. (*Beat*) I can't do this. I can't.

MOCKIS: What choice do they give you? (*Beat*) How can you let this go? It won't go away tomorrow, yes? (*Beat*) See how they wear the flag. America and them, America with them, all the way, yes?

WELLS: The flags were my choosing.

MOCKIS: They'd want you to believe that, yes? (*Snorts*) Oh, they are quick. (*Beat*) You and I, we could have been friends. We should be. Do they want that? (*Beat*) So here we stand, apart, because of them. What nonsense, yes? We've had it up to our eyes with them. Why do we, you and I, deserve it?

WELLS: What else can I do?

MOCKIS (*Pausing*): What can we, you and I, do, yes? Why should I let them embarrass you?

Long pause.

WELLS: You and I, we have to execute them.

MOCKIS: You have every right to stand by your decision, yes?

WELLS: We, you and I, have the right. We have to do it. (*Beat*) They did all of this, they are responsible, truly. You saw that from the start, didn't you?

MOCKIS: Yes, we did. You show them, now.

WELLS (*Pausing*): We will show them. Tomorrow morning. On schedule.

MOCKIS: Why should we let them embarrass us, you and me, together? (*Beat*) You and I, we want those flags off of them, yes?

WELLS (*Pausing*): Yes, how could I let them confuse me?

MOCKIS: They won't back you into any more corners, will they?

WELLS: They won't take advantage of you.

MOCKIS: You're in control, yes. That's the stuff.

WELLS: We're in control of this situation, you and I. This is our responsibility.

MOCKIS: Yes, it is.

WELLS (*Pausing*): I'll give you the flags. The flags come off.

MOCKIS (*Smiling*): That came from strength. I know that. (HE *steps to* WELLS, *offering a handshake*)

WELLS *looks at* MOCKIS, *smiles, turns and exits. Lights fade on* WELLS' *exit.*

Scene 2

A beach area adjacent to the veranda setting of the second scene.

A three-quarters moon in a starless, pitch blue-black sky.

An audio of a raucous party is heard in the dark. Reggae music, a section of Stones, Springsteen tunes, some Bartok sections fade in and out of the party noises. Shadows of characters move Upstage in the moonlight, silhouetted in the scene. At the beginning of the scene, the audio will abruptly cut off to silence.

Beer cans; bottles of champagne, rum, tequila, whiskey, red and white wine, some of them still capped or corked; trays and plates of appetizers and steaks, half-eaten; boxes of Churchill cigars; cartons of Benson & Hedges, Marlboros and Kools; and a huge three-tiered silver dish filled with sugar cubes and chocolates—all of this litters the setting. A long conference table, a stereo and speakers, record albums overturned in a heap.

JIMBO is sprawled out on the beach, canopied by an overturned beach chair. HE is shackled, except for his leg irons, and is sipping from a can of beer. HE is dressed in military pants, boots and a white T-shirt with the sleeves rolled up over his biceps. HE is tinkering with a rubber-tipped stick, hitting an occasional, sporadic note on the can. A GUARD is seated in a beach chair, sipping from a bottle of Appleton rum.

Lights up.

JIMBO: What the hell are you talking about, his "greatest"? So he gave him sight. That blind man didn't mean a thing to him. (*Strikes the beer can, once, for emphasis*) When he turned the water into wine, at the wedding feast, that was his top miracle!

GUARD: He let the blind man see for the first time! The wine trick was too easy.

JIMBO: He cured one guy. One. He could have healed the whole shitload of 'em. What's that show, huh? Cure the sick? (*Beat*) He could give a rolling shit about the blind. Disease? 'The fuck, huh?

GUARD: It's better today for them, much better than back then.

JIMBO: The best one he ever pulled off was when he fed all those thousands of people with one fish. (*Laughs*) One fish, one loaf of bread, can you figure that?

GUARD: Three fish.

JIMBO: What "three" fish?

GUARD: He used three fish. I am certain of that.

JIMBO: One damn fish.

GUARD: And several, not "one," loaves of bread.

JIMBO: Who do you think this guy was? What, he couldn't work it out from one fish, one loaf of bread? He could have pulled it out of the air.

GUARD: Three fish and several loaves of bread. He took what the people had with them. It's down on paper, for certain.

JIMBO: You're knocking my Jesus, boy.

GUARD: From his best writer, it was. Matthew. Matthew had the heart to get it down.

JIMBO: I give a fuck whose version it was. (*Beat*) Now, the water into wine, he did that one for sure. Did it to give us some fun. He wasn't trying to impress anyone with it. Sure, cure the blind, that might cut a lot of ice with people. But to make a party with all that wine, he did that for the soul. You ever been to a wedding without booze? "For Chrissakes," that's all you hear. (*Smiles*) I'll give you this much, healing the blind guy is in the top three, but it ain't number one. (*Beat*) Stay away from all the Matthews. The name says it all. (*Spits*) "Math-uuu . . ." (HE *tosses a pack of Kools to the* GUARD) Start integrating those sons of bitches for me, huh? Goddam boogie cigarettes anyway, ain't they? (HE *empties a beer over his head, cooling himself*)

GUARD (*Holding the pack of Kools out to* JIMBO): You want one?

JIMBO: Is there time to catch cancer?

GUARD *takes a cigarette, tosses the pack to* JIMBO.

JIMBO (*Continued*): Catch a goddam something tomorrow, huh?

Pause.

GUARD: I have a joke.

JIMBO: It's your party. Your "version" of one, huh? (*Laughs*)

GUARD (*Pausing*): How do you make love to a fat lady?

JIMBO: What? Where?

GUARD (*Looks askance*): Anywhere.

JIMBO: This a local joke?

GUARD: Anywhere!

JIMBO (*Shrugs his shoulders*): I give. How do you?

GUARD: You roll her in flour and check for the wet spot.

JIMBO: Yeah? Why? (*Brightening*) Oh, hell, I get it! (*Laughs*) That makes sense. (*Beat*) Oh, if this could pass. Some answer he got, huh? Some goddam answer. Play it out, son. Get your chin off the ground. Get out of this garden. Start the ball rolling. (HE *reaches out for a bottle of whiskey, sips*) What the hell else could he do? His own father says that to him. (*Smiles*) He goes to himself for an answer, and what does he find? An old man and a white bird. Some crowd, huh? He was bound to get a fucked-up answer. He, they, however many it was, it all comes up a little short. A little tight in the thinking, huh? (HE *knocks out a halfway decent rhythm on the empty beer can with the stick*) So much for talent. It always comes at a real wrong time. (HE *tosses the stick over his head, pauses*) The electric chair? Whoooweee . . . what an idea! (*Beat*) It can change your whole way of looking at furniture.

GUARD (*Pausing*): It'll be quick.

JIMBO: Quick? (*Snorts*) I appreciate that, yeah, don't I now. Matthew write that one down for you, too? (*Beat*) Catch a fucking something on that, yeah. (*Offers the* GUARD *the bottle of whiskey*)

GUARD *gestures with his bottle of rum.*

JIMBO (*Continued*): You ever play baseball?

GUARD: A long time ago. Soccer is our passion here now.

JIMBO: Soccer? Geezus, this fucking country of yours. (*Beat*) Once upon a time, it's always "once upon a time," ain't it? (*Whistles*) Why is that? (*Pause*) I was catching a game. I was a catcher. The umpire, this asshole, he's standing in back of me, giving me the shits. Every pitch, on every goddam pitch. My pitcher, he's a gunner. Arm on him like blue lightning. Boom, boom, boom, he's right down the heart of the plate. Wiseass in back of me, he's calling every one of those heartbreakers "outside." Outside? My ass, geezuschrist, every pitch was, zip, zip, splitting the goddam plate. What the fuck, I say, fuck this guy in back of me, I figure. (*Beat*) I turn to the guy, smile real wide, and I say, check out the curve ball on my pitcher. He ain't got a whole lot of control with it. (*Beat*) I set up outside for the pitch, asshole sets up right in back of me. He figures that I got it covered for him. (*Beat*) I call for a fastball. Just as the pitch is coming in, I move back inside, and boom! It caught the son of a bitch right in the throat. Knocked him out cold. Stone piss cold. (*Snorts, laughs*) Once upon a time. Ah, we're going to be splitting the heart of the plate, tomorrow. (*To* GUARD) Baseball is one helluva game. Don't let anyone tell you different.

GUARD: Your national sport, it is. It's a wonderful game.

JIMBO: It's the best in the whole world. Great fucking game. The absolute best, amen.

YOGI *comes bounding Onstage.* HE *is dressed in military pants and a sky-blue T-shirt.* HE *is wearing a black silk top hat. His pants cuffs are rolled up and dripping wet.* HE *is wearing gauze bandages over the flash burns from the accident in the electric chair, the bandages covering his wrists and shins.* HE *is shackled at the wrists.* DOCTOR *follows* YOGI *On, carrying her black medical bag, accompanied by* YOGI's GUARD. JIMBO's GUARD *quickly stubs out his cigarette, straightens to attention.*

YOGI: Jimbo? Come-a here, Jimbo. (*Belches*) I found a rabbit in this here hat. Where did it go?

JIMBO (*To* YOGI): How was your swim, boy?

YOGI (*Giggling*): The water is beautiful. So clear and warm, and something, you understand. (*Grabs a bottle of tequila, toasts the* DOCTOR) Tell 'em all that Yogi, he had to die twice. He was so fucking dumb that he couldn't get it right the first time! (*Laughs*) I'm a hairy man, Jimbo! I got some magic. I seen it. There ain't no angels, no bright colors. I didn't see heaven, but I didn't see hell. There ain't no hell, goddam!

SPIKE *comes Onstage, swaying drunkenly.* HE *is wearing the starched military uniform pants, boots, and wrist irons.* MOCKIS *follows, with* SPIKE's GUARD *in tow.*

SPIKE (*To* MOCKIS): I can't get over it! You're going to have us killed, and you still accept our invitation! Balls, mister, you got some pair of coconuts on you.

MOCKIS (*Belches drunkenly*): Some damn nerve, yes?

SPIKE (*To his* GUARD): Tell my buddy Jimbo where you've been, boy. Tell him! (*Laughs; to* JIMBO) He's been all round America! (*To his* GUARD) Tell him what you said. (*To* JIMBO) I ask him, where you been, "specifically"? He says, Houston. (*To his* GUARD) What'd I say then? (*To* DOCTOR) I said to your boy here, I ain't ever been to Houston. (*Laughs*)

MOCKIS (*Laughs*): What'd he say then?

SPIKE (*To* JIMBO): He's been to Chicago! I say, I ain't ever been to Chicago, either. Isn't that the bitch, Jimbo?

MOCKIS (*To* JIMBO): You've been to Chicago?

JIMBO: I've been to Houston.

SPIKE (*To his* GUARD): Houston, New York, Chicago, Los Angeles, Miami, Seattle. You've been all over my country, ain't you?

MOCKIS (*To* JIMBO): He's even spent some time in Wisconsin! (*Laughs*) That's your home, yes?

SPIKE (*To* MOCKIS): Tell Jimbo what you said to this colored boy then. (*To his* GUARD) What'd he say to you, fella?

SPIKE's GUARD: You shut your damn mouth!

DOCTOR (*To* SPIKE's GUARD): It's okay, it's nothing.

SPIKE (*To* MOCKIS): Tell him, Tony boy.

MOCKIS: I said, (*Clears his throat*) I said, "Son, it isn't where you've been in this world that counts, it's what you are."

SPIKE (*To his* GUARD): That blew the lights right out of you, didn't it? What are you, boy, huh? You'll never be anything. (*To* DOCTOR) You be sure to make the trip soon, honey! (*To* JIMBO) We're going home first class, Jimbo!

MOCKIS: I'm getting you full honors. That's a promise!

SPIKE: We'll be getting a parade in our hometowns! Our boy, Mockis, he's going to get us laid out with the flag. How's that for a bitch and a half?

MOCKIS: I'm committed to that, yes.

SPIKE: We're too much. We're too damn hot to be shipped back in an airplane. (*Laughs*) We'd melt the bottom right out of the plane. Get the refrigerators ready for us. (*To his* GUARD) We'll be back. Somebody will come back to get your ass!

JIMBO *grabs* MOCKIS *and locks him in a chokehold.* GUARDS *break* JIMBO *away from* MOCKIS.

JIMBO (*To* MOCKIS): What did I do wrong! I can't change water into wine? Is that it?

SPIKE: What the hell's the matter with you? He's taking us first class!

JIMBO (*To* MOCKIS): Call balls and strikes on me, huh? (*To* DOCTOR) Every pitch was right down the heart of the plate!

YOGI: We're getting a parade, Jimbo.

JIMBO (*To* MOCKIS): Show me the water into wine. Show me, goddammit!

SPIKE: You're a stupid drunk!

JIMBO (*To* MOCKIS): Go back home and take all this shit on the dinner circuit! Give the speeches, do the interviews, ain't that how it ends! Some payoff, huh? What's mine? Where is it, goddammit! (*To* DOCTOR) I've never been to New York or Seattle or Miami or any of that shit! (*To* MOCKIS) Tell 'em that, back home. Make it real, huh? Make it sad for them. (*Beat*) Tell the suckers that if I had my choice, I'd come back to kill them all! (*Beat*) Fuck any miracles! (*To* SPIKE) What medal you getting? (*To* YOGI) You got a parade, huh? Dance for the goddam thing. Step lively now. This is a party! (*Laughs*) Come on, magic man, dance, you son of a bitch! (HE *sings a bar of* "America, the Beautiful," *softly, delicately*) What a load of shit that is! (*Beat*) Dance, boys, keep yourself moving. Do something! No time for anything else!

Lights fade on the MERCS, JIMBO *swaying and dancing away from them. No music audio to bridge into next scene.*

Scene 3

The airplane hangar. The hangar is freshly painted; the entire floor has been waxed to a high gloss. The electric chair should be visible in the background, its construction completed, set upon a whitewashed wooden platform.

The lighting should be brilliant, almost blinding, so that the characters in this scene appear to be almost two-dimensional. The movements of the characters should be discernible, but the lighting should wash out sharp focus on the stage movements. The lighting should be pure white to make everything stark, muting the colors of the characters' faces and dress.

SPIKE *is bound and shackled at the wrists and ankles through the leather body brace.* HE *is bound in a manner which allows the* DOCTOR *access to the body areas that* SHE *will shave down.* SPIKE's *pants cuffs have been rolled up.* HE *is wearing a simple white T-shirt and is shoeless.* HE *is seated on a metal folding chair, and his feet are propped up on a wooden crate. The* DOCTOR *is standing near a small metal hospital cart, mixing up shaving cream in a mug. The small cart holds bottles of astringents, shaving soap, towels, a stainless bowl filled with water, and a straight razor.*

Lights up.

DOCTOR *begins to apply shaving lather to the crown of* SPIKE's *head.*

SPIKE: You be gentle up there, my darling.

DOCTOR *begins to shave* SPIKE's *head.*

SPIKE (*Continued*): What are you doing? (*Smiles*) Sounds like you're using sandpaper. You're gonna give me one of those monk's marks, huh? Make me a prayer boy? (*Laughs*)

DOCTOR *towels off the top of* SPIKE's *head, applies astringent.* SPIKE *shudders from the sting of the astringent.*

SPIKE (*Continued*): It's going to be a day today, huh? It's going to be a bitch of a day.

DOCTOR *resumes shaving the top of* SPIKE's *head.*

SPIKE (*Continued*): After this, after today, honey, you should take out a barber's license. Just say you shaved down a dead man. That ought to get you in the union. (*Giggles*) You're too damn overqualified for this, ain't you? Nothing but a bullshit job, ain't it?

DOCTOR *towels off the top of* SPIKE's *head, applies astringent.* SPIKE *shudders from the sting, reaches for the top of his head.* DOCTOR *pushes his hands away.* SHE *applies lather to* SPIKE's *wrist, begins shaving.*

SPIKE (*Continued*): You're damn good with that razor. Not too much, not too little. (*Beat*) Why don't you keep going? Cut it right down to the veins. Right to the bone, go ahead. No, you can't do that. That would fuck everything. No one wants any dying just yet. Not yet. It's all been set, right down to the second. (*Beat*) Go on, honey, right down to the veins, huh?

DOCTOR *towels off wrist, applies astringent.*

SPIKE (*Continued*): Ho, oh, that stings!

DOCTOR *resumes shaving* SPIKE's *wrist.*

SPIKE (*Continued*): One slip of that razor, just one slip, and you'll cheat them. Wouldn't that leave them sons of bitches high and dry. Yeah, they gotta get blood, every damn ounce of mine. They gotta get hyped for this one. Betcha I can, too. Betcha they get nervous. They'll get sweated up. They gotta lick their lips. (*Laughs*) They'll suffer, huh? It's a strut and pose. They gotta show that bullshit. That's their part of the show, huh? (*Beat*) It's a lie, goddammit. None of it's for me. They suck it up for themselves.

DOCTOR: Please, relax.

SPIKE: Making it tough on you, huh?

DOCTOR: However long you want this to take, that is up to you.

SPIKE: Years and years, honey. I got the hair if you got the time. (*Hums a few bars of the Miller beer commercial melody*) Sick man, sick. (*Laughs*)

DOCTOR *towels off* SPIKE's *wrist.*

SPIKE (*Continued*): Smooth as a new baby's butt, huh?

SPIKE *reaches to touch the* DOCTOR's *hair.* DOCTOR *flinches away.*

SPIKE (*Continued*): Ho, that's soft. You have soft hair.

DOCTOR (*Pointing the razor at* SPIKE): Don't do that.

SPIKE: Sorry. Really am, ma'am.

DOCTOR *moves to lather* SPIKE's *other wrist, moving the cart to the other side of him.* SPIKE *grabs the* DOCTOR's *thigh.* SHE *jumps away.*

SPIKE (*Continued*): Can't stop myself. (*Beat*) Can't. It's there for the taking. Right now. Can't stop my blood, and I ain't going to try.

DOCTOR *steps to the door.*

SPIKE (*Continued*): Go on, go for the goddam guard. What's he going to do? Beat me? He'd best beat my ass to death, honey. He can't, can he? No, none of you want it that way. You and the world, damn, you gotta have your countdown. Gotta have your rocks. You gotta shake it down. (*Sighs audibly*) I give up. I'm so goddam tired. (*Jerks his wrists out, extended*) Go ahead, silly bitch, cut them! Cut 'em right off! Get yourself a taste of it, huh, silly? Huh, bitch? I'm talking to you, slut! (HE *collapses against the back of the chair*) So damn tired. I give up. I give it up right now.

DOCTOR *splashes astringent on towel, places it to the back of* SPIKE's *neck.* SPIKE *is shocked by the cold of the astringent.*

SPIKE (*Continued*): Thank you. (*Beat*) They want to do it, don't they? They're going to do it, ain't they? All the way. They need it. They gotta have their ounce of blood. Clean. They gotta boil it clean. Gotta fry it. Gotta steam it. Cook it. Get it clean.

DOCTOR *splashes astringent down* SPIKE's *neck and back.* SPIKE *shudders, whistles.*

SPIKE (*Continued*): They gotta blow the bottoms right off my feet. Wheee . . . (*Laughs*) That's a taste.

SPIKE *moves his hand gently to the* DOCTOR's. SHE *moves away.*

SPIKE (*Continued*): Soft hands. Nice, soft hands.

DOCTOR *moves to the cart, picks up razor, resumes shaving* SPIKE's *wrist.*

SPIKE (*Continued*): I'll remember your hands. I do already. Gotta remember that touch. Gotta see that touch. I see it. Gotta get out of myself and see it. Now. Stand and breathe. I can't stand!
DOCTOR: Just stop it! (SHE *resumes shaving*)
SPIKE: You touch it first. Then the hits, the jolts, ho, yeah, they'll touch it. You got a smooth touch. You do it fast. (HE *reaches to stroke the* DOCTOR's *hair*) Soft, yeah. Electric.

DOCTOR *towels off* SPIKE's *wrist with astringent.* SPIKE *leans over and studies the* DOCTOR.

SPIKE (*Continued*): Nice ankles, nice calves, nice thighs. You got a pair of those, honey. Nice and firm. Nice hips. Ankles, calves, thighs, hips, and what in between?
DOCTOR: You keep still.
SPIKE: I gotta breathe, huh? (*Laughs*) What's in between? Something, huh? Is it nervous, huh? Nervous about me? Is it wet? Is it hot? It's going to be a hot one for everybody today. Going to be my goddam day, huh?

DOCTOR *moves to the cart, stands, nervously shifting the bottles and the shaving mug around.*

SPIKE (*Continued*): Ignore it. Don't let me bother you. (*Giggles*) The more you fight it, honey, the more you lose it. Don't you? (*Suddenly*) I gotta breathe. Where's the windows? Open a window.

DOCTOR *splashes* SPIKE's *face with some astringent.* SPIKE *revives, calming his breathing.*

SPIKE (*Continued*): Better. (*Beat*) Better than God, right from him. He never meant for you to stick a pillow under your ass. That's true. You're no sticks and bones, no skinny bones. (*Motions to his face*) More. I need more cold.

DOCTOR *towels* SPIKE *down.*

SPIKE (*Continued*): No, you don't need any pillow under you. It's all there. Natural as can be. A cradle, a saddle, a vise. Lock it around somebody? Good luck. (*Laughs*) To the end. To the damn end with that. Rock when it rolls. Roll when it rocks. The only way. I see that. I see it. Stay sane. Stay decent. Gotta stay awake. Stay awake. Go to sleep. You'll sleep with someone tonight.

DOCTOR: With no one, damn you!

SPIKE *laughs.* DOCTOR *steps away, begins to put the towel to her forehead, stops, wipes her forehead with the back of her hand.*

SPIKE: Come on, finish me up. You're making it take too long.

DOCTOR: You will go to hell!

SPIKE: You and me both, honey.

DOCTOR: Lift your legs! (SHE *grabs hold of one of* SPIKE'*s chains and lifts his leg off the crate, quickly lathers the underside of his leg, begins shaving*)

SPIKE: Take me home with you tonight.

DOCTOR *drops* SPIKE'*s leg down, begins shaving his shin.*

SPIKE (*Continued*): I'm gonna smoke you tonight, darling. Smoke you the rest of your days. I'm gonna give you a shot of me. Look at me. I gotta smoke you. (*Laughs*) I gotta catch. When someone else has you, has your favors. Gonna get you when your blood boils.

DOCTOR *moves cart to the other side, begins to lather and shave* SPIKE'*s shin.*

SPIKE (*Continued*): You got me clean. You got me smooth, huh? Gotta get you. I gotta say that. Gotta get me your honey. I gotta tell you that. No, I ain't saying that. I gotta leave you with that. I got you. I see it. No, I don't. Got you under me. Got you over me. No, I don't. Got you locked around me. No. Got me locked. No. Gotta die. Gotta be easy. Gotta be nice. (HE *motions to his face*) More cold!

DOCTOR *ignores* SPIKE.

SPIKE (*Continued*): I'm tired. No, I'm not. I'm getting there. No, I don't.

DOCTOR (*Towels off* SPIKE's *shins and ankles*): You're all set.

SPIKE (*Lifts* DOCTOR's *skirt, grabs her leg*): I need something. Stay with me.

DOCTOR (*Moves away from* SPIKE's *grasp*): Don't, damn you.

SPIKE: I have to, don't I? I gotta be that typical sorryass, don't I? Ain't I? (*Beat*) I can touch you nice.

DOCTOR: Oh, dear God, what is this? (SHE *exits quickly*)

SPIKE (*Calling after* DOCTOR): Get your ass back here. (*Laughs*) Get that ass back! (*Pauses, sighs, suddenly bangs his leg chains against the crate, kicking it over*) Killing me, huh? Killing is natural! (*Laughs*) Someone's gotta breathe. I can't! (*Beat*) Yes, I can. No, I won't. (*Beat*) Someone can!

Lights fade, silhouetting SPIKE's *head against the backdrop of the electric chair. Reggae music segue to the next scene.*

Scene 4

An anteroom adjacent to the airplane hangar. Remnants of an airplane interior, some seats, a window housing, the nose housing for a propeller, and an old wall calendar on the back wall. The steel plates from the first scene have been stacked against a side wall. Boxes and odd-sized crates of material and tools for the electric chair assemblage have been neatly stacked in the corners of the room. There is a long conference table, off center, with a few metal folding chairs set randomly around it. An aluminum pitcher of ice water and a stack of paper cups have been set on the table. The DOCTOR's *medical bag is also set on the table.*

SPIKE, YOGI and JIMBO are dressed in the starched military uniforms. The American flag patches have been removed from their upper sleeves, a few threads still showing from the ripped stitching. The MERCS *are shackled at the wrists and the ankles.* THEY *are wearing brown leather house slippers and white socks.* THEY *have been shaved down, their hair trimmed and blow-dried.* YOGI *is wearing the top hat and is seated on the edge of the table. The* DOCTOR *is scissoring off the gauze bandaging from his wrists and shins.* SPIKE *is seated on the nose housing of the propeller, playing with the rotor.* JIMBO *is seated at the table, in the throes of a violent migraine.* MOCKIS *is standing at the table, sipping some water.* GUARDS *are stationed around the room.*

Lights up.
Silent activity for a few seconds.

MOCKIS (*To* JIMBO): You should try shaking your head, side to side. That can help a migraine sometimes.

JIMBO (*Throws his head back*): It's behind my left eye. (*Laughs through the pain*) This is so silly. Right up to the end, huh? Goddammit.

MOCKIS (*To* DOCTOR): Give him something.

DOCTOR: I don't have that authority. (*To* JIMBO) I'm sorry.

MOCKIS: Is there anything you can give him? (*Beat*) An aspirin?
JIMBO: I can ask for my damn self!

Pause.

DOCTOR (*Checking* YOGI's *shins*): Let's see how well we're doing today.
SPIKE: I was born in 1953. A good year? (*To all*) You were there, weren't you?
(*Laughs*)

ALL *look to* SPIKE, *pause, resume their activity.*

MOCKIS (*Holds out a pack of cigarettes to* JIMBO): A cigarette? Sometimes that can
clear your head. I can go and get you something.
JIMBO (*Leans forward*): You're staying right here! You're wanted. We've "re-
quested" your presence.
DOCTOR (*Removing the gauze from* YOGI's *wrists*): These have healed very nicely.
(SHE *applies vaseline to* YOGI's *wrists*) This should help.
JIMBO: Give me something for this goddam head of mine!
DOCTOR (*To* JIMBO): I must have permission.
SPIKE: What happened in 1954? I was one, happy to be me, huh? (*Laughs*) 1955?
Who is two? Somebody?

WELLS *enters with a* GUARD *in tow.*

WELLS (*To* DOCTOR): Are we ready here?
DOCTOR: Yessir.

WELLS *motions to the* GUARD.

GUARD (*Reading from a sheet of paper*): Milliken. James Mark.
YOGI: Yes? (*Sighs*) Damn.

The GUARD *moves to* YOGI, YOGI's GUARD *joins him.* YOGI's GUARD *removes the
top hat.*

YOGI (*Continued*): Give me my hat!

YOGI's GUARD *looks to* WELLS, WELLS *nods,* GUARD *places the hat back on* YOGI.

YOGI (*Continued; to* JIMBO): Hey. (*Beat*) Hey, Jimbo?
JIMBO: Get the hell away from me. Not now!
YOGI: Something for the magic man, Jimbo? (HE *doffs his hat to* JIMBO)

ALL *turn away.*

YOGI (*Continued*): Spikey boy? (*Beat*) Hey, you! (*Pause, smiling*) It's all right for you, Spikey boy. You've made it out. You always were nuts, I understand. (HE *steps past his* GUARDS, *bops* JIMBO *with his hat*) Take care of that head, while you can, huh?

JIMBO: Don't shit all over that chair. Some people got it after you.

YOGI: I'll do my best. Goddam if I don't.

YOGI *exits with* DOCTOR *and the* GUARDS.

MOCKIS: I want something for a headache.

WELLS: Get your own damn aspirin!

MOCKIS (*Gestures to* JIMBO): You could give him something, yes? (*Beat*) Please.

WELLS (*To* JIMBO): For you, young man?

JIMBO: Keep your aspirin. Give me the gas. Gas me! Do it! (*Laughs*) Naw, save that for the Jews, huh?

WELLS (*Leaning over* JIMBO): Where are you sick? You feel nausea?

JIMBO: I got a hangover. Of all the things, huh?

SPIKE: When did 1953 come? (*Spins the propeller*)

ALL *pause, look at* SPIKE. *Lights dim, come up, dim, up, dim, up.* JIMBO *bolts out of his chair on the last "up."* MOCKIS *takes a cigarette, searches his pockets frenetically for a match. A* GUARD *steps forward, lights* MOCKIS' *cigarette.* MOCKIS *nods to the* GUARD, *smokes.* WELLS *opens the* DOCTOR's *bag, fishing through it.*

WELLS: We have something for a headache, young man.

DOCTOR *enters with* GUARD.

DOCTOR (*Stands, reads from paper*): Milliken, James Mark. He is deceased at 4:03 A.M. (SHE *hands the paper to* WELLS)

GUARD (*Reading from a second sheet of paper*): Whaley, Michael Robert. (*Pause*) Whaley, Michael Robert?

SPIKE's GUARD *moves over and takes* SPIKE *by the arm, easing him off the nose of the propeller.*

SPIKE: Where now? Is it 1953? Huh? It's a nice day, okay.

DOCTOR *and* GUARDS *begin to escort* SPIKE *out.*

JIMBO: Spike! Spikey boy!

MOCKIS (*To* DOCTOR): I want something for this young man's headache.

DOCTOR (*To* WELLS): Sir, he shouldn't have anything so close to the . . .

WELLS: . . . There is something that he could have?

DOCTOR (*Sighs, steps to the table, opens her bag, hands* WELLS *some pills*): These should do.

MOCKIS: What are they? I have a right to know. (*Beat*) He does.

DOCTOR (*To* WELLS, *irritated*): It has simple caffeine and a muscle relaxant.

MOCKIS: Muscle relaxers, what? I prefer the aspirin for him.

DOCTOR (*To* WELLS): These are just as good?

MOCKIS: How do I know that?

DOCTOR (*To* WELLS): Can we just get on with this! (*Breathes heavily and angrily*)

WELLS (*To* DOCTOR): I'm sorry. Go on. (*Pause*) Don't you look at me that way!

DOCTOR *exits,* GUARDS *following with* SPIKE *in tow.* JIMBO *reaches to touch* SPIKE, WELLS *eases* JIMBO's *hand away.*

WELLS (*Continued*): We have your medicine, son. Take your medicine.

WELLS *opens the vial, dumps out some pills, pours a cup of water, hands the water to* JIMBO. JIMBO *begins to hyperventilate, wheezing, drops the cup of water.* WELLS *quickly pours a cup of water, holds it in* JIMBO's *hands.* WELLS *holds a pill to* JIMBO's *mouth.* JIMBO *opens his mouth,* WELLS *pops a pill in.* JIMBO *tries to bring the cup of water to his mouth.*

WELLS (*Continued; to* MOCKIS): You can do something!

MOCKIS *steps over, stubs the cigarette, attempts to help guide the cup of water to* JIMBO's *mouth.*

WELLS (*Continued*): Steady, young man. Easy as it goes.

JIMBO *opens his mouth to drink. The pill falls out.* WELLS *retrieves it from the floor, puts it to* JIMBO's *lips.*

MOCKIS: That one is dirty, yes?

WELLS: Yes. I have another one, somewhere. (*Grabs a second pill from the table, holds it to* JIMBO's *lips*) Maybe if you were seated, young man.

JIMBO: No, no.

MOCKIS: He has a suggestion, yes?

JIMBO: I'll be sitting soon enough, goddammit!

WELLS: You can stand.

MOCKIS: Sure, stand, if you'd like.

JIMBO (*To* MOCKIS): Now you care? It's too late! (*To* WELLS) 'The fuck with you, too!

WELLS: Son, the medicine.

Lights dim, up, dim, up, dim, up. JIMBO *collapses.* MOCKIS *and a* GUARD *ease* JIMBO *into a chair.*

JIMBO: Too many whiskeys last night. (*Laughs*) Too many sugars. Too damn much.

JIMBO *opens his mouth.* WELLS *pops the pill into* JIMBO's *mouth.* MOCKIS *guides* JIMBO's *hands as* JIMBO *gulps the water. Pause as* JIMBO *settles the pill down his throat.* HE *shakes his head, side to side.*

JIMBO (*Continued*): We did all this out of love for you! (*Laughs, to* WELLS) We believe that! It was suppose to be, goddam! (*Shakes his head again, side to side*) It ain't working. I need more pills.

DOCTOR *and* GUARDS *reenter.* DOCTOR *stands, tears in her eyes.*

DOCTOR (*Her voice trembling*): Whaley. Michael . . .
WELLS: What . . .
DOCTOR: . . . Nothing! (*Pausing, trying to compose herself*) Whaley, Michael . . . (*Pause*)
WELLS: Something went wrong . . .
DOCTOR: . . . That, the bastard is dead! (*Pausing*) Whaley. Michael Robert. He is now deceased at . . .
WELLS (*To* DOCTOR): It's not necessary for you to . . .

GUARD *jams a sheet of paper into* WELLS' *hands.*

JIMBO (*Laughs*): It makes you sick! That's it! You ain't shit!
GUARD (*Reading from a third sheet of paper*): Ryan. Gerald O.
JIMBO: You're fucking with me, ain't you? You can't be doing this. Something got settled, huh?

ALL GUARDS *cluster around* JIMBO. JIMBO *bolts from the table away from the* GUARDS.

JIMBO (*Continued; jabbing his finger at them all*): You, you, and you! You and you! You can't do it! It's got you sick!

GUARDS *grab hold of* JIMBO.

JIMBO (*Continued*): No! Let me sit! I need more pills! Okay? (*Beat*) Okay, dammit! Okay, how long? How much longer do you have? Get me now? No, you're fucked! (*Laughs*) All of youse? It took all of you! What's coming after me, after me and the boys, hell, this ain't shit! You know it! I'm tame, you bastards. Compare what's to come, this ain't shit! We got you beat!

GUARDS *begin to haul* JIMBO *out.*

JIMBO (*Continued*): Get God to love you! (*Laughs*) Get him, he ain't shit either!

GUARDS *exit with* JIMBO, DOCTOR *following. Silence.* MOCKIS *pours a cup of water, offers it to* WELLS. WELLS *looks, pauses, accepts the water.* BOTH *sip water, slowly, audibly.*

MOCKIS: Headaches. They come up when you least expect them, yes? They make you say funny things. (*Smiles*)

WELLS *smiles, nodding in agreement.* MOCKIS *nods, easing himself into a seat at the table.*

MOCKIS (*Continued*): Headaches come up all the time.
WELLS: Yes. (HE *grabs a chair, sits away from the table*)
MOCKIS: How are you going to handle the bodies?
WELLS: Excuse me?
MOCKIS: I don't know whose responsibility that is, primarily, but I think we can reach some agreement that is satisfactory.
WELLS (*Pausing*): Can the young man die first!
MOCKIS: Oh, yes, of course. I'm not trying to rush you on any decisions. (*Pause, sips water*) They got what they wanted, yes?
WELLS (*Pausing*): And you have what you wanted.
MOCKIS (*Slams his paper cup on the table*): Do something with your water! (HE *steps away from the table*) Things take their course. It's for the best, yes? One way or another. Always. (*Beat*) How I work to make the world forget all the crap, yes? How I have to. (*Beat*) Add some fluoride to your water. You would do a service for your country.
WELLS (*Pausing*): You want their bodies? You'll go with their bodies then, is that clear? I want their bodies out with you!
MOCKIS: Work something out, would you?
WELLS: On your departure then! With your luggage!
MOCKIS: Today was to be big? For you, perhaps. (*Sighs*) Tomorrow?

Lights dim, come up.

MOCKIS (*Continued*): How we love all our distractions, yes?

Lights dim, come up.

MOCKIS (*Continued*): We can get back to normal things now. For awhile.
WELLS: For the time being.
MOCKIS: Yes.

Lights dim, come up, and then fade on MOCKIS *and* WELLS.

END OF PLAY

About TCG

Theatre Communications Group, the national organization for the nonprofit professional theatre, was founded in 1961 to provide a national forum and communications network for the then-emerging nonprofit theatres, and to respond to the needs of both theatres and theatre artists for centralized services.

Today, TCG is a unique national arts organization, creatively combining the activities of both service organization and national professional association by addressing artistic and management concerns, serving artists and institutions, and acting as advocate and provider of services for a field diverse in its aesthetic aims and located in every part of this country. TCG's Constituent and Associate theatres, as well as thousands of individual artists, participate in nearly 30 programs and services. TCG participants encompass artistic and managing directors, actors, playwrights, directors, designers, literary managers, trustees and administrative personnel. Institutions and individuals are served through casting and job referral services, management and research services, publications, literary services, conferences and seminars, and a wide variety of other programs.

TCG's goals are to foster cross-fertilization and interaction among different types of organizations and individuals that comprise the profession; to improve the artistic and administrative capabilities of the field; to enhance the visibility and demonstrate the achievements of the American theatre by increasing the public's awareness of theatre's role in society; and to encourage a nationwide network of professional theatre companies and individuals that collectively represent our "national theatre."

TCG gratefully acknowledges the generous support of the following foundations, corporations and government agencies: Actors' Equity Foundation, Alcoa Foundation, American Telephone & Telegraph Company, Atlantic Richfield Foundation, Robert Sterling Clark Foundation, Dayton Hudson Foundation, The Equitable Life Assurance Society of the United States, Exxon Corporation, The Ford Foundation, The General Electric Foundation, Home Box Office, Inc., The Andrew W. Mellon Foundation, Metropolitan Life Foundation, National Endowment for the Arts, The New York Community Trust, New York State Council on the Arts, The Scherman Foundation and Warner Theatre Productions, Inc.

Other TCG Publications

American Theatre
Recently expanded from *TheatreCommunications*, the national monthly forum for news, features and opinion.

Theatre Profiles
The biennial illustrated reference guide to America's nonprofit professional theatre.

Theatre Directory
The annual pocket-sized contact resource of theatres and related organizations.

Subscribe Now!
Danny Newman's landmark work on building arts audiences through dynamic subscription promotion.

New Plays USA 1
TCG's 1982 collection of current scripts from America's professional theatres includes *A Prelude to Death in Venice*, by Lee Breuer; *Dead Souls*, adapted by Tom Cole; *FOB*, by David Henry Hwang; *Still Life*, by Emily Mann; *The Resurrection of Lady Lester*, by OyamO; and *Winterplay*, by Adele Edling Shank.

Plays in Process
A subscription service providing immediate circulation of new plays, translations and adaptations produced at theatres across America.

Computers and the Performing Arts
The special report on TCG's 1980 National Computer Project for the Performing Arts.

Dramatists Sourcebook
The annual guide to opportunities for playwrights, translators, composers, lyricists and librettists.

Theatre Facts
The annual report on the economic health of the nonprofit professional theatre in the United States.

Graphic Communications for the Performing Arts
A richly illustrated compendium of outstanding examples of graphic design for the performing arts.

ArtSEARCH
The bi-monthly national employment bulletin for the performing arts.

Performing Arts Ideabooks
A series of monographs by working professionals outlining innovative approaches to telemarketing, touring and volunteer groups.